Valentino Monticello

Opera & Wine
Wine in Opera

Collage of 'The National Gallery' in London, where the collection of Valentino Monticello, as illustrated in this book, was exhibited.

Valentino Monticello

Opera & Wine
Wine in Opera

Text Luciano Citeroni

Cantor Holding
ART PUBLICATIONS

Contents

Introductions to the wine labels

These works of art – for such they are – in this extraordinary book are unique in two respects: first, for revealing the many and various ways in which wine features as an integral part of so many operas; secondly, for the medium used: wine labels painstakingly selected and even more painstakingly cut, trimmed and mounted to illustrate the opera in question.

For a man with such unusual imagination and creative gifts, as well as the fortuitous possessor of such a romantic sounding name, Valentino Monticello is the most modest and unassuming of men. Yet, lurking beneath his self-effacing exterior, and now exposed, is his extraordinary triple-passion, for music, art and wine.

Imagine the task, knowing the opera, first to visualise the most appropriate scene, next to select from an enormous collection of wine labels, accumulated over many years, those not only of the right colour but, more importantly, those labels which adorned the bottles of wine produced in the country featured by the opera. For example, Valentino used labels of champagne for the scene from La Traviata, German wine labels for Weber's Der Freischütz; perhaps, more surprisingly, labels of English wines to illustrate Shakespeare's famous bucolic character depicted in Verdi's Falstaff.

Even at a superficial level these scenes are colourful and evocative. But look at them more closely, better still with a magnifying glass, and the brilliance, ingenuity and complexity of detail is breathtaking.

I first came across Valentino and his work at Christie's. For many years I was not only the head of Christie's Wine Department but, as a draughtsman and water colourist, served as Chairman of the Wine Trade Art Society. Conveniently, and appropriately, our annual exhibitions were held at Christie's and it was here that his suitably wine-related pictures first caught my eye and those of the many visitors. The work he exhibited was of poster size, yet, even reduced in scale for this book, the detail is quite clearly amazing.

As a lover of wine, music and art myself, I am lost in admiration for the patient genius of a man who has managed to encapsulate for our delectation all three, and in such a novel, ingenious and attractive way.

Michael Broadbent – M.W.
Christie's, London

I see Valentino Monticello often at the Opera House as he is seen at other establishments for opera. His passion for the art form is in abundance and his love of wine is obvious when you talk to him about what to drink with a meal or dish.

Research and knowledge of opera is seen in the selection for each country, and craftsmanship, skill and patience seen in each of these works of art. For this is what they are.

The selection of the wine labels has been carefully thought through down to the smallest detail. The results are simply outstanding. In some cases the fun is to spot each opera house, without cheating, from the proscenium.

Sir Colin Southgate
Chairman of the Royal Opera House

There are two sorts of artists; those who wish only to innovate and those that thank the muse for another revelation. The desire to impress is not the key that opens the door to the divine; it is the humility.

It is good to still find passion and craftsmanship in a picture. Valentino Monticello's collages are a tribute to his three loves – wine, opera and the fine arts.

Behind his Uccello-like compositions lie anthropomorphous landscapes. Nymphs spill out of trees, crouching nudes become mountains and Nereids race with the waves through inundated palaces.

Valentino's strict rules on his subject matter and his choice of materials has made his imagination work all the harder. What should just be a set of charming illustrations has become a surreal body of work showing us the private world of Valentino Monticello.

Emma Sergeant

L'Ombre (Also the studio of J. Ward)

Music **Friedrich van Flotow**
Libretto **Jules-Henri Vernoy de Saint-Georges and Adolphe de Leuven**
First Performance **7th July 1870, at the Paris Opéra-Comique**

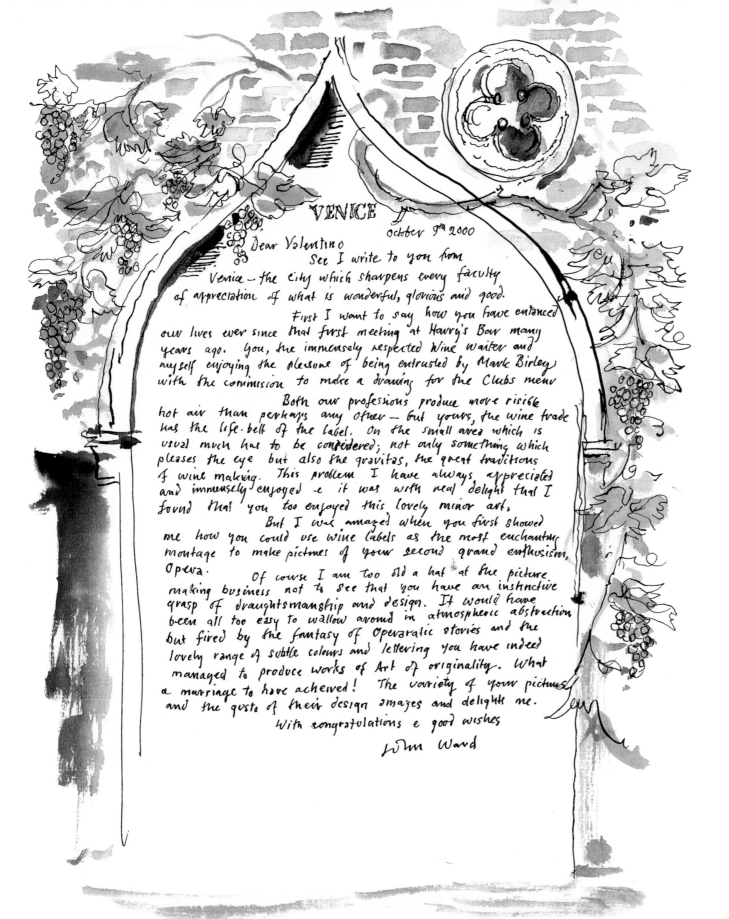

VENICE
October 9th 2000

Dear Valentino
See I write to you from Venice – the city which sharpens every faculty of appreciation of what is wonderful, glorious and good.

First I want to say how you have enhanced our lives ever since that first meeting at Harry's Bar many years ago. You, the immensely respected Wine Waiter and myself enjoying the pleasure of being entrusted by Mark Birley with the commission to make a drawing for the Clubs menu

Both our professions produce more risible hot air than perhaps any other – but yours, the wine trade has the life-belt of the label. On the small area which is usual much has to be considered; not only something which pleases the eye but also the gravitas, the great traditions of wine making. This problem I have always appreciated and immensely enjoyed & it was with real delight that I found that you too enjoyed this lovely minor art.

But I was amazed when you first showed me how you could use wine labels as the most enchanting montage to make pictures of your second grand enthusiasm, Opera.

Of course I am too old a hat at the picture making business not to see that you have an instinctive grasp of draughtsmanship and design. It would have been all too easy to wallow around in atmospheric abstraction but fired by the fantasy of Operatic stories and the lovely range of subtle colours and lettering you have indeed managed to produce works of Art of originality. What a marriage to have achieved! The variety of your pictures and the gusto of their design amazes and delights me.

With congratulations & good wishes
John Ward

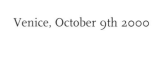

Venice, October 9th 2000

Dear Valentino,

See I write to you from Venice – the city which sharpens every faculty of appreciation of what is wonderful, glorious and good.

First I want to say how you have enhanced our lives ever since that first meeting at Harry's Bar many years ago.
You, the immensely respected wine waiter and myself enjoying the pleasure of being entrusted by Mark Birley with the commission to make a drawing for the Clubs' menu.

Both our professions produce more risible hot air than perhaps any other – but yours, the wine trade has the life-belt of the label. On the small area which is usual, much has to be considered; not only something which pleases the eye, but also the gravitas, the great traditions of wine making. This problem I have always appreciated and immensely enjoyed and it was with real delight that I found that you too enjoyed this lovely minor art.

But I was amazed when you first showed me how you could use wine labels as the most enchanting montage to make pictures of your second grand enthusiasm, Opera.

Of course I am too old a hat at the picture making business not to see that you have an instinctive grasp of draughtsmanship and design. It would have been all too easy to wallow around in atmospheric abstraction, but fired by the fantasy of Operatic stories and the lovely range of subtle colours and lettering, you have indeed managed to produce works of Art of originality.
What a marriage to have achieved! The variety of your pictures and the gusto of their design amazes and delights me.

With congratulations and good wishes,

John Ward – C.B.E. – R.A.

Dedication and acknowledgements

I dedicate this book to my wife Silvana, my children Michele and Claudia, and our family friend Charles P. Russell.

The inspiration for this book was borne out of my love and fascination for music, wine and art, all of which have transported me to a different plane.

But my excitement for this work was challenged by many seemingly insurmountable problems; the difficulty of obtaining appropriate labels, finding a suitable operatic text or scene, and most of all, the dilemma of creating something worthwhile.

However, the appreciation and encouragement I received for my collages from Michael Broadbent, Emma Seargent, David Maude-Rosby-Montaldo di Fragnito and Lucien Freud gave me the incentive and inspiration to continue, in spite of the difficulties. In particular, John Ward, who is one of the most remarkable men I have had the good fortune to meet, spent many unforgettable, precious hours, explaining the movement of the human figure and the importance of perspective.

His kindness has always been unstinting and I have been totally charmed by his warm smile and manner; I learnt from him how beautiful the universe is!

The moral support I had from Phillip Adkins, Clark and Elisabeth Swanson, Ambassador Charles Price and his family will stay in my heart forever.

I would also like to thank all the wine producers that so kindly helped me with the material and the various chambers of commerce, trade centres, associations of wine-makers and Embassies Attachés d'Affaires, for providing me with the historical and latest information on the state of wine-making in their respective countries or regions.

Also Casa G. Ricordi, maestro Hans Werner-Henze, maestro Giorgio Battistelli, maestro Ikuma-Dan, the librarian of the Museo alla Scala for allowing me access to previously unpublished musical scores and texts.

In addition, H. Watanabe, Paul Taylor, Virginia Orazi, Paul Valois, Susan Mitchelmore, John Rice and Colin Russ for the general help with the script, transcriptions and translations.

Jan-Dirk Paarlberg, Oscar van Overeem for making the publication of this book possible.

Finally, a very special thank you to Mark Birley for being so patient with me, and most of all for enlightening me on the art of elegance and perfection.

Valentino Monticello

Luciano Citeroni

Portrait by Valentino of Luciano Citeroni.

Many years ago, on a flight back from the Verona Wine Fair, I found myself sitting next to Luciano Citeroni. Throughout the journey we passed the time by talking about wine and music and I was greatly impressed by his considerable knowledge on both subjects.
We subsequently became very good friends.

When I came up with the idea to produce a book of collages made with wine labels representing the many operatic pieces about wine, I thought that Luciano would be the ideal person to write the script. We discussed the idea but he had at first some reservations about undertaking the project, considering himself well versed in opera but only an amateur where wine was concerned.
When I explained that he could seek information from me concerning the wine element, Luciano agreed to take on the time consuming task.

A chemistry teacher by profession, it is natural that Luciano is a perfectionist.
As an opera lover with a collection of over one thousand recordings of complete operatic works, he has lectured on the subject a number of times. The Anglo-Italian Cultural Circle of Sutton has received lectures in Italian on 'Great singers of the past', 'Discovering rare unperformed operas', 'Verdi's first hundred years' and 'Bellini's bicentenary', the last two also being given in English to the Wallington Gramophone Society. Luciano has also given an operatic talk to the Cultural Association of the Castelli Romani in Genzano di Roma, Italy.

The accompanying text he has written is clear, concise and thoroughly researched. As for the section on wine, although relying on my expertise as a consultant, his notes are extremely comprehensive and as far as possible up to date. I feel fortunate to have found this partnership and hope that the reader will enjoy this book as much as I have.

Valentino Monticello

Luciano Citeroni about Valentino

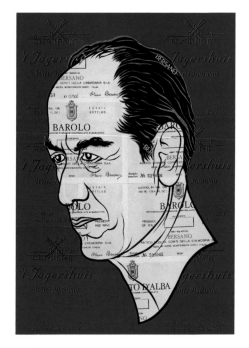

Self-portrait.

Dealing with art and good wine have always been amongst Valentino Monticello's greatest loves. In this, he has certainly followed a family tradition; his grandfather was a wine producer, his mother ran an inn called 'Dalla Lucia' and his father was the owner of a hotel in Piovene Rocchette, near Vicenza.

In 1959 he decided to move to London, commencing his career as sommelier at the 'Twenty One Club', where he developed his professional skill and experience. In 1983 he was engaged as head sommelier by the prestigious 'Harry's Bar', one of England's most exclusive club restaurants where he still acts as consultant, despite having retired two years ago.

Wine, however, is not his only love; music, particularly opera and figurative art, even though cultivated as hobbies, have been equally important to him. Valentino has drawn and painted since boyhood and in spite of not having undertaken any artistic studies, his early works, accomplished using a variety of techniques, reveal the presence of a notable talent.

With unusual ingenuity, Valentino discovered a way of combining his three pursuits; that is to depict scenes from various operas in which wine is drunk, mentioned or alluded to by using collages made up of wine labels. These would be from the countries or regions where the opera was set, created or first performed. "Many books have been written about opera and love, politics and tragedy," Valentino explains, "but no one has examined the relationship between opera and wine." This union invented by Valentino Monticello is without question original as well as stimulating. The artist wishes to emphasise that his invention is not intended to publicise any particular product but to indirectly promote wine itself by using this unusual vehicle of cultural communication.

The amalgamation of figurative arts, fine wine and opera started in 1985, when Valentino made his first collages using this material. By cutting, superimposing and glueing the small pieces of paper and by combining their colours and inscription patterns, Valentino succeeds in creating remarkable effects. Each collage takes him several months to complete and incorporates as many as 600 labels. There is no drawing; every last detail is cut from the material used. As interest in Monticello's project began to grow, people started to send him wine labels from all over the world. Nevertheless, the huge work was beset with difficulties. In fact, although it was easy to assemble the necessary material for countries such as France, Italy, Germany and Spain, there appeared to be insurmountable problems for some other nations. Particular difficulty was experienced in obtaining wine labels from Russia, a nation with a rich operatic tradition but which hardly sells any wine to Western Europe, and conversely finding an opera set in New Zealand, a strong wine exporter. Unfortunately, the latter has not been fully resolved.

Originally, Valentino's preferred subjects were interiors, vases with flowers and characters from the Italian 'Commedia dell'Arte'. During this period the artist's imagination and creative ability were evident. This brought about results which were not only complex but also extraordinary, as for example, flowers obtained through an intertwining of feminine nudes in movement. These pictures present an evolution in the artist's style. The space is ample and filled with numerous figures and the colouring, scenic and perspective effects, together with the movement of forms and volume results in such complexity that it is difficult to believe they have been obtained by means of such an unlikely method. Now, in his latest works, an extremely personal figurative language and a fresh spontaneous creativity have emerged. These are combined with great precision and accuracy of detail as well as a complete mastery of technique.

Monticello's artistic career has developed rapidly. In 1989, the selection committee of the Royal Academy accepted one of his pictures for its summer exhibition. In 1990, a presentation of his work took place at the Ergon Gallery near Bond Street in London. In spite of a deep national recession at the time, nearly all the pictures were sold within a few hours.

Opera & Wine

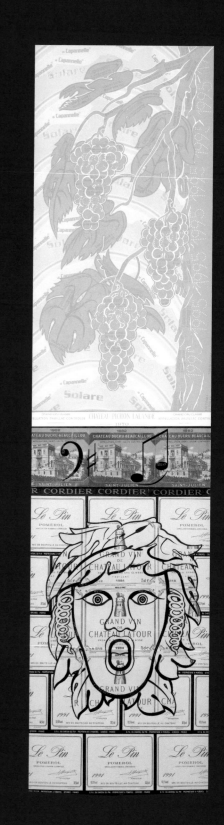

As was typical of Mozart, composition was rapid and the opera was completed in a mere four months. The première took place two months later, but in that time the composer had written and seen the first performance of his last opera, 'La Clemenza di Tito'. Thus, Die Zauberflöte was to be Mozart's last work to see the stage; he died just over two months later. The opera enjoyed great success with a run of nearly two hundred performances in just two years. Not even 'Le Nozze di Figaro' or 'Don Giovanni' had captured the public's favour for such a long continuous period.

The plot is very complex. The action takes place in no particular country and at no specific time. The setting could be described as that of a fantastic fairy tale, very much in the style of 'naïve' art. However, the story, in simple terms, concerns the triumph of the good Sarastro over the evil Queen of the Night. The former has abducted the latter's daughter, Pamina, in order to free her from her wicked mother's influence.

In addition to the positive points above, it is significant that the work had been composed to a German libretto for performance at the people's opera house while the Da Ponte works had been commissioned for showing at a court theatre and had been composed to Italian librettos. It is therefore no surprise that the opera did so well with its popular audience. However, there are a number of other reasons that explain its immediate success. The comic quality of the naïve element, the charming character of the strange setting, the conflict between good and evil and the superb music combine to give just the right product to captivate all but the most highbrow of audiences. In fact it has continued to enthral millions and is still a favourite in the repertory today.

The collage represents a scene taken from the first act. The Queen of the Night's three ladies-in-waiting have been searching for Tamino, a prince; he is to be the agent they will use in their attempt to 'rescue' Pamina. They appear as he is in conversation with Papageno, a bird catcher in the service of the wicked Queen. Papageno introduces them to his companion...

Die Zauberflöte
Music **Wolfgang Amadeus Mozart** • Libretto **Emanuel Schikaneder**

First Performance **30ᵗʰ September 1791, at the Theater auf der Wieden, Vienna**

The action concerns the futile attempt by the forces of darkness to get her back. Strangely, the Queen of the Night, grieving at the loss of her daughter, appears as good in the beginning of the work, while one is led to believe that the abductor, Sarastro, is actually evil. That the opposite is true becomes clear pretty quickly, but the switch creates an original and interesting situation nevertheless. The opera has strong Masonic connections. This is hardly surprising, since both composer and librettist were members of the brotherhood at the time. It would appear that a possible moral of the work is to cast Freemasonry as good and its detractors as bad.

Musically, the opera, a 'Singspiel' with spoken dialogue, is one of Mozart's very best; it has everything one would wish for. There is biting coloratura in the Queen of the Night's two arias, lyrical beauty in the melodies for Pamina and Tamino and solemn, dignified music to accompany Sarastro.

There is also the charming simple element where Papageno and Papagena are concerned, the celebrated patter duet towards the end of the opera being an utter delight. The choir plays its part, 'O Isis und Osiris' in the second act being a memorable contribution. The finale, a thanksgiving and rejoicing chorus, is also beautifully done.

"Wer sind diese Damen?"

"Das sind die Damen, die mir täglich meine Vögel abnehmen und mir dafür Wein, Zuckerbrot und süsse Feigen bringen."

"Sie sind vermutlich sehr schön?"

"Ich denke nicht."

"Papageno!"

"Denn wenn sie schön wären, Würden sie doch ihre Gesichter nicht bedecken."

"Papageno!"

TAMINO
"Who are these ladies?"

PAPAGENO
"These are the ladies who collect my birds every day and in exchange bring me wine, cake and sweet figs."

TAMINO
"I presume they are very beautiful?"

PAPAGENO
"I don't think so."

THE THREE LADIES
"Papageno!"

PAPAGENO
"For if they were beautiful "they surely wouldn't cover their faces."

THE THREE LADIES
"Papageno!"

Operas for Africa and the Middle East

Samson et Dalila
Music **Camille Saint-Saëns** • Libretto **Ferdinand Lemaire**

First Performance **2ⁿᵈ december 1877, at the Grand Ducal Theatre, Weimar**

As an admirer of Mendelssohn's 'Elijah' and Handel's religious works, the composer had planned Samson et Dalila to be an oratorio and it was his librettist who convinced him to write an opera instead. Saint-Saëns had started work in 1868 but a general lack of enthusiasm on the part of all around him led to discouragement and self-doubt. In 1870 he visited Franz Liszt in Weimar and although the latter gave a positive reaction and even offered to produce the opera, once completed, his indecision remained and the project was put aside. Then, in 1872, the successful outcome of his new composition, 'La Princesse Jaune', provided the spark for him to resume and by 1877 the opera had been completed.

As promised by Liszt, the première was staged in Weimar at the end of that year. It was next shown in Hamburg in 1882. However, apart from the odd concert or private performance, (at which little interest was shown and severe criticism was given), there was no sign of it being performed in public in France where the theatrical staging of a biblical subject appeared to be totally unacceptable. After many years it was presented in Rouen (1890) and at last, in 1892, the Paris Opéra staged it with considerable success. In retrospect, it is an interesting paradox that none of Saint-Saëns' other operas struggled so much to gain recognition yet none have since endured such an eminent position in the French operatic repertory!

The work itself, based on the conflict between Israelites and Philistines as related in the Book of Judges, deploys a large orchestra, and although in only three acts (four tableaux), is written in the spectacular French 'Grand Opera' manner with a ballet ingrained within the story. The score, a blend of symphonic form and some significant set numbers, is highly dramatic and the orchestral palette is full of rich, sensuous colours, especially in the second act. As correctly foreseen by Lemaire, the feel for theatrical emotion is natural in the story, and indeed is imaginatively employed by both himself and the composer.

The collage depicts the second act after the seduction scene. Delilah has used all her wiles and feminine charm to extract the secret of Samson's strength. The Philistine soldiers are about to enter...

"Mon coeur s'ouvre à ta voix
Comme s'ouvrent les fleurs
Aux baisers de l'aurore!
Mais, ô mon bien-aimé,
Pour mieux sécher mes pleurs,
Que ta voix parle encore!
Dis-moi qu'à Dalila tu reviens pour jamais!
Redis à ma tendresse
Les serments d'autrefois,
Ces serments que j'aimais!
Ah! Réponds à ma tendresse!
Verse-moi, verse-moi l'ivresse!"

"Dalila! Dalila! Je t'aime!"

"Ainsi qu'on voit des blés les épis onduler
Sous la brise légère,
Ainsi frémit mon coeur, prêt à se consoler
A ta voix qui m'est chère!
La flèche est moins rapide à porter le trépas
Que ne l'est ton amante à voler dans tes bras!"

"A moi! Philistins! A moi!"

"Trahison!"

DALILA
"My heart opens to your voice
as do the flowers
to the kisses of the dawn!
But, oh my beloved,
in order to better dry my tears,
let your voice speak again!
Tell me that you come back to Delilah for ever!
Repeat to my affection
the one-time promises,
those promises I loved!
Ah! Answer my tenderness!
Fill me, fill me with ecstasy!"

SAMSON
"Delilah! Delilah! I love you!"

DALILA
"Just as one can see the ears of corn rippling
in the gentle breeze,
thus flutters my heart ready to take comfort
from your voice which is dear to me!
The arrow is less swift in bringing death
than is your lover to fly into your arms!"

(SLOWLY, SHE MOVES TOWARDS HER AIM, DEMANDING HIS SECRET AS PROOF OF HIS LOVE AND TRUST, AND BECOMES MORE AND MORE INSISTENT AS HE REPEATEDLY FRUSTRATES HER. AT THIS POINT DELILAH PRETENDS TO BREAK OFF THEIR RELATIONSHIP AND LEAVES. HE HURRIES AFTER HER INTO HER HOUSE, WHERE ALL IS REVEALED. SHE NOW SUMMONS THE PHILISTINE SOLDIERS WHO ENTER THE HOUSE. SAMSON, SHORN OF HIS HAIR, IS OVERPOWERED.)

DALILA
"To me! Philistines! To me!"

SAMSON
"Treachery!"

L'Incontro improvviso is Haydn's sixth opera and the fifth written for the court of the Hungarian prince, Eszterházy. Widely adapted from the plot of Gluck's 1764 opera, 'La Rencontre Imprevue', it was composed for a special occasion, that is, the visit to the Eszterháza Palace by the Austrian Archduke Ferdinand and his Italian wife.

The opera has an interesting history. Although successful at the outset, it went out of favour and was lost except for one soprano aria, 'Or vicina a te, mio cuore', which continued to be performed occasionally as a concert piece. It was not until the middle of the twentieth century that a Danish Haydn scholar found the original score in the Saltykov-Shchedrin library in St. Petersburg, Russia. This was then published in the early 1960's.

L'Incontro Improvviso

Music **Franz Joseph Haydn** • Libretto **Karl Friberth**

First Performance **29th August 1775, at the Eszterháza Palace, Hungary**

A forerunner to Mozart's 'Die Entführung aus dem Serail', Haydn's work, together with its original Gluck model, features a harem enslavement, an abortive rescue attempt and a final pardon leading to a happy ending.

The opera, the most ambitious Haydn had composed at that time, contains forty-seven numbers divided into three acts. The work, tuneful in a classical manner, is typical of the composer. There are many attractive pieces, of which the Act II coloratura aria mentioned above is particularly notable. Also in the second act, the love duet, 'Son quest'occhi', and the martial tenor solo 'Il guerrier con armi avvolto', are very fine. In addition, there is an interesting soprano trio in the first act. Overall the opera can hardly be described as memorable but is still a very melodious work with a number of interesting features. The collage depicts the very first scene. A calender beggar and his henchmen are drinking a toast to their mendicant exploits and to the store of provisions (seen in the background) which they have accumulated by dishonest means...

"Che bevanda, che liquore!
La dolcezza ed il sapore
Fanno rallegrar il cor.
Su beviamo, evviva Bacco,
Viva il vino ed il tabacco,
Viva il magazzino ancor!"

(SCENE: A STORE WITH VARIOUS KINDS OF MERCHANDISE AND EDIBLES. THE CALENDER AND HIS DERVISHES ARE SITTING AROUND A TABLE, SMOKING AND MERRILY DRINKING WINE.)

CALENDER AND DERVISHES
"What a drink, what liquor!
Its sweetness and flavour
enlighten the heart.
Come, let's drink, long live Bacchus,
hurrah for wine and tobacco,
hurrah for the storehouse too!"

Problems with the libretto caused the production of L'Africaine to be an intermittent and extremely long drawn-out affair. Composition had started as early as 1837, but the work had to be repeatedly shelved. In the meantime, Meyerbeer had also worked on and finished three other operas, 'Le Prophète', 'L'Étoile du Nord' and 'Dinorah'. At last, in 1864, he completed the work, which he had in the intervening period re-named 'Vasco da Gama'. Tragically, he died very soon afterwards – an event that had serious consequences. It had been Meyerbeer's practice to substantially modify all his operas during extensive rehearsals, which he had always ensured took place before the première, but this could now no longer be done in this case. In the event the revision was entrusted to François-Joseph Fétis, who restored the original title, L'Africaine to the work.

The plot is very complex and difficult to simplify. Briefly, Ines is wooed by Don Pedro, but loves Vasco da Gama, whom, however, she believes is dead. Unexpectedly Vasco appears, back from his travels, together with two native captives, Selica, who is in love with him and Nelusco. However, to complicate matters, Nelusco loves Selica, who is his Sovereign. After sea adventures that take all those involved around the Cape of Good Hope and then onto Queen Selica's territory, Don Pedro, who had tried to kill Vasco and usurp his glory, is himself killed.

At the end of the opera, Selica renounces her love in order to allow Vasco and Ines to return home together. She then breathes the poisonous perfume of the mancenilla tree and dies in the arms of Nelusco who, electing to die with her, takes the poison as well.

Although this last opera, which Meyerbeer considered would be his masterpiece, does contain some of the composer's finest music, it is dramatically weak. This is due to the wavering character of Vasco da Gama and other generally unconvincing characterisations, as well as the rather loose way in which the plot is knit together. As explained above, the opera contains a number of love triangles, all of which involve the Portuguese explorer. It is in the finales to acts II and IV, where these come into play powerfully, that L'Africaine contains its most interesting and dramatic scenes. It is a pity that these high spots could not be more typical of the work as a whole. Musically, Vasco's celebrated aria, 'O Paradis', Selika's coronation at the beginning of Act IV, and her death at the end of the opera are particularly memorable.

The opera's most interesting character, the Indian captive Nelusco, is pictured in the collage. The ship has just rounded the Cape successfully but the wind is changing. He wishes to wreck the vessel against dangerous rocks where he knows his warriors will be waiting. He thus calls upon the crew to turn north, a disastrous manoeuvre. He then invokes Adamastor, the tempest giant to the consternation and terror of the sailors who feel they are now certain to meet their doom...

L'Africaine

Music **Giacomo Meyerbeer** • Libretto **Eugène Scribe**

First Performance **28th April 1865, at the Opéra, Paris**

NELUSCO

"Holà! Maltelots, le vent change.
Courez aux voiles,
Hâtez-vous donc, car le vent change,
Tournez au nord,
Voyez à l'horizon les signes
Précurseurs du terrible typhon!
Tournez au nord! Tournez au nord!
Ou, si non, le trépas!"

NELUSCO

"Hey there, sailors, the wind changes.
Run to the sails,
hurry then, for the wind is changing,
turn to the north,
see on the horizon the warning
signs of a terrible typhoon!
Turn to the north! Turn to the north!
Or otherwise it's certain death!"

(THE SAILORS STEER NORTHWARDS. NELUSCO, NOW CERTAIN THAT THE SHIP WILL RUN INTO A STORM, DECIDES TO TAUNT THE SAILORS BY SINGING THE LEGEND OF THE SEA GIANT ADAMASTOR TO THEM. THEY ARE CURIOUS AND WANT TO HEAR MORE. NELUSCO IS ONLY TOO HAPPY TO OBLIGE.)

"Adamastor, roi des vagues profondes,
Au bruit des vents s'avance sur les ondes.
Et que son pied heurte les flots,
Malheur à vous navire et matelots!
Le voyez-vous? Le voyez-vous?
A la lueur des feux et des éclairs,
Le voyez-vous! C'est le géant des mers.
Jusqu'au ciel il soulève les cieux.
Mort à l'impie!
Et la mort sans tombeaux!"

NELUSCO

"Adamastor, king of the deep waves,
advances over the waves to the sound of the wind.
And if his foot should ruffle the waves,
it is woe to you, ship and sailors!
Do you see him? Do you see him?
By the glimmer of fires and lightning,
do you see him? It's the giant of the seas.
He lifts the seas up to the skies.
Death to the impious!
And death without burial!"

(THE SAILORS TAKE ALL IN GOOD HEART, AND EVEN PROVIDE A CHORUS TO THE SONG. HOWEVER, AS THE REAL MEANING OF THE WORDS TAKE EFFECT, THEY DRAW BACK IN FEAR AND SLOWLY DISPERSE. NELUSCO HAS ACHIEVED HIS AIM.)

Operas for America

Porgy and Bess

Music **George Gershwin** • Libretto **DuBose Heyward**

First Performance **10ᵗʰ October 1935, at the Alvin Theatre, New York**

Gershwin first became acquainted and fascinated with the story of Porgy in 1926, but eight years were to elapse before he could put it to music. In the meantime, the novelist and future librettist, DuBose Heyward had, with his wife Dorothy, dramatised the book into a successful play; only afterwards could the composition of an opera commence.

Gershwin, having previously lived in Harlem, New York, was already familiar with Negro life and counted many black musicians among his friends. Nevertheless, he decided to spend much time in South Carolina in order to gain first hand local experience while writing the score. The opera took just over eighteen months to complete and was premièred in New York towards the end of 1935. Unhappily, it lost money and was considered a flawed composition by most critics in spite of running for no less than 124 performances. Subsequent productions saw a slow but positive revival in its fortunes. Alas, this was achieved by a number of deletions, resulting in the work being considered more a popular operetta than a serious opera. It took three full-length productions in 1976, a triumph in Houston, Texas and two successful recordings for Gershwin's masterpiece to finally get the acclaim it deserved.

The action takes place in South Carolina in the early part of the twentieth century. The main location is a Negro tenement on a waterfront called 'Catfish Row'. The complex story involves a love triangle consisting of the two principals and a stevedore called Crown. A fourth important individual is Sporting Life, a local alcohol and drugs dealer whose evil influence tends to condition the turn of events in the plot. A host of other characters contribute more or less important parts, both from a musical and dramatic point of view, making up the Negro community around which the action revolves.

The opera uses leitmotifs, large choral ensembles, dramatic scenes and declamatory passages and so could be said to be rather reminiscent of Wagner, an opinion reinforced by the fiercely menacing fugue accompanying the fight between Crown and Robbins. On the other hand, the work is full of appealing and in some cases haunting solo numbers, songs expressing a great variety of moods, ranging from exultation through to stark desolation. These are tunes capable of standing on their own, out of context of the work as a whole. It is probable that this paradoxical mixture confounded the critics when the opera first appeared. Now, at last, it is fully established, a masterpiece and the greatest of American operatic works.

The picture depicts the Act I scene in Catfish Row. A game of crap is in progress. Porgy enters on a goat cart and is greeted by the crowd...

JAKE
"Here's the ol' crap shark!"

MINGO
"Now we'll have a game!"

PORGY
"Evenin' ladies, hello boys!
Luck been ridin' high with Porgy today.
I got a pocket full of the Buckra money,
and it's goin' to any man what got the guts
to shoot it off me."

MINGO
"Get on down, son, we'll take it."

SPORTING LIFE
"Lay it down."

ROBBINS
"All right, mens, roll'em.
We done wait long enough."

JIM
"You bes' wait for Crown. I see him
comin', takin' the whole sidewalk, and he
looks like he ain't gonna stand no foolin'."

PORGY
"Is Bess with him?"

JAKE
"Lissen to Porgy.
I think he's soft on Crown's Bess."

(MEN LAUGH.)

(CROWN ARRIVES, BUYS A FLASK OF DRINK FROM SPORTING LIFE AND TAKES HIS PLACE IN THE GAME OF CRAP...)

The opera, Puccini's 7th , is set in California during the 1849 gold rush. Minnie, the camp girl, has fallen in love with Dick Johnson who is really Ramerrez, a notorious bandit being hunted by the sheriff Jack Rance and the mining community.

The plot has points in common with Tosca, Puccini's 5th opera, in that in both cases the heroine's honour is at stake as is the life of her lover. There is also a similarity in the third member of the love triangle, the evil police chief in the earlier work and the hard drinking, gun slinging and gambling sheriff in the later one. At this point any comparison ends, however, as sheriff Rance, although far more coarse than Scarpia, is less cunning than his Tosca counterpart. Also he is a man of some honour, as he makes no attempt to seduce Minnie and even withdraws on losing a vital poker game to her. Indeed, unlike any of his previous works the opera has a happy ending. This certainly distinguishes it from Tosca where all three principals die in violent manner.

La Fanciulla del West

Music **Giacomo Puccini**
Libretto **Guelfo Civinini & Carlo Zangarini**
First Performance **10ᵗʰ December 1910, at the Metropolitan, New York**

The work features an attempt at innovation and has some excellent music. Much use is made of the whole tone scale, mainly in association with violent or frightening events. An example is the tune accompanying the wounded Johnson's painful attempt to climb the stairs to Minnie's loft when trying to hide from Rance. However the opera is uneven and the new musical language doesn't fully fit into Puccini's style. Consequently, although the opera obtained over 50 curtain calls at its Toscanini-conducted première, subsequent performances have been received less enthusiastically. The work is still in the repertory but has had only mixed success.

The collage scene occurs just after Dick Johnson has entered the 'Polka' bar. Having ordered whisky and water he sits at a table, where Minnie joins him. They remember having met before (she does not know his true identity) and reminisce over their previous meeting. Rance is at the bar, becoming increasingly jealous...

"Vi ricordate di me?"

JOHNSON
"Do you remember me?"

"Si, se anche voi mi ricordate..."

MINNIE
"Yes, if you remember me too..."

"E come non potrei?"

JOHNSON
"And how couldn't I?"

"Fu pel sentier che mena a Monterey..."

MINNIE
"It was on the road that leads to Monterey..."

(THE CONVERSATION BECOMES MORE INTIMATE...)

*"Si che lo ricordate:
Dissi che da quell'ora..."*

JOHNSON
*"Oh yes, you do remember:
I said that from that moment..."*

"...Non m'avreste scordato."

MINNIE
"...you wouldn't have forgotten me."

"...Nè v'ho scordata mai, mai, mai!"

JOHNSON
"...nor have I forgotten you, ever, ever, ever."

*"Quanto tempo sperai di rivedervi...
E non vi vidi più!"*

MINNIE
*"How long I had hoped to see you again...
and I never did!"*

RANCE
(INTERRUPTING, AND UPSETTING
JOHNSON'S GLASS.)

*"Mister Johnson, voi m'avete seccato!
Sono Rance, sceriffo.
Non mi lascio burlare.
Che venite a far qui?
Ragazzi? Uno straniero ricusa confessare
Perche si trova al campo!"*

*"Mister Johnson, you have annoyed me!
I'm Rance, the sheriff.
I don't let anyone fool me.
What's your business here?
Boys? A stranger refuses to say
why he is at the camp!"*

C arousel was composed immediately after the highly successful Oklahoma with Oscar Hammerstein II again providing the libretto. All leading parts were written for trained singers, with the result that it is possibly the musical composed by Rodgers which comes closest to being a modern operetta. Compared to its predecessor, it has a text which delves more deeply into human emotions and is far richer in musical terms with a host of beautiful and memorable melodies.

The première was immensely successful, the show running for 890 performances, a fact that must have given the composer, who favoured Carousel above his other works, great satisfaction. It has always enjoyed great success in London and a number of highly favourable revivals in the U.S.A.

Carousel

Music **Richard Rodgers** • Libretto **Oscar Hammerstein II**

First Performance **19ᵗʰ April 1945, at the Majestic Theatre, New York**

The action takes place in New England in the last quarter of the nineteenth century. Billy Bigelow, now in purgatory, is told that all is not well with his daughter back on Earth. A flashback follows. This relates to his love affair with Julie Jordan, the loss of both their jobs, their marriage and her pregnancy, a hostile town, his friendship with a criminal, his attempt to get money by stealing and his death due to falling onto his own knife when the robbery goes wrong. He is allowed to go back on Earth for one day on the condition that he can help his daughter, who is now fifteen, and whose unhappiness he has caused. This he does, showing himself only to her and through good fatherly advice is able to give her strength and assurance to meet the future.

In the score, set numbers abound. There is a heartfelt soliloquy and a number of other fine solos and duets. The choral work is also of a very high standard. It is interesting that the memorable final hymn, which has been adopted as an anthem by Liverpool Football Club supporters, should end the work on a note of hope rather than happiness, an unusual feature for a stage musical.

The collage represents a composite illustration of the carousel itself and townsfolk setting out for the clam-bake at the end of Act I...

TOWNSFOLK

"We're all wore out and done up!
And what's more we're hungry as goats!
You'll get no drinks er vittles 'till we get
Across the bay.
So pull in yer belts and load them boats
And let's get under way.
The sooner we sail,
The sooner we start
The clam-bake 'cross the bay!"

Astor Piazzolla was born in 1921 during the time the tango was the rage in Argentina. He quickly fell in love with the genre and matured into a very gifted bandoneon player. He progressed rapidly from musical arrangement to composition and was a leading band conductor by the age of twenty-six. Unsatisfied with the traditional tango form, he went to Paris to study under Nadia Boulanger in order to perfect his composition. Then, turning innovator, he created a new style of tango writing by instilling both new harmonies and rhythms into his music.

There is surely a connection with the composer's own renovation of the tango in the mid 1950's in the work's theme. The similarity of the two cases can hardly be mere coincidence!

The picture features the scene in the magic bar in which the inebriated goblin expresses his pain at Maria's loss. The three marionettes look on...

Maria de Buenos Aires

Music **Astor Piazzolla** • Libretto **Horacio Ferrer**

First Performance 8th May 1968, at the Sala Planeta, Buenos Aires

Piazzolla first met the Uruguayan poet, Horacio Ferrer, a great admirer of his, in 1948, when the latter was only fourteen years old. Subsequently they became good friends as Piazzolla admired Ferrer's poems just as Ferrer admired his music. Then, in 1967, the composer suggested they work together to produce something for the musical theatre. Two months later Ferrer handed Piazzolla the Maria de Buenos Aires libretto. Rapid completion followed and so the 'Tango Operita' was born. The première took place in the first half of 1968 and no less than 120 performances were given between May and September of that year. The partnership had proved an immediate success.

In the plot, Maria personifies the tango itself. A goblin (a speaking narrator part, played by Ferrer himself at the première), loves Maria, who is now dead, and conjures up past images of Maria's rise and fall: her rise from the country to the suburbs and thence to the cabarets and bordellos of the city centre, her subsequent decline and death. Now her shadow wanders aimlessly through the city. At length the drunken goblin comes across three marionettes, also drunk, in a magical bar. He asks them to find the shadow and tell it that Maria will be reborn, changed, but Maria nevertheless. And so it comes to pass...

The work is scored for eleven musicians, the violin being given a particularly prominent role. Much of the libretto is spoken, but with telling effect as the musical background is highly evocative and truly exquisite. Four instrumental scenes are beautifully integrated into the work. These are, in order, Maria's theme where she is presented, her progress from the suburbs to the city, her burial and the desolate wandering of her shadow and lastly the search for her by the three marionettes. The music is both sad and captivating. Maria's piece, 'Yo soy Maria' (I am Maria), is particularly haunting, both in its lyrics and its orchestration. The rebirth is accompanied by a sustained crescendo and the work ends on a note of reverent prayer.

"Desde esta copa que El Duende
Por triste, se está fajando
Tres Marionetas Borrachas
De Cosas, lo campaneamos."

"Aquí donde mañana sabe a antaño,
Buscando a Dios yo ví, de escalofrío,
Que estaba en lo que quiero y lo que extraño,
Cortado a esa sazón, como el tamaño
Del grano da el tamaño del estío."

"Aquí, en cada botella, cabe un río;
Y al fondo de ese río hay otro estaño;
Y, en curda, en ese estaño, un verso mío,
Y, en él, la plata triste de otro río
Que me hizo Duende, me hizo...
!Hace mil años!"

"Al Duende – que en la operita
Venía el cuento contando -
Se le ha perdido una sombra
Y, en curda, la va llamando."

THREE MARIONETTES
"From this glass that the goblin,
so sad, is gulping,
three marionettes inebriated
on things, are observing him."

THE GOBLIN
"Here, where tomorrow seems like long ago,
seeking God I saw, in a shiver,
that he was in what I love and what I miss,
cut to measure, as the size
of the grain indicates the size of the summer."

"Here, in each bottle fits a river;
and at the bottom of this river there's another bar;
and drunk, on this counter, a poem of mine,
and in it, the sad silver of another river
that made me a goblin, made me...
a thousand years ago!"

THREE MARIONETTES
"The goblin – that in the little opera
came relating a story –
has lost a shadow
and drunken, keeps calling it."

South America's most important opera composer, Antonio Carlos Gomes, was born in 1836 to a musical family in Campinas, about 80 kilometres from São Paulo in Brazil.

His first major work, 'A Noite do Castelo', was performed in 1861 with great success. Two years later a second opera, 'Joana de Flandres', followed and also triumphed. Gomes was awarded the title of Cavalliero da Orden do Rosa and also given a generous grant to travel to Italy in order to perfect his composing technique. Having arrived in Milan, he composed two musical comedies before writing the music to Il Guarany, which turned out to be his masterpiece. The work was performed at La Scala and received immediate acclaim. Other operas followed but with more mixed results. These were 'Fosca', 'Salvator Rosa', 'Maria Tudor', 'Lo Schiavo' and 'Odaléa'. Finally, he composed a symphonic vocal poem, 'Colombo', in 1892, as part of the four-hundredth anniversary celebrations for the discovery of the New World. He died on 16th September 1896, embittered with the new republican government that had deprived him of the grant he had continued to receive since 1863.

Il Guarany   Music **Antonio Carlos Gomes** • Libretto **Antonio Enrico Scalvini and Carlo D'Ormeville**

First Performance   **19ᵗʰ March 1870, at Teatro alla Scala, Milan**

Unfortunately and in the opinion of the writer, disgracefully, the operas of Gomes are all but forgotten. Yet, during his lifetime, Boito regarded him to be Verdi's successor, while the latter considered him a true musical genius.

The plot of 'Il Guarany' is complex, but in simple terms can be explained as follows: Cecilia, the daughter of Don Antonio, a wealthy Portuguese nobleman, is in love with Pery, an Indian Guarany tribe chieftain. At the same time she is wooed by a Portuguese settler, Don Alvaro, her father's choice, but also by Gonzales, a scheming Spanish adventurer who has designs on Don Antonio's silver mine. Don Alvaro is killed and in the finale, in order to save Cecilia from Gonzales, her father entrusts her to Pery and then blows up his castle with himself and Gonzales and his men in it.

The collage depicts a scene in the forest in which Gonzales and his fellow adventurers drink and sing a song praising the life of the fortune seeker...

"Senza tetto, senza cuna,
Vita abbiamo nel gioir;
Lieta o avversa la fortuna
Non c'importa di morir.
Chi ne impera sola ed una
È la donna del sospir.
Si nel duol che nel diletto
Non si teme il rio destin;
È la mira del moschetto
Che ci guida nel cammin.
Sovra il capo maledetto
Non imbianca il nostro crin."

GONZALES

"Without shelter, without refuge,
we enjoy life;
whether fortune be happy or adverse
we don't care about dying.
The only one to rule us
is the woman of our sighs.
Both in sorrow and delight
we do not fear evil destiny;
it's the aim of the musket
that guides us on our path.
Upon our accursed heads
our hair does not go white."

Operas for Asia

In 1916, having completed his opera Arlecchino, Busoni was looking for a companion piece as the work was too short for a full night's theatre entertainment. He quickly decided to turn the incidental music he had composed eleven years previously to Carlo Gozzi's play 'Turandot' into an opera. He achieved this by reducing the orchestration and inserting new music, mainly arias for the principal roles. These alterations took him three months to complete and both works received their joint première as a double bill in mid 1917.

Turandot   Music **Ferruccio Busoni** • Libretto **Ferruccio Busoni**

First Performance **11ᵗʰ May 1917, at the Stadttheater, Zürich**

The basic plot is the same as in the far better known Puccini opera. Princess Turandot will marry any suitor of royal blood who is able to solve her three riddles. However, the axe awaits he who attempts the challenge and fails. There are a few other similarities between the two works. The two central characters, Turandot and Kalaf (Calaf for Puccini,) are identical as is the Emperor Altoum, who however has a rather more important role in the Busoni opera. Also, Turandot is here less icy and distant than her Puccini counterpart, and is constantly fighting her own emotions as the drama unfolds. There is one important distinction in that Busoni's composition contains spoken dialogue and has a German text. Many other differences lie in the plot itself. First and foremost, Puccini's sweet and faithful slave Liù (who dies to avoid revealing the Prince's identity), is replaced by Turandot's scheming confidante, Adelma who wants Kalaf for herself and doesn't hesitate to reveal his name to Turandot at the appropriate time. Second, the ministers Ping, Pang and Pong are absent, and instead we have three masks from the Italian Commedia dell'Arte in Truffaldino, Pantalone and Tartaglia. Third, Kalaf's father, Timur, although mentioned in the libretto, is not seen and Kalaf's companion is Barak, his old retainer who now lives in Peking and has spotted him on his arrival in the city. Finally, the answers to the three riddles are completely different to those in Puccini's opera.

Busoni's Turandot is, of course, much shorter than Puccini's, but was composed some six years earlier. Although not on a par with the latter's masterpiece, it is an attractive and interesting work in its own right, with much charming music of Chinese and Arabic influence. In addition, the opera contains an interesting riddle scene and some fine choral work.

The collage represents the opera's finale, in which preparations for the wedding between Turandot and Kalaf are being made. The happy couple, together with the chorus ask and reveal the answer to a fifth and final riddle: what is that force that unites all men? It is love!...

"Was ist's, das alle Menschen bindet,
Vor dem jedwede Kleinheit,
Jede Kleinheit schwindet,
wogegen Macht und List zerschlägt
Und das Geringe zum Erhabnen prägt;
Das treibt den Kreislauf
Der ew'gen Weiten,
Umschliesst die Gegensätzlichkeiten,
Das überdauert alle Triebe,
Das uns vereinte:
Ist die Liebe! Liebe!"

KALAF, TURANDOT AND CHORUS
"What is the force that unites all mankind?
humbles itself
before all modesty,
against which power and cunning come to nothing,
yet which elevates the humblest peasant;
which propels the course
of men's ambitions,
which embraces all opposition,
which outlasts all instincts,
and unites us all:
it is love! Love!"

Madama Butterfly

Music **Giacomo Puccini** • Libretto **Giuseppe Giacosa and Luigi Illica**

First Performance **17th February 1904, at Teatro alla Scala, Milan**

In the year 1900, while in London for a production of Tosca, Puccini went to see a play by David Belasco and so become acquainted with the story of Madama Butterfly for the first time. The subject immediately captured his imagination; the idea of juxtaposing two distinctive and very different musical environments appealed to him as a novelty and therefore as a challenge.

The seeds of Puccini's sixth opera had been sown. His original plan had been to set the work in two acts, the first taking place in the U.S.A. and the second in Japan. However this was soon changed to a three-act piece set totally in Japan, but, in order to inject some western atmosphere into the work, a part of the second act was made to occur in the house of the American Consul. Well over a year went by with good progress being made, when Puccini suddenly had a change of mind. He became adamant that this very scene should be dropped, and the opera revert to two acts. Indeed this was how Madama Butterfly was presented at its première at la Scala, with disastrous consequences.

A number of alterations were now made. These resulted in cutting down the first act and supplying new music for the second, which was split into two parts divided by a musical interlude with a sailors' chorus at nightfall and a bird chorus at dawn. In particular, the tenor's aria, 'Addio fiorito asil', was added. When the revised work was performed in Brescia on 28th May 1904, the opera had at last started on a sequence of triumphs that have continued up to the present day.

The opera is set near Nagasaki at the turn of the century. Pinkerton, an American Naval Officer is making arrangements for a Japanese wedding. His consul warns him that the fifteen year-old girl is very serious about the matter but he insists on going through with the ceremony. Unfortunately, he is taking the union flippantly as a light-hearted adventure. The wedding takes place and the act closes with an extended love duet. The second act takes place three years later. Pinkerton has sailed back to America and Butterfly, now with child, awaits his return with a stubborn certitude, refusing other more genuine marriage offers. Eventually, he does return, but with an American wife. He doesn't have the courage to show himself, but Butterfly meets his wife. She is broken-hearted and as a last gesture to preserve her honour she gives up her child to be reared by its father in the U.S.A. She then commits suicide and dies as Pinkerton at last arrives to claim the child.

The opera is very endearing, having a wealth of beautiful music, that accompanying the extended fifteen minute-long love duet that concludes the first act being especially sumptuous.

Also, the title role is an extremely challenging part, requiring a childlike innocence and ingenuousness in the first act and a tragic maturity in the suicide scene. The aria 'Un bel di vedremo', in which she wishfully expresses the certainty that Pinkerton will return to her, is justly famous and the part has proved a vehicle for great sopranos throughout the opera's history.

The collage shows the small party that takes place just before the Japanese wedding in the first act. Butterfly has arrived with some of her friends and relatives, including her uncle, Yakusidé, a reputed drunkard. Pinkerton points them out to Sharpless, the American consul. Soon Yakusidé is looking for wine...

PINKERTON
(TO SHARPLESS.)

"Che burlata la sfilata
Della nuova parentela, tolta in prestito,
A mesata!"

"What a farce is the procession
of my new relations, taken out on a month's loan!"

"Certo dietro a quella vela
Di ventaglio pavonazzo la mia suocera si cela."

"Certainly behind the veil
of that dark violet fan hides my mother-in-law."

"E quel coso da strapazzo...
...È lo zio briaco e pazzo."

"And that worthless creature...
...is the drunk and crazy uncle."

(SHORTLY AFTERWARDS.)

UNCLE YAKUSIDÉ

"Vino ce n'è?..."

"Is there any wine?..."

BUTTERFLY'S MOTHER AND AUNT

"Guardiamo un po'."

"Let us see."

FRIENDS
(TO YAKUSIDÉ.)

"Ne vidi giá color di thè,
E chermisì!"

"I've already seen some the colour of tea,
and some crimson."

Yu-Zuru

Music **Ikuma Dan** • Libretto **Jiyunji Kinoshita**

First Performance **30ᵗʰ January 1952, at the Asahi Hall, Osaka**

Yu-Zuru (Twilight Crane) is Japan's best-loved opera. It features the ancient folklore story of Tsuu, a crane which had turned itself into a woman to become the wife of Yohyo, a poor and simple-minded young farmer who had saved her life as a bird by removing an arrow from her wing.

Tsuu weaves Yohyo rich and rare fabrics by using her own feathers. Hearing this and fully knowledgeable of the true value of this cloth, two villains approach the farmer promising wealth and riches if more material is woven and sold. The ingenuous Yohyo, caught up in a web of human greed, accepts. Tsuu, knowing that the removal of more of her feathers would kill her, at first protests. Finally, however, she succumbs to her husband's insistence and resolves to sacrifice herself for his happiness. The fabric is made and Tsuu transforms herself back to a crane, flying off on her final journey.

Yohyo is left with the villains. He has the expensive cloth but has lost his loving wife's priceless care and affection for ever.

The collage is a composite scene. In the foreground the cloth is being offered and sold in the city, whilst a geisha is offering drinks to the traders. On the opposite side, a weaving loom and the crane-woman are visible. The country huts where Yohyo lives can be seen in the background.

The libretto extract covers part of the scene where the villains Sodo and Unzo convince the gullible Yoho to have his wife weave more of the rare material from her feathers, while at the same time deceiving him on the real value of the cloth...

ソード
"ちょっと待って、ウンズ、今いい儲けができるよ。
え、ヨーヒョ、きれいな服についてちょっと前に言ったのは…
え、ウンズ、彼に残りを話してよ。"

ウンズ
"ちょっと聞け、ヨーヒョ、
この服を京都に持っていったら簡単に千両になる。"

ソード：
"ばかな、よく聞け、ヨーヒョ、
もっと妻に服を織らせたら百両に売れるよ。"

ヨーヒョ
"えっ？百両？"

ソード：
"そう！百両？"

(ウンズへ)：
"その通り"

ウンズ
"そう？百両！"
"百両儲かるよ！"

ヨーヒョ：
"すごい！百両！"

SODO
"Wait and see Unzu, we'll make a nice little fortune now!...
Hey, Yohyo, as I was saying a moment ago about that beautiful cloth...
Hey, Unzu, you tell him the rest!"

UNZU
"Listen to me, Yohyo!
If we take this cloth of yours to Kyoto, we can easily make a thousand Ryo!.."

SODO
"Id...i...ot! Now listen, Yohyo!
If you can get your wife to weave more of that cloth of hers, we can sell it for a hundred Ryo."

YOHYO
"What? A hundred Ryo?"

SODO
"Yes! A hundred Ryo.

(To UNZO)
"That's right!"

UNZU
"Yes, a hundred Ryo!
You'll make a hundred Ryo!"

YOHYO
"My! A hundred Ryo!"

Operas for Europe

On the 24th of February 1776, the Regio Ducal Teatro of Milan was giving a performance of Tommaso Traetta's opera 'La Merope'. A few hours later the building had been completely gutted by fire and the city needed a new opera house.

Construction was started as soon as Maria Theresa of Austria had given her permission, and two years later the new theatre was complete. It was then called the Regio Ducal Teatro alla Scala, after the church Santa Maria della Scala that had existed previously on the site.

Gluck had been asked to write an opera on Verazi's libretto for the opening night, but had declined due to pressure of work. However he generously passed the commission on to his most prominent follower, Salieri, who quickly took it on. Thus, Europa Riconosciuta was performed as a double première, for both opera and opera house, on August 3rd 1778.

Europa Riconosciuta

Music **Antonio Salieri**
Libretto **Mattia Verazi**
First Performance **3ʳᵈ August 1778,
at the Teatro alla Scala, Milan**

The opera turned out to be innovative in several respects. It is full of dramatic effects, particularly in the many action ensembles. Also, the choral writing is prominent for a work of that time. The music and libretto are vivid and also full of pathos, while the characters are interesting and complex. Unfortunately, although the production proved successful at the time, posterity has been unkind and the opera has not been given the recognition it appears to deserve.

The complicated plot concerns the return of the abducted Europa, Queen of Tyre, to her homeland. Her captor, Asterio, King of Crete, who is now her husband and their child accompany her. Shipwrecked near home, they are captured by Egisto who intends to further his aspirations to the throne by putting Asterio to death. They are saved by Isseo, the fiancé of Europa's niece, Princess Semele. Egisto is killed and Semele recognises Europa, who with Asterio, in return cedes her and Isseo the throne.

The picture represents the final scene of general celebration. Europa is portrayed allegorically on the set as Europe, surrounded by the three continents, America, Asia and Africa. On stage, Semele, next to the figure of justice, gives her recognition...

---

*"A regnar su questa sede,
Torni al fin la vera erede."*

*"Ed in mezzo a' suoi contenti
Del destin più non rammenti
Il rigor, la crudeltà."*

*"Ed in mezzo a' suoi contenti
Piu l'offese non rammenti
Della nostra infedeltà."*

*"Chi a scordar gli oltraggi apprende
Degli Dei qual sia comprende
La piu gran felicità.
Che sia ver l'intendo adesso,
Che felice a voi d'appresso
Questo cor godendo sta."*

*"Quella man, che noi difese
Che a me rese il soglio mio,
Se a mia voglia dar poss'io
Oggi a Semele sarà."*

"Non la sdegni: e a lei la dono."

"Io vi aggiungo il serto, e il trono."

CHORUS
*"May the rightful heir at last
return to reign on this throne."*

CRETAN MAIDENS
*"And in all her happiness
may she no longer remember
the rigour and cruelty of past destiny."*

CRETAN MAIDENS AND
DIGNITARIES OF THE REALM
*"And in all her happiness
may she no longer remember
the offence of our faithlessness."*

ASTERIO
*"He who learns to forget the wrongs
of others gets to know, by the Gods,
the greatest happiness.
That this is true I now understand
since happy in your presence
this heart is full of joy."*

EUROPA
(POINTING TO ISSEO.)
*"That hand that defended us
and that restored me my throne,
if I could give it as I would wish
it would today belong to Semele."*

ISSEO
(OFFERING HIS HAND TO SEMELE.)
"Don't disdain it: I do give it to her."

ASTERIO
(REMOVING HIS CROWN TO PLACE IT ON ISSEO)
"I will add the crown and throne."

Verdi's first opera, Oberto, had been composed in 1839. Now, some fifty years later, while living in retirement, the great librettist Arrigo Boito twice successfully tempted him to compose again. The first, a masterpiece, premièred in 1887, had been from the Shakespeare tragedy 'Othello'. The second, presented to Verdi in 1889, was to be from the comedy 'The Merry Wives of Windsor', again by Shakespeare.

This was indeed a special challenge. The Italian Opera Buffa tradition had grown completely out of fashion and had been fallow since the days of Rossini and Donizetti some forty-five years previously. Now, a retired 76 year-old veteran was contemplating a renewal of this long neglected art form, an undertaking as bold as it was unexpected, particularly since he himself had composed only one other comic work, 'Un Giorno di Regno', and that had been over fifty years earlier!

Falstaff

Music **Giuseppe Verdi** • Libretto **Arrigo Boito**

First Performance **9ᵗʰ February 1893, at Teatro alla Scala, Milan**

The opera was eventually premièred in 1893, proving to be a masterpiece, possibly even greater than Otello. Again Verdi was fortunate in having a superb libretto to work on, fully the equal to Shakespeare's original text. The music itself is similarly inspired. There are arias but the style is more symphonic in nature than that of other Verdi operas, including Otello, which itself, compared to previous works, shows a movement towards that direction. Yet, the short melody to the words, 'Bocca baciata non perde ventura, anzi rinnova come fa la luna', split between tenor and soprano and heard only fleetingly three times, remains one of the most hauntingly beautiful he wrote. Verdi's touch of genius is also shown by the sarcastic inflection behind the single word 'Reverenza!', which appears three times in Act II and once in Act III of the opera. Foremost, however, are the many fine baritone solos, such as 'Quand'ero paggio' and 'Mondo ladro!', respectively in the second and third acts of a work that has indeed been a vehicle for great baritones since its inauguration over one hundred years ago.

The story concerns the amorous adventures of Sir John Falstaff, a licentious and hard-drinking knight who is trying to seduce the wives of two rich burghers as a means of getting at their husbands' money. Needless to say, he gets his just deserts in the end but does so in a good-hearted and philosophical manner, leading the company in a finale that treats the whole thing in a manner that is light-hearted and full of jest.

The collage scene takes place in the first act. Here, we see the Garter Inn at Windsor, where Falstaff, as usual, is filling himself with wine. Naturally he is asking for more! ...

"Oste! Un'altra bottiglia
Di Xerez."

"Sei la mia distruzione!
Spendo ogni sette giorni dieci ghinee!
Beone!
So che se andiam, la notte,
Di taverna in taverna,
Quel tuo naso ardentissimo
Mi serve da lanterna!
Ma quel risparmio d'olio
Tu lo consumi in vino.
Son trent'anni che abbevero
Quel fungo porporino!
Costi troppo."

"E tu pure."

"Oste! Un'altra bottiglia!"

FALSTAFF
"Innkeeper! Another bottle
of Sherry."

(...AND SHORTLY AFTERWARDS, FIRST TO BARDOLFO AND THEN TO PISTOLA, HIS TWO RETAINERS...)

(TO BARDOLPH.)
"You're the ruin of me!
I'm spending ten guineas a week!
Drunkard!
I know that if we go, at night,
from tavern to tavern,
that extremely fiery nose of yours
serves me as a lantern!
But what is saved in oil
you consume in wine.
For thirty years I've been soaking
that purple fungus!
You cost too much."

(TO PISTOL.)
"And you do too."

(TO THE INNKEEPER.)
"Innkeeper! Another bottle!"

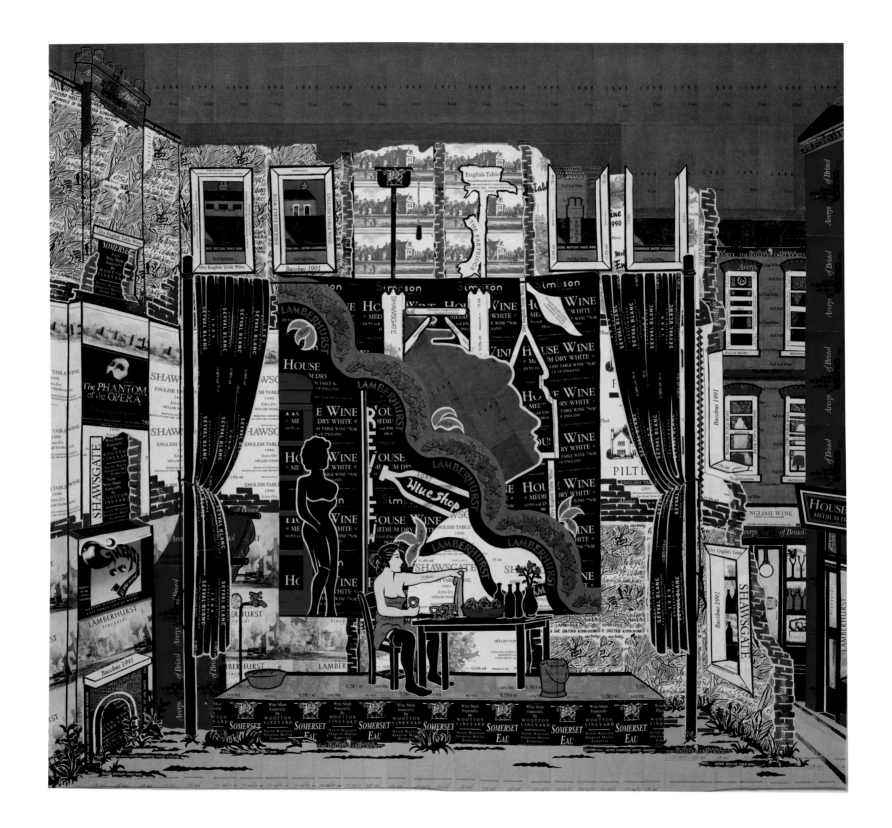

The Threepenny Opera is based on John Gay's 'The Beggar's opera', first performed almost exactly two hundred years before Weill's version was first shown to the public.

As in Gay's work, the plot concerns the women, exploits, arrest, pardon and elevation to a peerage of the gangster-hero Macheath. Also, in common with John Gay's opera, the libretto, written by Bertolt Brecht, a poet with strong left-wing convictions, is full of popular clichés that are used to pour scorn at the capitalist society of the time. However, Gay's work had drawn its music from contemporary operatic tunes, ballads and folk songs. On the other hand, Weill's opera is written in a jazz inspired idiom.

Die Dreigroschenoper
Music **Kurt Weill** • Libretto **Bertolt Brecht**

First Performance **31ˢᵗ August 1928, at the Berlin Schiffbauerdamm Theatre**

Although some of the music is rather harsh, generally it is quite tuneful, possessing a German cabaret 'Songspiel' style that is strongly nostalgic and deeply moving. This tends to mollify Brecht's politically motivated, heavily sarcastic and astringent text. In fact, the work proved to be an immediate popular success. When it was first staged in New York in 1933, it had already been shown ten thousand times in Europe, having been performed in no less than eighteen different languages.

In spite of its international success, there remains a real problem in staging the work, which calls for singing actors rather than operatic stars. Nevertheless, it requires actors with voices capable of meeting the demands of Weill's 1920's German cabaret style music. Consequently, the choice of appropriate performers is limited, thus making a cast with all the right attributes not easy to find. This is in spite of the fact that the action is discontinuous to a degree that some songs can be independently raised or lowered in pitch, in order to suit a singer deemed to be essential for a particular role.

The artist's chosen scene depicts Jenny, a prostitute and former lover of Macheath, now turned kitchen maid, washing glasses in a dingy little brothel bar. She is imagining herself becoming the lover of a powerful pirate, and in consequence respected and feared by the clients who at present take her for granted and even despise her...

JENNY

"Meine Herren, heute sehen Sie mich
Gläser abwaschen
Und ich mache das Bett für jeden.
Und Sie geben mir einen Penny,
Und ich bedanke mich schnell
Und Sie sehen meine Lumpen
Und dies lumpige Hotel
Und Sie wissen nicht, mit wem Sie reden.
Und Sie wissen nicht, mit wem Sie reden.
Aber eines Tags wird ein Geschrei
Sein am Hafen
Und man fragt:
'Was ist das für ein Geschrei?'
Und man wird mich lächeln
Sehn bei meinen Gläsern
Und man fragt:
'Was lächelt die dabei?'
Und ein Schiff mit acht Segeln
Und mit fünfzig Kanonen
Wird liegen am Kai."

"Gentlemen, today you see me
washing glasses
and for each one I am making the beds.
And you give me a penny
and I thank you at once
and you see my rags
and this shabby hotel
and you do not know to whom you're talking
And you do not know to whom you're talking.
But one day there'll be a shout
by the harbour,
and you'll ask:
'What is this shouting for?'
And you'll see me
smiling by my glasses.
And you'll ask:
'Why is she smiling now?'
And a ship with eight sails
and with fifty cannons
will be lying at the quay."

The Rake's Progress
Music **Igor Stravinsky** • Libretto **W.H. Auden & Chester Kallman**

First Performance **11th September 1951, at the Teatro La Fenice, Venice**

The inspiration for this opera came to Stravinsky when he saw Hogarth's paintings at the Chicago Art Institute in 1947. The last picture, with its mental asylum scene, particularly impressed him and he started composition in December of that year, even before receiving the libretto. The opera was completed in the spring of 1951 and the première staged later that year in Venice, with the La Scala orchestra and chorus, conducted by the composer.

The story relates the adventures of the lazy and weak-willed Tom Rakewell. Informed by Shadow, the Devil in disguise, that he has inherited a fortune, he is enticed to leave his fiancée, Anne, for a life of pleasure and debauchery in a London brothel. The Devil promises to serve him pending repayment after one year and a day. However, Tom is soon bored with this and is urged by Shadow to free himself from pleasure as well as duty by marrying a grotesque 'bearded lady' artist. This too proves to be a disaster.
Meanwhile the loyal Anne tries unsuccessfully to persuade him to mend his ways. Eventually, the day of reckoning arrives. Due to a combination of extravagance and poor investments, Tom is bankrupt, with creditors closing in on him. The Devil takes him to a graveyard and explains it's his soul he wants and not his money. However, Tom succeeds in cheating death by correctly guessing three cards the Devil cuts for him. Furious at losing his prey, the Devil makes him go insane. Confined to an asylum, he is visited by Anne for the last time. She sweetly puts him to sleep, but he dies of grief when he wakes up to discover she has left. The opera ends with the five principals, including Anne's father, singing a moral to the audience.

The Rake's Progress borrows some ideas from previous operas. The pact-with-the-Devil 'Faust' connection is obvious, as is that of 'Carmen', 'La Fanciulla del West' and Tchaikovsky's 'Queen of Spades' in the card game. Also, the final moral bears comparison to a similar ending in 'Don Giovanni'. Indeed, its detractors have unfairly dismissed the work as a 'pastiche'. That the opera has been composed in a Mozart idiom is an accepted fact due to the composer's own admission. A harpsichord is employed to accompany some of the recitatives and is used to particular effect in the graveyard scene. However, all this was done to make the eighteenth century action more realistic. Moreover, every generation has borrowed from and built on what has been achieved before and this is no exception; it is not avant-garde but is modern nonetheless, and Stravinsky through and through. Aided by a superlative libretto, the opera has proved immensely successful so far. Only time will tell whether its place in the operatic repertoire will be permanent or otherwise.

The collage represents the second scene in Act I. Tom has just been introduced to the brothel. Mother Goose the hostess, and Shadow the disguised Devil, are in the process of initiating him into the business. For a moment Tom has doubts. So he is given more wine...

MOTHER GOOSE
"More wine, love?"

RAKEWELL
"Let me go."

SHADOW
"Are you afraid?"

(AS THE CUCKOO CLOCK COOS ONE, RAKEWELL RISES.)

RAKEWELL
"Before it is too late."

SHADOW
"Wait."

(SHADOW MAKES A SIGN AND THE CLOCK TURNS BACKWARD AND COOS TWELVE.)

"See. Time is yours.
The hours obey your pleasure.
Fear not. Enjoy.
You may repent at leisure."

(RAKEWELL SITS DOWN AGAIN AND DRINKS WILDLY.)

Composed over a two-year period, Korngold's third opera is probably his masterpiece, thanks to a combination of an originally managed plot and some inspired music.

The action centres round Paul's inner struggle between the memory of his dead wife, Marie and his love for a young, vivacious dancer, Marietta, who greatly resembles her. In the whole of the second and most of the third act, a prolonged dream sequence of nearly an hour sees the conflict intensify. Here, the girl uses her resemblance to Marie in order to step up her efforts to seduce Paul, who, at the same time increasingly desires, yet repudiates her. The climax takes place as the dream shifts from a desolate quay in Bruges back to Paul's house. Here, Marietta adorns a plaid of Marie's hair, which Paul had jealously preserved in a glass showcase. The man can take no more and enraged, strangles the girl with the plaid. Promptly, the vision ends and Paul returns to reality; the hair is in the case, untouched. Presently, Marietta is announced, but he ignores her and she leaves. Paul now realises he was attracted to the girl only because of her similarity to his wife. Indeed, the past can't be brought back and at his friend Frank's suggestion he prepares to leave the city of death and his past behind.

"Brav so. Machs nu recht toll!
Gibts Sekt?
Wollt ihr bei mir gedeckt?
Doch nein, hier draussen –
Das ist neu!"

"Die kunst ist frei"

"Schach Brügge!
Und Schach der dumpfen Lüge!"

MARIETTA
"Bravo! Do it impressively!
Is there any wine?
Shall we have it at my place?
But no, let's stay here, outside;
that is different!"

THE COUNT
"Art is free"

(FRITZ HAS FETCHED A BASKET OF SPARKLING WINE AND GLASSES FROM THE BOAT AND SIGHS LANGUISHINGLY AT MARIETTA. VICTORIA POURS AND DISTRIBUTES THE GLASSES. ALL IS DONE IN AN UNREAL DANCE SEQUENCE.)

MARIETTA
"Down with Bruges!
And a curse on its false image!"

Die Tote Stadt Music **Erich Korngold** • Libretto **Julius and Erich Korngold (pseudonym Paul Schott)**

First Performance **4ᵗʰ December 1920, simultaneously at the Stadttheater, Hamburg and the Opernhaus, Cologne**

The music is reminiscent of Richard Strauss with a number of Puccini-like touches and is impassioned throughout. Nevertheless, a number of highlights are worth noting. Paul's narrative in Act I where he tells Frank about Marietta is a superb mixture of lyrical contemplation and passionate exhilaration. Also in the first act, Marietta's beautiful aria 'Glück, das mir verblieb', is skilfully turned into an equally endearing duet as the tenor joins in. In Act II, Marietta is serenaded in a lovely baritone aria, which is embellished at the end by an offstage soprano chorus. The third act boasts a marvellous passage for soprano and children's chorus. Finally, a modified reprise of 'Glück, das mir verblieb', sung by Paul, concludes the opera in masterly fashion.

The picture depicts the dream vision scene in the second act. Paul is hiding behind a tree. A boat bearing Marietta and her fellow actors and dancers arrives along the canal. They alight with a case of wine, then drink and make merry...

Der Fliegende Holländer
Music **Richard Wagner** • Libretto **Richard Wagner**

First Performance **2nd January 1843, at the Royal Saxon Court theatre, Dresden**

Wagner had originally intended the Flying Dutchman to be a one-act curtain raiser to a new ballet, to be composed by himself, for the Paris Opéra. It is our good fortune that the scheme didn't materialise. To Wagner, in financial difficulties at the time, this was a severe blow, but it had the effect of his rewriting the work and adding both length and depth to it. It was turned into a full-scale opera in its own right and eventually performed at Dresden, but with limited success.

It appears that Wagner had still intended the opera to be in a single act, with each part following the previous one without an interval. However, the composer then opted for a three-act version and in none of his subsequent major revisions of 1846, 1852 and 1860 did he revert to his original intention. A recent trend of combining the three acts into one seems to be based on a critical edition vogue rather than a more substantial reason.

It is said that Der Fliegende Holländer is Wagner's first mature work. Certainly, it was the first step towards his movement of eliminating operatic numbers and instead creating a synthesis of words and music involving the use of leitmotifs, that is, musical themes used to identify a character, event, idea or feeling which would recur throughout a work.

An interesting point is that in 1840 there was a period when Wagner was working on his previous opera Rienzi and the Flying Dutchman at the same time. He was able to do this successfully in spite of the fact that the former work still belonged to the old school in which idiom he was still composing and yet rejecting in the latter opera. The question is how could he change his style so immediately? There are a number of factors that made this possible. Primarily, Wagner was much more deeply touched by the suggestive and mysterious world of myth and legend than by down to earth historical subjects. Also, he had just escaped from his creditors in Riga in a clandestine and hair-raising manner. His journey to England (en route to Paris) by sea, had taken him through some very rough weather in a small ship. This, together with his passage through the Norwegian fjords, had left a lasting impression on him. Lastly his lack of success in finding a lady companion who could communicate and share his musical experiences with him had somewhat embittered him. All these had the effect of enabling him to associate deeply with the Dutchman, a man condemned to roam the seas until the day of judgement, unless delivered by a woman who would love and be faithful to him forever.

Musically, the Flying Dutchman is clearly a gigantic step forward from Rienzi. However, dramatically the opera still retains some traditional elements.

The strange and unreal natures of the Dutchman and of Senta, the girl who dies to redeem him, must not let one forget the practical everyday world of Daland and Eric, the other two main characters in the work. It can be argued that Der Fliegende Holländer is essentially a transition between styles, a transition that would become complete with Wagner's next opera, Tannhäuser.

The picture relates to the beginning of Act III. The Norwegian and Dutch ships are anchored side by side. The Norwegian sailors are drinking and making merry. Girls arrive, carrying baskets of food and drink. In sinister contrast to this happiness, the Dutch ship is shrouded in unnatural darkness and deathly silence...

Norwegian Sailors
(Drinking.)

"Steuermann, lass die Wacht!	*"Steersman, leave your watch!*
Steuermann, her zu uns!	*Steersman, come with us!*
Ho! He! Je! Ha!	*Ho! Hey! Ye! Ha!*
Hisst die Segel auf! Anker fest! Steuermann, her!	*Hoist the sails! Anchor fast! Steersman, here!*
Fürchten weder Wind noch bösen Strand,	*We fear no wind nor treacherous coast.*
Wollen heute mal recht lustig sein!	*Today we'll be just merry!*
Jeder hat sein Mädel auf dem Land,	*Each has ashore his girl,*
Herrlichen Tabak und guten Branntewein!	*Grand tobacco and good brandy!*
Hussassahe! Klipp' und Sturm drauss' –	*Hussassahey! Rocks and storms outside –*
Jollohohe! Lachen wir aus!	*Yollohohey! We laugh at them*
Hussassahe! Segel ein! Anker fest!	*Hussassahey! Furl sails! Anchor fast!*
Klipp' und Sturm lachen wir aus!	*Rocks and storms, we laugh at them!*
Steuermann, lass die Wacht!	*Steersman, leave your watch!*
Steuermann, her zu uns!	*Steersman, come with us!*
Ho! He! Je! Ha!	*Ho! Hey! Ye! Ha!*
Steuermann, her, trink mit uns!	*Steersman, here, drink with us!*
Ho! He! Je! Ha! Klipp' und Sturm, he!	*Ho! Hey! Ye! Ha! Rocks and storms, hey!*
Sind vorbei, he!	*Are over, hey!*
Hussahe! Hallohe! Hussahe!	*Hussahey! Hallohey! Hussahey!*
Steuermann! Ho!	*Steersman! Ho!*
Her, komm und trink mit uns!"	*Here, come and drink with us!"*

(They drink and dance...)

Rossini composed the opera William Tell at the age of thirty-seven. He was still comparatively young and had already produced nearly forty stage works and yet having written this, his masterpiece, he abandoned the operatic scene and composed very little else in the second half of his life. Various reasons have been suggested for this, ill health and his state of having already attained financial security for life, among others. Probably, it was a combination of factors that caused this strange turnabout of events. The capricious nature of the man himself, as typified by the mood that is prevalent in much of his music, is another possible cause.

Guillaume Tell
Music **Gioacchino Rossini** • Libretto **Étienne de Jouy, Hippolyte Bis & Armand Marrast**

First Performance **3rd August 1829, at the Opéra, Paris**

The opera relates the drama surrounding Tell's leading the successful uprising of the Swiss nation against the Habsburg domination in the thirteenth century. It is a powerful dramatic work in which the aria takes a secondary position to some strong declamatory recitative and much fine choral writing. Indeed, the chorus, representing the Swiss people, whose armed insurrection is bubbling beneath the surface, takes a central role in the work. Also, the title part is given to a baritone and not a tenor. Moreover, in order to gain authenticity, the composer utilised Swiss sources in writing the music. All these factors certainly make it the least Italian of all Rossini's operas. The presence of some very fine ballet music in the work emphasises the true nature of this composition; that of French grand opera at its best, composed by an Italian! The strong ballet tradition in France meant that the French were very favourably disposed to the insertion of dance into opera. Naturally, in order to gain favour with the establishment, Rossini had been happy to oblige...

The scene in question takes place in the first act. Here, the most venerated member of the community, the old shepherd-sage, Melchthal, has just acted as officiator at a ceremony at which three bridal couples are to be blessed. The couples sing and dance and the general atmosphere is one of festivity... Although wine is not mentioned in the libretto, one presumes it would have been present in liberal amounts!...

"Hyménée, ta journée
Fortunée luit pour nous.
Ton beau jour luit pour nous, etc.
Des couronnes que tu donnes,
Ces époux sont jaloux.
D'allégresse, de tendresse,
Leur jeunesse s'embellit, etc.
Sur nos têtes
Les tempêtes sont muettes, etc.
Tout nous dit –
Hyménée, ta journée, etc.
Par tes flammes dans nos âmes
Tu proclames notre espoir;
Ton ivresse joint sans cesse
La tendresse au devoir, etc.
Hyménée, ta journée, etc.
...Ces époux sont jaloux."

YOUNG PEOPLE
(DANCING.)

"Hymen, your happy day
dawns for us.
Your glorious day dawns for us, etc.
These couples are envious,
of the crowns that you give.
Their youth grows in beauty,
with joy and tenderness, etc
Over our heads
the tempests are dumb, etc.
Everything tells us –
Hymen, your happy day, etc.
Through your flames in our souls
you proclaim our hope;
your rapture increasingly joins
tenderness to duty, etc.
Hymen, your happy day, etc.
...these couples are envious."

C omposed in less than two months, Bellini's seventh opera is the first showing the composer's fully mature style.

Written for two of the greatest singers of the day, Giuditta Pasta and Giovanni Rubini, the original score was pitched at a high level. Subsequent modifications resulted in much of the tenor part being lowered, as can be seen in the now generally performed Ricordi score. For example, the aria 'Prendi, l' anel ti dono' is now sung one note below the original version interpreted by Rubini. Bellini composed other operas for each of the two singers but they never again appeared together in one of his works. It is significant that the première and subsequent performances were so enormously successful that they have been described as the highest point of nineteenth century Italian opera.

La Sonnambula   Music **Vincenzo Bellini** • Libretto **Felice Romani**

First Performance **6ᵗʰ March 1831, at the Teatro Carcano, Milan**

The theme of the work, a girl found in a compromising position because of her sleep-walking, was a favourite of the time. Many operas have been composed on this idea, but none remotely as successful. In the present case all ends happily as the somnambulism is discovered and all doubts regarding Amina's virtuosity are dispelled. She is able to marry her fiancé, who had earlier repudiated her.

Apart from the tenor's cavatina mentioned above, there are many numbers of great beauty. Of particular note are the Soprano's brilliant cabaletta in the aria 'Sovra il sen la man mi posa', sung against a choral background and 'Son geloso del zefiro errante', a duet in which the principals unite in a closely knit vocal coloratura. The sleepwalking aria 'Ah! Mi credea mirarti' is yet another beautifully written masterpiece in a score full of delicately melodic music. Strong dramatic declamation is absent in the work, in keeping with its lyrical sweetness and idyllic pastoral nature.

La Sonnambula has, throughout its existence, been a major vehicle for many famous prima donnas. Pasta apart, Maria Malibran, Jenny Lind, Giuseppina Strepponi, Adelina Patti, Luisa Tetrazzini, Amelita Galli Curci, Toti Dal Monte, Maria Callas, Renata Scotto and Joan Sutherland have all been closely associated with the role of Amina, Bellini's captivating heroine.

In the picture, Count Rodolfo, the village Lord, has returned after a very long absence. He is entertained at the local inn by Lisa the hostess (who is jealous of Amina). She has recognised the Count and makes him feel at home...

COUNT RODOLFO

"Davver non mi dispiace
D'essermi qui fermato: il luogo è ameno,
L'aria eccellente, gli uomini cortesi,
Amabili le donne oltre ogni cosa.
Quella giovane sposa
È assai leggiadra...e quella ostessa?
È un po' ritrosa; ma mi piace anch'essa.
Eccola: avanti, avanti,
Mia bella albergatrice."

"Indeed, I'm not sorry
for having stopped here: the place is agreeable,
the air is excellent, the men are courteous,
above all else the women are amiable.
That young bride
is very pretty...and that hostess?
She is a little shy; but I like her too.
Here she is: come in, come in,
my lovely innkeeper."

LISA

"Ad informarmi
Veniva io stessa se l'appartamento
Va a genio al signor Conte."

"I came in person
to ensure that the apartment
is to his Lordship's satisfaction."

Tannhäuser

Music **Richard Wagner** • Libretto **Richard Wagner**

First Performance **19ᵗʰ October 1845, at the Hoftheater, Dresden**

Wagner's fifth opera marks an important point in the composer's career. For the first time he uses a teutonic and knightly hero as his main protagonist, a trend continued more or less in all his subsequent works. At the same time, the standard style of composition incorporating traditional set pieces has been pretty well abandoned. Instead, Wagner uses long and complex scenic units, that is, vast tracts of continuous flowing music. These are linked by recurring leitmotifs that impart a sense of symphonic unity to the work.

This new style of composition set the path for future operas. The old traditions never recovered from the influence of Wagner's style. It is true that the best of the older works are still being performed and doubtless will continue to be so. However modern operatic composition is heavily influenced by Wagner's ideals, which continue to have a lasting effect up to this day.

The opera represents the conflict between love that is sensual on the one hand and pure and virtuous on the other. The action takes place in the Wartburg in Germany in the 13th Century. At this time, the Landgraves of the Thuringian Valley were lovers of poety and music and held frequent singing contests at which troubadour knights, the 'Minnesingers', came to compete. Tannhäuser is a minstrel knight who for one year has given himself up to lustful pleasures at the court of Venus in the Venusberg. Eventually, sated and tired of these physical delights, he repents and aided by an appeal to the Virgin returns to the outside world. There he takes part in a singing contest for the hand of Elisabeth, the Landgrave's niece. The theme of the song is to be love and at this point Tannhäuser's contribution, a sensuous praise of the profane love for Venus, betrays his past. The other knights try to attack him, but he is protected by Elisabeth, who is deeply in love with him.

Tannhäuser is now forced to undertake a pilgrimage to Rome in order to seek expiation from the Pope, and although Elisabeth prays for his forgiveness, he returns without absolution. Repudiated by all he prepares to go back to the Venusberg. Meanwhile Elisabeth dies of a broken heart. Her selfless love and Tannhäuser's self sacrifice by throwing himself on her bier and dying with her, finally redeems him. At the cost of death, the sacred has won over the profane.

The collage depicts Tannhäuser in the Venusberg at the beginning of the opera. The Wartburg can be seen in the distance.
The Nymphs and the Sirens dance. Only Venus and Tannhäuser take no part...

(SIRENS.)

"Naht euch dem Strande!
Naht euch dem Lande,
Wo in den Armen
Glühender Liebe
Selig Erbarmen
Still'eure Triebe!"

"Approach the beach!
Draw near the land,
where in the arms
of glowing love
blessed compassion
will ease your cares!"

(LATER, TANNHAUSER EXPRESSES HIS DOUBTS...)

TANNHÄUSER

"Dank deiner Huld!
Gepriesen sei dein Lieben!
Beglückt für immer, wer bei dir geweilt!
Ewig beneidet, wer mit warmen Trieben
In deinen Armen Götterglut geteilt!
Entzückend sind die Wunder deines Reiches,
Die Zauber aller Wonnen atm'ich hier;
Kein Land der weiten Erde bietet gleiches,
Was sie besitzt, scheint leicht entbehrlich dir.
Doch ich aus diesen ros'gen Düften
Verlange nach des Waldes Lüften,
Nach unsres Himmels klarem Blau,
Nach unsrem frischen Grün der Au',
Nach unsrer Vöglein liebem Sange,
Nach unsrer Glocken trautem Klange.
Aus deinem Reiche muss ich fliehn—
O Königin, Göttin! Lass mich ziehn!"

"Thanks be to your grace!
Praised be your love!
Happy forever is he who dwells with you!
Eternally fortunate who with warm excitement
savours godlike pleasure in your arms!
The wonders of your realm are delightful,
and here I breathe the magic of all pleasures;
no country in the wide earth offers such bliss,
and all your riches flow in excess.
Yet here I languish amidst the scent of roses,
longing for the clear air of the forest,
the clear blue of our earthly sky,
the fresh green of our meadows,
the dear song of our little birds,
the comforting peal of our bells.
Out of your realm must I go—
O Queen, Goddess! Let me depart!"

Der Freischutz is possibly the only German opera of the first half of the nineteenth century to have been continuously included in the standard repertory. This is easily explained by the inspired music in this early romantic work. The opera is strongly nationalistic, both musically and dramatically, and embodies a style of composition well ahead of its time, embarking on a path which Wagner was to follow to fulfilment some twenty years later. A particular point worth mentioning is the atmosphere evoked in the Wolf Glen scene, especially at the climax, when the magic bullets are being cast.

This is a truly expressive rendering of the gruesome and macabre, and has hardly been bettered by any other composer right up to the present day.

Der Freischutz

Music **Carl Maria von Weber**
Libretto **Johann Friedrich Kind**
First Performance **18th June 1821,
at the Schauspielhaus, Berlin**

The story runs as follows. The head forester in the service of the ruling Prince wishes to give his loyal assistant, Max, the hand of his daughter Agathe and also appoint him as his successor. The Prince agrees but the young man is required to undergo a severe shooting test. Max, normally an excellent shot, misses everything in a preliminary competition and in despair, is enticed by the malicious Kaspar to go with him into the wolf's glen where they can cast seven magic bullets together. The first six will find their mark but in return, the seventh will belong to and be guided by the Devil. The point is that Kaspar also has his eye on the girl and in previously casting these bullets, has already sold his soul to hell. He now hopes, by this ruse, to get Max to replace him as the Devil's victim.

At the shooting contest, the first six bullets, three fired by each Max and Kaspar, have found their mark. The seventh bullet is to be unwittingly fired by Max. He aims it at Agathe whom the Devil has caused him to mistake for a dove. However, Agathe is protected by heaven through the intervention of a hermit and it is Kaspar who falls, mortally wounded, to be claimed by hell.

The collage scene depicts a drinking toast offered by Kaspar to Max just before sealing the agreement to go into the wolf's glen. Max refuses to join Kaspar in the coarse song...

"Hier im ird'schen Jammertal
Wär' doch nichts als Plack und Qual,
Trüg' der Stock nicht Trauben:
Darum bis zum letzten Hauch
Setz' ich auf Gott Bacchus' Bauch
Meinen festen Glauben!
Du musst aber auch mitsingen."

"Lass mich!"

"Jungfer Agathe soll leben!
Wer die Gesundheit seiner
Braut ausschlüge,
Wär' doch wahrlich ein Schuft!"

"Eins ist eins und drei sind drei!
Drum addiert noch zweierlei
Zu dem Saft der Reben;
Kartenspiel und Würfellust,
Und ein Kind mit runder Brust
Hilft zum ew'gen Leben!"

"Wie kannst du mir zumuten,
In so etwas einzustimmen?"

"Unser Herr Fürst soll leben!
Wer nicht dabei ist,
Wär' ein Judas!"

"Ohne dies Trifolium
Gibt's kein wahres Gaudium
Seit dem ersten Übel.
Fläschchen sei mein Abc,
Würfel, Karten, Katherle meine Bilderbibel."

KASPAR

"Here in this earthly misery
there would be nothing but exasperation and pain,
if the vine were not to bear a cluster;
so until my last breath
I'll put my faith
on God Bacchus' belly!
But you must sing with me."

MAX

"Leave me alone!"

KASPAR

"Here's to Mistress Agathe!
The man who would refuse
to drink his own bride's health
would be a scoundrel indeed!

"One is one and three is three!
So add two other things
to the juice of the vine.
Cards and the pleasure of dice,
and a girl with rounded breast
assist one to eternal life!"

MAX

"How can you expect me to join you
in something like that?"

KASPAR

"Here's to the Prince our master!
He who doesn't participate in this
would be a Judas!

"Without this trio
there's been no real merrymaking
since the primal Fall.
The bottle is my ABC,
dice, cards and kitty my illustrated bible."

Les Contes d'Hoffmann

Music **Jacques Offenbach** • Libretto **Jules Barbier**

First Performance **10ᵗʰ February 1881, at the Opéra-Comique, Paris**

Having obtained great fame in writing pleasant and popular operettas with incredible rapidity, Offenbach became determined to win recognition as a 'serious opera' composer and so the idea of Les Contes d'Hoffmann was born. Starting in 1877, he found the task a demanding one, particularly as he was concurrently still writing operettas as a rapid source of much needed income. Tragically, he died in 1880, leaving the work unfinished, a fact that was to have serious repercussions in the future.
Although completed by Ernest Guiraud, the opera has been subjected to drastic changes of all kinds throughout its hundred-year existence. Significantly, the most authoritative versions so far were not produced until the late twentieth century. These were by Fritz Oeser in 1976 and Michael Kaye in 1988. Indeed, up to this day no definitive edition exists and alterations are still made. In particular, the second and third acts are often interchanged.

The plot is based on an 1851 play in which the poet E.T.A.Hoffmann, appearing as a participant in the action, narrates a number of unhappy past love experiences.
In the opera he relates and relives the stories of three loves while awaiting the arrival of his latest conquest, Stella, a prima donna who represents a combination of the others.

The opera opens in a German tavern where Hoffmann tells his tale. This is the prologue. Each past love experience is represented by one act of the action. Olympia, a mechanical doll, which the poet mistakes for the inventor's daughter, is seen in the first act, Antonia, a singer, in the second and Giulietta, a Venetian courtesan, in the third. The arrival of Stella from her triumph in the theatre and her departure with Lindorf, Hoffmann's present love-rival, forms the epilogue.

In order to emphasise the connection between the four ladies, the same singer (a Soprano) is intended to take all four roles, just as one Baritone should sing the part of all four rivals (Coppelius, Dr.Miracle, Dapertutto and Lindorf) who are similarly linked.

Although celebrated for his operettas, Offenbach had composed some fairly serious works before. Nevertheless 'Les Contes d'Hoffmann' is his greatest achievement, both musically and dramatically. It is significant, however, that some of the most engaging musical numbers have a distinctly operetta-like flavour, reminding one of some of his most popular lighter works.

The collage shows the beginning of the epilogue, together with an image of the Venetian Giulietta episode. In the tavern, Hoffmann and his companions are drinking and smoking. The poet has just finished recounting his tales. Stella, fresh from her triumph in the theatre, is about to appear...

HOFFMANN

"Voilà, mes amis, quelle fut l'histoire de mes trois amours. Buvons!"

"There, my friends, that was the history of my three loves. Let's drink!"

NICKLAUSSE

"Un dernier coup, messieurs. A Olympia, à Antonia, à Giulietta!"

"A final toast, gentlemen. To Olympia, Antonia and Giulietta!"

STUDENTS

"Vivat!"

"Hurrah!"

(APPLAUSE OFFSTAGE.)

LUTHER

La représentation est terminée, messieurs."

"The performance is over, gentlemen."

NICKLAUSSE

"Pardieu! C'est la diva qu'on acclame!"

"Heavens! That's the applause for the diva!"

LINDORF

"A moi, la belle."

"That beauty's mine!"

(HE GOES OUT.)

HOFFMANN

"Oui, Stella, sous les trois aspects de sa vie! Artiste, courtisane et jeune fille!"

"Yes, Stella, under the three aspects of her life: artist, courtesan and young girl!"

NICKLAUSSE

"Buvons à cette aimable synthèse!"

"Let's drink to that pleasant mixture!"

(THE STUDENTS BURST OUT LAUGHING.)

Faust

Music **Charles Gounod** • Libretto **Jules Barbier & Michel Carré**

First Performance **19ᵗʰ March 1859, at the Théâtre-Lyrique, Paris**

Although the idea of composing a work based on Goethe's Faust had come to him in 1839, nothing materialised until sixteen years later when he met his future librettists. Michel Carré had already written a three-act play, 'Faust and Marguerite' and it was on this that Jules Barbier, with Carré's help, based the Gounod opera's libretto. The composition was completed in 1858 and the première took place early in the following year.

Barbier had expanded Carré's play and had made his libretto very close to the Marguerite episode of Goethe's original work. However the opera turned out to be four-and-a-half hours long and Léon Carvalho, the director of the Théâtre Lyrique, insisted on extensive cuts before the opening night, thereby mauling Barbier's excellent text and weakening the work dramatically. Further cuts and modifications (the ballet music was added in 1869) have led to a large number of different versions with no definitive one in existence. Unfortunately, Gounod's original score is unavailable, so the uncertainty cannot be resolved.

Although Faust has the title role in Gounod's work, the character of Marguerite is far more interesting and it is around her that the opera revolves. She is portrayed with very real emotions: innocence, sensuality, motherly love, remorse and nobility. These are all displayed during the course of the action. On the other hand the character of Faust is rather stolid while Mephistopheles is hardly a serious devil.

Gounod's opera is one of at least four on the subject, the others being by Louis Spohr ('Faust',1813.), Hector Berlioz ('La damnation de Faust', 1846.) and Arrigo Boito ('Mefistofele', 1875). The Spohr opera bears hardly any resemblance to Goethe's work while that by Boito is the most faithful. Gounod's composition, although it misses the essential point of the redemption of Faust, is a fine dramatic work. It may not possess the interest of the principal male roles shown in the Boito opera, but does not suffer from the disjointed quality of the latter, and its music is more consistently inspired.

The collage scene takes place at the end of Act I or in Act II, depending on the version of the opera. Mephistopheles has just tasted some wine given to him by the townspeople. Finding it poor he uses his powers to offer some of his own...

WAGNER
(OFFERING MEPHISTOPHELES A GLASS.)

"Nous ferez-vous l'honneur
De trinquer avec nous?"

"Will you do us the honour
of making a toast with us?"

MEPHISTOPHELES
"With pleasure!"

"Volontiers!"

(MEPHISTOPHELES SEIZES WAGNER'S HAND AND CARRIES OUT SOME PALM READING. HE ALSO READS THE PALMS OF SIEBEL AND MARGUERITE'S BROTHER, VALENTINE. HE THEN TAKES THE CUP FROM WAGNER AND DRINKS.)

MEPHISTOPHELES
"To your health!
Ugh!...Your wine's awful!
Allow me to offer you
some from my cellar!"

"A votre santé!
Peuh!...que ton vin est mauvais!
Permettez-moi de vous
En offrir de ma cave!"

(STRIKING THE BARREL, SURMOUNTED BY A FIGURE OF BACCHUS, WHICH SERVES AS A SIGN FOR THE INN.)

"Holà! Seigneur Bacchus! à boire!"

"There! Sir Bacchus! To drink!"

(TO THE TOWNSPEOPLE, AS WINE POURS FROM THE BARREL.)

"Approchez-vous!
Chacun sera servi selon ses goûts!"

"Draw near!
Each will be served according to his taste!"

(RAISING HIS GLASS.)

"A la santé que tout à l'heure vous portiez,
Mes amis, à Marguerite!"

"To the health of whom you were drinking to
just now, Marguerite!"

Undine
Music **Albert Lortzing** • Libretto **Albert Lortzing**

First Performance **21ˢᵗ April 1845, at the Magdeburg National Theatre**

The ancient water nymph legend seems to appear in the operatic world in two basic versions. One is of the girl, who jilted, drowns herself, turns into a water spirit and spends her existence in taking revenge on all men. Her victims are made to drown as punishment. The other is of the water spirit who becomes mortal in order to experience the love of a man, is betrayed and drowns as a consequence, reverting to a nymph. She then exacts similar revenge on her former lover.

Many composers have written operas on one or other of the above. The best known, Lortzing apart, are E.T.A.Hoffmann ('Undine',1816), Aleksandr Dargomyzhsky ('Rusalka', 1856), Max Bruch ('Die Loreley',1863), Alfredo Catalani ('Lorelei', 1880) and Antonin Dvorak ('Rusalka', 1901). Tchaikovsky started composing an opera called Undine in 1869, but the work remained unfinished and was destroyed by the composer.

Lortzing's work, as Hoffmann's, follows the second of the above versions. Undine, a Rhine water sprite longs to become mortal and participate in human love. This is allowed to happen but she is betrayed and the fatal course of the events, which would destroy her and her lover, inexorably takes place...

A master of operatic comedy, Lortzing found himself on foreign ground while composing this romantic tragedy. He undertook the project with uncertainty, making modifications as he went along. Nevertheless he succeeded in presenting the work, musically more complex than any of his previous operas, as a well-structured composition. Undoubtedly the use of leitmotif for particular characters helped him to achieve this. However, either because he wasn't happy with a tragic finale, or because he feared this would be adversely received by the audience, he sweetened the ending by creating a fairy-tale realm beneath the waters where a generous pardon enables Undine and Hugo to be reunited forever. Unfortunately this has the effect of weakening the opera dramatically, which is a pity as there is much fine music to admire in the work.

The picture portrays the penultimate scene of the opera. Hugo and Bertalda's wedding feast is in progress. The clock has just struck the last stroke of midnight...

"Füllt die Pokale!
Fröhlichkeit strahle
Aus jedem Aug',
Aus jeglichem Blick;
Preisend die Schönen
Lasset ertönen
Schallende Lieder
Von Liebesglück."

"Ha, nun erkenn'ich – mein Traum wird wahr –
Du kommst zu richten – nimm mich hin!
Doch lass noch einmal, eh ich sterbe,
Dein lieblich Angesicht mich schaun."

"O holdes Bild, das mich hoch beglückte,
Noch einmal gönne mir die Seligkeit,
Dich liebend zu umfangen."

"Du winkest mir. Ich komme!"

"So lass mich sterbe."

HUGO AND THE CHORUS
"Fill the goblets!
Let gaiety shine
from every eye,
from every glance:
in praise of beauties
let songs resound
with the happiness
of love."

(ALL DRINK, BUT HUGO EXPRESSES ANXIETY AS MIDNIGHT APPROACHES. BERTALDA IS CONCERNED AND ALARMED AT HUGO'S AGITATION. NEVERTHELESS, THE GUESTS TAKE UP THEIR POSITIONS TO DANCE. AS THE CLOCK STRIKES TWELVE, HUGO'S APPREHENSION INCREASES. AT THE TWELFTH STROKE UNDINE APPEARS, VEILED.)

HUGO
"Ah, now I realise my dream was true.
You come in judgement – take me!
But allow me once more, before I die,
to perceive your lovely face."

(UNDINE THROWS BACK HER VEIL.)

"O lovely image, that made me so happy,
grant me once more the bliss
of lovingly embracing you."

(UNDINE HOLDS OUT HER ARMS.)

"You beckon me. I come!"

(HE HURRIES INTO HER ARMS.)

"Now let me die."

(EMBRACED, THEY SINK BENEATH THE WATERS THAT HAVE RUSHED INTO THE PALACE. THE COMPANY FLEES IN TERROR FROM THE RAGING TORRENT.)

Although this remarkable composition is the most famous of all Viennese operettas, its origin is French. Strauss originally planned the work to be an Austrian translation of 'Le Réveillon', an 1872 Parisian vaudeville. However it was soon realised that this would have proved to be too audacious for Austrian audiences of the day. Consequently the more indelicate parts were removed or modified and the names of characters changed. A midnight supper party was, in fact, turned into a Viennese ball.

The plot is based on the revenge of Doctor Falk on his friend Eisenstein, for having once left him to walk home in full daylight from a party, dressed as a bat! Falk convinces Eisenstein to secretly go to a ball given by the Russian Prince Orlofsky. There he meets and flirts with his own wife Rosalinde who has also gone to the ball, but disguised as a Hungarian countess. During this courtship she is able to appropriate her husband's repeater watch, which she later produces unexpectedly at the pay-off scene at the end of the work. Falk's revenge is indeed complete!

Die Fledermaus   Music **Johann Strauss** • Libretto **Carl Haffner & Richard Genée**

First Performance **5th April 1874, at the Theater an der Wien**

Composed in a mere six weeks, the operetta is truly inspired, with an endless array of melodies and catch tunes from start to finish. The lilt and vitality of the music represents the best in Viennese tradition and the work has deservedly gained a permanent place in the full operatic repertoire.

The collage shows the ballroom scene in the second act. Prince Orlofsky explains how he, although bored himself, insists that his guests enjoy themselves. He then turns his attention to drinking...

"Wenn ich mit andern sitz' beim Wein,
Und Flasch' um Flasche leer',
Muss jeder mit mir durstig sein,
Sonst werde grob ich sehr!
Und schenke Glas um Glas ich ein,
Duld'ich nicht Widerspruch.
Nicht leiden kann ich's, wenn sie schrei'n:
'Ich will nicht, hab' genug!'
Wer mir beim Trinken nicht pariert,
Sich zieret wie ein Tropf,
Dem werfe ich ganz ungeniert
Die Flasche an den Kopf.
Und fragen Sie, ich bitte,
(stürzt seinen Wein hinunter)
Ach, meine Herr'n und Damen,
Hier gibt es einen Spass!"

PRINCE ORLOFSKY

"When I sit with others drinking wine,
and empty bottle after bottle,
everybody must be thirsty with me,
or else I become very rude!
And when I pour out glass after glass,
I tolerate no refusal.
I cannot suffer when they cry out:
'No more. I've had enough!'
He who can't keep up with me at drinking
and makes a fuss like a dullard –
I will unceremoniously throw
the bottle at his head.
And if you should ask, I beg you,
(He gulps down his wine.)
Oh, Ladies and Gentlemen,
This is really so amusing!"

Dvě Vdovy

Music **Bedřich Smetana** • Libretto **Emanuel Züngel**

First Performance **27ᵗʰ March 1874, at the Provisional Theatre, Prague**

Having received Züngel's libretto to Jean Pierre Mallefille's play, Smetana began composition of 'The Two Widows' in July 1873, completing the work in January of the following year. Although the opera was fairly successful, the composer decided to improve it by replacing dialogue with recitative, adding two minor characters and making a few changes to the original score. A second première, in 1878, proved an unqualified triumph. Nevertheless, the opera was performed only fifteen times during Smetana's lifetime and became continually plagued by ill-conceived modifications. For example, in a three-act adaptation, the action was restored to the French location of the original play. Happily, the 1878 two-act rendering, with its Czech setting, has been accepted as the definitive version and is the one performed today.

The plot involves two widowed cousins, Karolina, of bright and cheerful disposition and Anežka, who believes that her status will forever exclude her from the pleasures of life. This situation is upset by the arrival on the scene of Ladislav, a young man whom Anežka had been secretly in love with while her husband was alive. Resolutely fighting her inner feelings, she spurns his advances. However, her jealousy is aroused by Karolina, whom she finds wooing Ladislav, a ploy used in order to push her to this very reaction! Anežka confesses her love and the opera ends happily with a banquet to celebrate the engagement between the happy couple.

Apart from the three principals mentioned, the opera includes a second courting couple, two peasants called Toník and Lidunka. Some particularly fine lyrical music accompanies the two scenes where their courtship is featured. Also, Karolina's gamekeeper, Mumlal, a busybody and pompously self-righteous character, is featured in a comic bass role.

The work opens with a lively overture, followed by an equally vivacious chorus. This seems to set the tone for Karolina's aria, 'Samostatně vládnu já,' in which she expresses how her newly obtained independence and power has given her a positive role in life. There are two fine arias for Ladislav, 'Aj, vizte lovce tam,' ('Ah, see the hunter here,') and 'Když zavítá máj,' ('When Maytime arrives,') and an intense heartfelt soliloquy for Anežka, 'Odcházejí spolu k radosti!' ('Seeking pleasure, they've left together!'). However, the opera abounds in superb ensembles. A beautiful quartet in the first act is followed later by an equally splendid duet between Anežka and Ladislav just before her great soliloquy. The final quartet in which Anežka at last surrenders her feelings is truly marvellous. The opera ends with a lively polka and a spirited chorus that honours the happy occasion.

The collage represents the celebration banquet in the finale. The two ladies are seated with Ladislav while the gamekeeper leads the merrymaking...

"Oznamuji slavnou novinu,
Že již pripravili hostinu!"

"Ó, tot' sem s ní!"

"Vy pak po cestě
Rámě podejte své nevěstě!"

"Nevěstě? Dá říc'se slovy,
Jaké nestvůry jsou vdovy?!
Pro ten život světský
Duši dají všecky!"

"Musí nás mít Pán Bůh rád,
Že nás živí napořád!
Vše dobré nám dává,
Radosti popřává,
Nepřátelům brání,
Od zlého nás chrání.
Za zdraví naší pajmámy,
Která se raduje s námi,
Za zdraví celého domu
I pana ženicha k tomu!"

MUMLAL
"I now solemnly announce,
that the festive banquet is prepared!"

KAROLINA
"Oh, serve it here!"

(TO LADISLAV.)
"Now you may offer
your arm to your adored bride!"

MUMLAL
(ASIDE.)
"She said bride? Are there words with which
to say what monsters widows are?!
For all worldly living,
they all give up their souls!"

VILLAGE YOUTH
(MERRILY.)
"Our Lord must surely love us,
because he always sustains us!
He thinks only of our good,
wishes us worldly joy,
protects us from all enemies,
and also from all evil.
Let's drink the health of our lady,
who shares all our joys and pleasures;
let's drink the health of her entire house,
including the brand new bridegroom!"

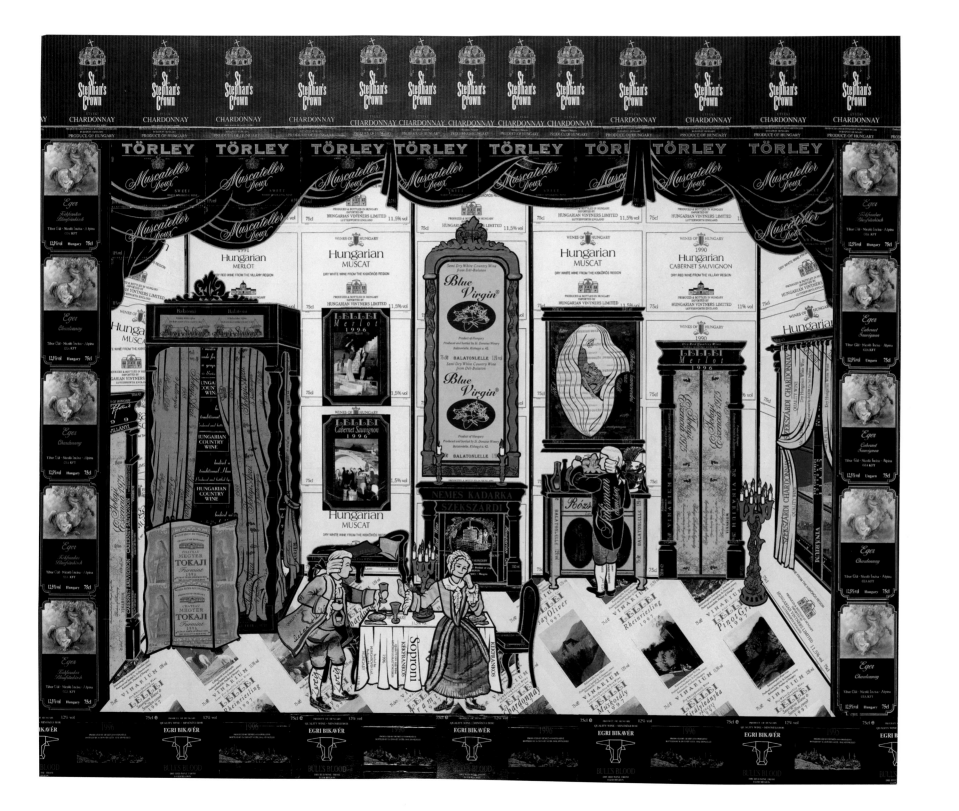

D er Rosenkavalier is Richard Strauss' fifth opera, composed in just less than one and a half years.

In the plot, the young nobleman, Octavian, lover of the Feldmarschallin (Field Marshall's wife), a woman fifteen years his senior, outmanoeuvres the licentious and much older Baron Ochs to win the hand of the young Sophie. The Feldmarschallin sees herself as getting old at thirty-two and realises that her liaison with Octavian cannot last. She imagines herself young again and sees Sophie's position as a reversal of roles, where she herself might have similarly been coerced into a loveless union with a much older man.

Thus, although being a rival to Sophie, she nobly sides with Octavian and ensures he is successful in wooing the girl. The Baron is forced to retreat, frustrated and defeated.

Der Rosenkavalier

Music **Richard Strauss**
Libretto **Hugo von Hofmannstahl**
First Performance **26ᵗʰ January 1911,
at the Königliches Opernhaus, Dresden**

It is clear that the characters of the Feldmarschallin and Octavian are inspired by the Countess and Cherubino in Mozart's 'Marriage of Figaro'. Also, the class-conscious but coarse and lecherous Baron Ochs brings Verdi's 'Falstaff' to mind. Yet, these are the most interesting personages in the work. The Feldmarschallin, in particular, is the most complex and the part has become one of the great soprano roles. The opera can be considered, at least in its conception, as a kind of dramatic pastiche, influenced by a number of sources, literary as well as operatic. It is interesting that the only tenor aria in the opera is itself a pastiche of Mozart's Italian songs.

A first class libretto and Strauss' memorable score result in a superb portrayal of eighteenth century Vienna. The dialogues, with their light chamber music accompaniments are in contrast to and yet blend beautifully with the opulent orchestration that permeates most of the work. Der Rosenkavalier remains Strauss' greatest achievement and maintains a firm foothold in all the major opera houses in the world today.

The picture illustrates the scene at the start of the third act. Ochs has been tricked into a meeting with Octavian who has disguised himself as a chambermaid. Typically, the baron tries to seduce his prey using wine, which Octavian refuses...

"Halt, was woll'n die Maikäfer da?"

BARON
"Wait, what do these busybodies want?"

WAITERS
(AT THE DOOR.)
"To serve, your Grace."

"Servier'n, Euer Gnaden."

BARON
(WAVES THEM AWAY.)
"Don't need anyone."

"Brauch' niemand nicht."

(WHEN THEY DON'T GO, VEHEMENTLY.)
*"You clear out!
My valet here will do the serving.
I myself will pour. Does he understand?"*

*"Packt's Euch!
Servieren wird mein Kammerdiener da.
Einschenken tu' ich selber. Versteht Er?"*

(THE BARON POURS ONE. OCTAVIAN SIPS. THE BARON KISSES OCTAVIAN'S HAND. OCTAVIAN WITHDRAWS THE HAND. THE BARON WAVES TO THE VALET TO LEAVE AND HAS TO REPEAT IT SEVERAL TIMES BEFORE THE SERVANT FINALLY GOES.)

OCTAVIAN
(PUSHING HIS GLASS AWAY.)
"No, no, no, no! I drink no wine."

"Nein, nein, nein, nein! I trink' kein Wein."

BARON
*"Come on, my sweet, what now?
Don't make such a fuss."*

*"Geh, Herzerl, was denn?
Mach' doch keine Faxen."*

OCTAVIAN
"No, no, I'm not staying here."
(JUMPS UP AS IF TO GO.)

"Nein, nein, i bleib' net da"

BARON
(GRABS HIM WITH HIS LEFT HAND.)
"You're making me desperate."

"Sie macht mich deschparat."

OCTAVIAN
*"I already know what you're thinking.
Oh you naughty gentleman!"*

*"I weiss schon, was Sie glaub'n.
O Sie schlimmer Herr!"*

Nozze Istriane
Music **Antonio Smareglia** • Libretto **Luigi Illica**

First Performance **28ᵗʰ March 1895, at the Teatro Comunale, Trieste**

Antonio Smareglia was born in Pola (now Pula) of an Italian father and Croatian mother on 5th May 1854. He took up musical studies at an early age, undergoing most of his training in Vienna and Milan. His first opera, 'Preziosa', was premièred in 1879 and he wrote four more before arriving at the present work, composed in a few months of intense activity between 1893 and 1894. He went on to compose three more, his last opera, 'L'Abisso', dating from 1911, by which time he had been blind for eleven years. He died in the spring of 1929.

Nozze Istriane is, with his penultimate opera, 'Oceania', one of the composer's two most successful works. In the tragic plot, Marussa and Lorenzo are secretly engaged and exchange trinkets as a mutual pledge of love and trust. Unfortunately, the girl's miserly father is persuaded by the scheming Biagio to match his daughter with Nicola, a wealthy young man. Together, they find the token that Lorenzo has given Marussa and have it returned to him with a false message, prompting him to send back the golden heart she gave him. Desperate and feeling betrayed, she consents to wed Nicola, and marriage promises are made. Soon afterwards, however, the conspiracy is discovered and Marussa beckons Lorenzo, informing him of the facts. The couple are reconciled and together decide to enlighten Nicola about the trick used to get her acceptance. The girl begs him to free her from her promise, but he refuses. Lorenzo appears and is killed in the ensuing fight between the two suitors. As the opera ends she curses her father and his fellow conspirator.

The authentic nature of protagonists and plot and also the tragic ending bring the verismo of Mascagni's 'Cavalleria Rusticana' to mind. However, the violent drama that pervades the whole of Mascagni's opera is here replaced by a greater sublety as the events unfold. Also, although the composer shows his Italian background in lyrical passages involving Lorenzo and Marussa, his use of sensitive, profound and elaborate orchestral accompaniment involving sombre harmonies shows a leaning towards Wagnerian ideals. As a subject about his native Istria that was close to his heart, Smareglia gave his best to the work. Yet, perhaps because the man himself as well as his style involved a mixture of cultures, he failed to get the backing of either of the two great Milan publishers, Ricordi and Sonsogno, for any of his works. His operas have been admired far more in Austria and Germany than in Italy, where Nozze Istriane has hardly ever been performed. Happily, this romantic composer, a fine lyricist and excellent orchestrator, is still remembered in his native Istria, where his best works are still occasionally staged.

The picture features the second scene in the first act. Biagio, the local marriage broker, has just spoken to Marussa's father, who is leaning out of a window. Meanwhile, the village youth are drinking at the tavern and admiring the girls as they pass by on their way to church...

BIAGIO
(TOWARDS THE WINDOW.)

"Fate il comodo vostro, fate!"   *"At your convenience!"*

(HE APPROACHES THE YOUNG MEN.)

"Be', giovanotti, a' vespri non andate?"   *"Well, lads, aren't you going to the vespers?"*

YOUNG MEN

"Qui ci sostiamo ad aspettare
Le ragazze che devono passare
E un gotto ne beviamo.
Se ne beve un bicchiere
E le stiamo a guardare;
Così doppio piacere,
È bere ed ammirare."

"We stay here waiting for
the girls who must pass by,
while drinking a mug of wine.
We drink a glass
and watch them pass;
thus it's a double pleasure,
to drink and to admire."

The Bassarids is a singular work in that it was composed to an English libretto by a German permanently living in Italy. The première was sung in German but the libretto is readily available in all three languages.

The opera is one long act, divided into four movements, the third of which is broken up by an intermezzo on the judgement of Calliope as to the relative rights of Venus and Persephine to be accepted as the lover of Adonis. The whole work is indeed imbued in Greek mythology. It relates the story of the Bacchae of Euripides in which Pentheus, the King of Thebes, who believes in one universal good God attainable via human reason, loses his life in his bitter struggle against the resurgence of the cult of Dionysius, characterised by bacchanalian revelries and orgies.

The Bassarids
Music **Hans-Werner Henze** • Libretto **W. H. Auden and Chester Kallman**

First Performance **6ᵗʰ August 1966, at the Grosses Festspielhaus, Salzburg**

The four movements, in symphonic form, are an attempt by Henze, urged by his librettists, to come to terms with the post Wagnerian tradition. The opera marks a deviation from the traditional Italianate operatic forms, which had dominated the composer's previous works. The first movement is in sonata form with marked contrasts between the austere, classical Pentheus music and the sensuous and voluptuous Bassarid orchestration. The second movement is a sequence of baccanalian dances in scherzo form. The third, a slow adagio, is divided into two by the extended intermezzo, while the fourth consists of a long theme that builds up to a grand passacaglia finale.

In spite of the Wagnerian influence, some traditional operatic forms are still present in the arias and ensembles ingrained in the structure of the work. Henze has succeeded, using the symbolism of mythological tragedy, in marrying the conventional operatic forms with his personal style of contemporary music.

In the picture, Pentheus has just asked his prisoner, the disguised Dionysius, to tell him how he came upon his God. Dionysius now relates his story...

STRANGER (DIONYSIUS)

"Ich fand ein Kind, das schlief, schöner
Als je ein Kind ich sah.
Naxos! rief es erwachend.
Naxos! war mein Befehl;
Mein Schiff lief aus."

"I found a child asleep, more beautiful
Than any child I'd seen.
Naxos, he cried awakening.
Naxos, I told my crew
And we set sail."

"Er erwacht und weint';
Naxos ist weit zurück!
Ich war ihr Gefangener.
Naxos ist weit voraus, klang ihr Lachen.
Der Bug stand steil
In der geteilten Welle."

"He woke and wept;
Naxos is far astern!
I was their prisoner.
Naxos is far ahead, they laughed.
The bow stood poised
In the divided wave."

"Reben klommen hoch am Mast
Und banden die Ruder.
Ein Leopard strich um das Deck.
Die Mannschaft sprang wild in die See,
Delphin, nicht Mensch.
Der Gott war überall."

"Vines clambered up the mast
And roped the oars.
A leopard pawed the deck.
The maddened crew leapt in the sea,
Dolphins, not men.
The God was everywhere."

"Die Eichen des Kytheron schwingen.
Ich folge dem Gott, Pentheus. Du auch."

"The oaks of Cytheron sway, sway.
I follow the God, Pentheus. You shall."

Les Troyens
Music **Hector Berlioz** • Libretto **Hector Berlioz**

First Performance   **(Acts III-V only) 4ᵗʰ November 1863, at the Théâtre Lyrique, Paris**
(Acts I-II only) 6ᵗʰ December 1890, at the Grossherzogliches Hoftheater, Karlsruhe
(Full Opera)   6ᵗʰ June 1957, at the Covent Garden Opera House, London

The foundations of Berlioz's masterpiece were laid long before its creation. As a boy he had studied Virgil's Aeneid as part of Latin lessons given to him by his father, whose passion for the subject (Berlioz's Christian name, Hector, is no coincidence!) was quickly passed to his son. One assumes that Berlioz must have toyed with the idea of turning the story into an opera throughout the intervening years. However, since the subject was in contrast to the operatic fashion of the time, he realised that the chance of acceptance, let alone a performance by the Paris Opéra, was very remote, so he continually hesitated to attempt it. At last, a successful oratorio and the prompting of a friend, Princesse Carolyne Sayn-Wittgenstein, were sufficient to allow his burning desire to get the better of him and in 1856 he started on the work. He wrote his own libretto, naturally heavily based on Virgil's epic poem, and in just two years had completed the whole opera.

The huge work is very long, (yet shorter than a number of Wagner's great operas) and is written on a grand scale in two complementing parts. The first relates to the fall of Troy and the second to Aeneas' relationship with Dido, the Queen of Carthage, where he had stopped on his journey towards Italy. In deciding whether or not to perform the work, the Paris Opéra dragged its feet for five long years and eventually Berlioz gave it to a smaller theatre whose resources were inadequate for the task. Fearing another refusal, he accepted the suggestion to stage his opera as two separate works, each conforming to the two parts mentioned above. In actual fact, only the second half was performed and remained the only part the composer ever heard.

This state of affairs continued after Berlioz's death. For nearly ninety years the opera was misrepresented, being divided into two parts and performed as 'La Rose de Troie' and 'Les Troyens a Carthage' on successive nights, or else cut to pieces and performed as a single work in a drastically reduced form. It was not until 1957 that the opera was at last staged as intended with only a few minor cuts. The complete, uncut original was first performed in Glasgow in 1969!

We now know that Les Troyens is a masterpiece of epic proportions. The two halves complement each other. Although they relate to the personal tragedies of two very different women, Cassandra and Dido, the underlying aim, the destiny of the Trojan nation in the birth of Rome, unifies them into a coherent whole. The musical invention is extraordinary and richly varied.

The first part is exciting, almost electrifying, while the second is overwhelming in a lyrical sense. Common melodic motifs run throughout the work. The splendour of Aeneas' vision of the creation of Rome and his burning mission to achieve it is constant throughout; this is the foundation upon which the whole opera is built. Berlioz loved Virgil; he also loved Shakespeare and the love duet in Act IV was inspired by 'The Merchant of Venice'. There are other instances of Shakespeare's influence in the work: Cassandra's thoughts of doom during the crowd's triumphal procession at the end of Act I and the appearance of Hector's ghost at the start of the second act are examples.

The picture shows the scene at the very beginning of the opera. Shown is the site of the abandoned Greek camp on the plains before the city of Troy, with Mount Ida bearing an allegorical vision of the judgement of Paris in the background. The abandoned horse is in the foreground left. The people of Troy are spread over the plain, rejoicing, citizens and soldiers alike; some are drinking. The Royal party is seen in the foreground right. Cassandra is raising her arms in dismay, but the crowd takes no notice and continues to celebrate...

CHORUS OF THE TROJAN PEOPLE

"Ha! Ha!
Après dix ans passés dans nos murailles,
Ah! quel bonheur de respirer
L'air pur des champs,
Que le cri des batailles
Ne va plus déchirer."

"Ha! Ha!
After ten years spent within our walls,
Ah! what delight to breathe
the pure air of the fields,
that will never again
be rent by the shouts of battle."

(YOUNG BOYS AND CHILDREN RUN UP WITH THE REMAINS OF WEAPONS IN THEIR HANDS.)

"Que de débris! – Un fer de lance!
Je trouve un casque! – Et moi, deux javelots!
Voyez, ce bouclier immense!
Il porterait un homme sur les flots!
Quels poltrons que ces Grecs!"

"Look at these remains! – A spearhead!
I've found a helmet! – And I two javelins!
Look at this huge shield!
A man could float on it over the waves!
What cowards are these Greeks!"

Otello

Music **Giuseppe Verdi** • Libretto **Arrigo Boito**

First Performance **5ᵗʰ February 1887, at Teatro alla Scala, Milan**

Verdi's opera Aida had received its première in 1871 and his Requiem Mass had followed three years later. The year was 1880 and he was rich and famous. An old man, he was resting on his many laurels and living in retirement; it seemed he had given up composition for good. However, his publisher, Ricordi, wanted him to write a new opera to a libretto by the poet Arrigo Boito on Othello, the tragedy by Shakespeare. However, Verdi was suspicious of Boito, who had annoyed him with some of his writings many years previously. Also, his age and his recent inactivity had eroded his confidence in his ability to write an opera conforming to the demands of the day and which would not be considered too old fashioned. Two factors finally intervened to make him change his mind. The diplomacy and continual prompting of Ricordi played a part, but the need to revise one of his earlier works was probably the main reason. Verdi had been very fond of his opera Simon Boccanegra and had not taken kindly to its failure, mainly because of an over-complex and ambiguous libretto, to find a place in the standard repertory. He agreed to Boito revising the Boccanegra text as a 'trial' and was so impressed by the results that he at last decided to initiate work on Otello. Even so, his uncertainty continued to hamper progress and the composition proceeded with a number of interruptions and numerous corrections. No opera had ever taken him so long to write and alterations continued right up to the première, which turned out to be a resounding success.

It must be pointed out that Boito had constructed a taut and economical drama by compressing the Shakespeare tragedy in a brilliant manner. The Venetian first act was discarded, references to it being made in an early dialogue between Jago and Roderigo and in the love Duet. The result was the stunning sea-storm opening to the opera as well as the presentation of the whole work in Cyprus and the elimination of a number of unnecessary characters from the action. Thereafter Shakespeare was followed quite accurately although further compressions and one notable interpolation were made. In Shakespeare's play Jago's motives for his machinations against Othello are rather obscure. The conception of demonic malignity in Jago's credo, inserted by Boito, is a positive improvement and far more convincing than any jealousy-motivated desire for revenge he might also have had. Verdi's music and Boito's words, both inspired, have resulted in one of the greatest operas ever written.

The story of how the evil Jago poisons the mind of the jealous and gullible Othello in making him believe some subtly fabricated evidence that his wife Desdemona is being unfaithful to him, thus leading him to murder her, is well known. The scene depicted occurs in the first act. Othello's ship has just braved the storm and set anchor. In his intention to plot Othello's downfall, Jago has already put his plan into action. Knowing that Cassius, whom he intends to smear as Desdemona's lover, can't take his wine, he uses the pretext of Othello and Desdemona's wedding to initiate a celebration thus getting him drunk prior to provoking a fight that will lead to his disgrace...

JAGO

"Ingoia questo sorso..."

"Swallow this sip..."

CASSIO

"Cessa. Già m'arde il cervello
Per un nappo vuotato."

"Stop. My brain's already on fire
for having drunk one cup."

JAGO

"Sì, ancora bever devi,
Alle nozze d'Otello e Desdemona!..."

"Yes, you must drink again
to the marriage of Othello and Desdemona!..."

(AS EVERYBODY IS MAKING MERRY, JAGO TELLS HIS FRIEND RODERIGO TO HELP GET CASSIUS DRUNK. HE THEN ADDRESSES THE TAVERNERS.)

"Qua, ragazzi, del vino!..."

"Here lads, some wine!..."

(TO CASSIUS, HANDING HIM A GLASS.)

"Inaffia l'ugula! Trinca, tracanna
Prima che svampino canto e bicchier!..."

"Wet your whistle! Drink, gulp
before both song and glass disappear!..."

(TO EVERYBODY.)

"Chi all'esca ha morso del ditirambo
Spavaldo e strambo,
Beva con me, beva con me,
Beva, beva, ecc....
...Beva con me!"

"Who has taken the bait
of the bold and strange Bacchanal,
drink with me, drink with me,
drink, drink etc...
...drink with me!"

Die Entführung aus dem Serail

Music **Wolfgang Amadeus Mozart**
Libretto **Gottlieb Stephanie the Younger**
First Performance **16ᵗʰ July 1782, at the Burgtheater, Vienna**

Although some parts of this three-act 'Singspiel' opera, Mozart's thirteenth, were completed within a matter of hours, the work as a whole took the composer a record ten months to finish. In spite of this, and the obvious enthusiasm Mozart had for the opera, there are serious dramatic flaws to it. The text to the libretto is hardly inspiring, but worse, the part of Pasha Selim, fundamentally important to the twists and turns of the plot, is taken by a spoken role. Thus his changes of mood, which control the fate of the action, go without music. Yet the opera's strength, its fresh engaging and inventive music, laden with beautiful arias and duets, a trio and a particularly memorable quartet, has ensured its lasting success, from the première right up to the present day.

The story relates how the Spanish nobleman, Belmonte, helped by his ex-servant Pedrillo, attempts to rescue his fiancée Konstanze and her maid Blonde from a Turkish harem, where they have been held captive since pirates had abducted them from their home in Spain. The attempt almost succeeds but then fails. Unexpectedly, Pasha Selim, who had wanted Konstanze for himself, has a sudden and total change of attitude and gives the two couples their freedom to go. The opera ends in general rejoicing. Only Osmin, guardian of the Pasha's palace and desirous of Blonde is unhappy with the outcome.

The picture shows the palace garden in the second act. Pedrillo successfully entices Osmin to drink in order to get him drunk. The path will then be clear for him and Belmonte to penetrate Pasha Selim's palace, enter the harem and carry out the rescue...

PEDRILLO
"Long-live Bacchus! A toast to Bacchus!
Bacchus was a gallant man!"

"Vivat Bacchus! Bacchus lebe!
Bacchus war ein braver Mann!"

OSMIN
"Should I risk it? Should I drink?
Supposing Allah can see?"

"Ob ich's wage? Ob ich trinke?
Ob's wohl Allah sehen kann?"

PEDRILLO
"What's the point in hesitating?
Drink it down, drink it down,
without further question!"

"Was hilft das Zaudern?
Hinunter, hinunter!
Nicht lange, nicht lange gefragt!"

OSMIN
"Well , I've done it, now it's down!
That's what I call bold!"

"Nun wär's geschehen, nun wär's hinunter!
Das heiss'ich, das heiss'ich gewagt!"

OSMIN AND PEDRILLO
"Hurrah for girls, blondes and brunettes,

here's to their health!"

"Es leben die Mädchen, die Blonden,
die Braunen!
Sie leben hoch!"

PEDRILLO
"That tastes wonderful!"

"Das schmeckt herrlich!"

OSMIN
"That tastes excellent!"

"Das schmeckt trefflich!"

OSMIN AND PEDRILLO
"Ah! I call that the drink of the gods!"

"Ah! Das heiss' ich Göttertrank!"

The Tempest had been attributed to Purcell until fairly recently (1964), when research undertaken by Dr. Margaret Laurie suggested that John Weldon, a pupil of Purcell's, might have written most of the work instead.   It is known that Weldon did compose an opera on the subject but there remains no trace of the work, unless, of course, this happens to be it. Certainly, one song, 'Dear pretty youth', in Act IV, is definitely by Purcell. On the other hand, Weldon's claim to authorship is based on the fact that the music, although very much better than anything else he is known to have written, is Italianate in manner and much closer to his style than Purcell's.

It is a known fact that a number of people supplied music towards revisions of an original version of this piece. Several other composers amended the work well after the deaths of both Purcell and Weldon. The present rendering then took over but at an uncertain date. All this does not preclude the possibility that some of the music might have been brought over from the first version of the opera. The Act III Ariel aria 'Come unto these yellow sands' is a case in point. Thus it is probable that the opera is a composite work with contributions made by a number of composers at different times.

The Tempest

Music **Henry Purcell, John Weldon and others**
Libretto **William Davenport, John Dryden and Thomas Shadwell**
First Performance **7ᵗʰ January 1712 (?)**

The story is based on Shakespeare's homonymous play. In the original, Prospero, Duke of Milan, had been deposed and set adrift with his infant daughter. Arriving at a Mediterranean island, he attained magical powers. Many years later he has the opportunity to gain revenge by using these powers against his usurpers who have been shipwrecked on the island. The opera contains airs, choruses and dances featuring devils, demons and spirits conjured up by Prospero in order to achieve his objective. All ends happily as Prospero regains his lost dukedom and forgives his enemies.

The collage consists of a composite scene incorporating the dance of the winds at the end of the second act together with Ariel's air 'Dry those eyes', which takes place in Act III...

ARIEL

"Dry those eyes which are o'erflowing
All your storms are overblowing.
While you in this isle are biding
You shall feast without providing
Ev'ry dainty you can think of,
Ev'ry wine that you can drink of,
Shall be yours and want shall shun you,
Ceres' blessing too is on you."

La Bohème

Music **Giacomo Puccini**
Libretto **Giuseppe Giacosa & Luigi Illica**
First Performance **1ˢᵗ February 1896, at the Teatro Regio, Turin**

The rights to Murger's novel, 'Scenes de la vie de Bohème', were claimed by Ruggero Leoncavallo as well as by Puccini. Both men refused to back down and the composition of an opera on the subject became an open race. Nevertheless, Puccini's version took about three years to complete. Typically of him, the opera underwent numerous alterations before it was staged. Even then he was unsatisfied, and further changes were made before the final version was produced. Yet, in spite of all the delays Puccini still won the race, as Leoncavallo's opera wasn't premièred until 1897, over a year later.

Leoncavallo's work differs from Puccini's in a number of ways, notably in the casting. Rodolfo, the tenor in the Puccini opera is a baritone in Leoncavallo's, while Marcello, Puccini's main baritone is the Tenor in the other version. Musetta, a light soprano in Puccini's work, is taken by a coloratura mezzo in Leoncavallo's opera. Also, Leoncavallo's version is more closely allied to the principles of verismo than Puccini's. It's a very fine opera in its own right, not deserving the relative neglect it has received.

In the Puccini opera, the basic story – boy meets girl, each relating to the other about themselves, the resulting love duet, the friendly separation and the tragic reconciliation when the girl is terminally ill – is set against an atmospheric and evocative portrayal of everyday life in Paris in the 1830's. The carefree bohemian life of poverty and unpaid bills set amidst the Parisian bustle is in stark contrast to the sombre tones of the ultimate tragedy. Throughout the work, the interplay between the frivolous lifestyle of the four friends and the serious problems surrounding love, illness and death is very poignant, each complementing the other. The bohemians are made to 'grow up' and become more and more responsible as the action proceeds.

Puccini's opera, also rich in expansive, unforgettable melodies throughout, must be considered as being one of the finest ever written. It was Leoncavallo's misfortune to come up against such a work, which today, just over one hundred years on, has been translated into countless different languages and is one of the three most performed in the whole operatic repertoire.

The picture shows the scene at the Café Momus in the second act. It is Christmas Eve. Rodolfo has just presented his new girl, Mimì, to his friends. At the next table, accompanied by an elderly gentleman, is Marcello's ex-girlfriend Musetta, who unashamedly tries to gain his attention...

"Allegri, e un toast!"

"Qua del Liquor!"

*"E via i pensier, alti i bicchier!
Beviam!"*

"Beviam!"

"Ch'io beva del tossico!"

*"Quando me n'vo soletta
Per la via,
La gente sosta e mira,
E la bellezza mia
Tutta ricerca in me,
Ricerca in me da capo a piè."*

*"Ed assaporo allor la bramosia
Sottil che dagli occhi traspira
E dai palesi vezzi intender sa
Alle occulte beltà.
Così l'effluvio del desio
Tutta m'aggira.
Felice mi fa, felice mi fa."*

*"E tu che sai, che memori e ti struggi,
Da me tanto rifuggi?
So ben: le angoscie tue
Non le vuoi dir,
Ma ti senti morir."*

SCHAUNARD AND COLLINE
"Let's be merry; a toast!"

MARCELLO
(TO THE WAITER.)
"Bring some drink here!"

MIMI, RODOLFO AND MARCELLO
*"Away with sad thoughts; raise the glasses!
Let's drink!"*

ALL
"Let's drink!"

(MARCELLO SPOTS MUSETTA WHO ENTERS LAUGHING.)

MARCELLO
"Let me drink poison!"

(AS THE SCENE PROCEEDS, MUSETTA INTENSIFIES HER EFFORTS TO GET MARCELLO BACK. THIS CULMINATES WITH THE FOLLOWING ARIA:)

MUSETTA
*"As I walk alone
Through the streets
the people stop and stare
and my beauty
they seek in me,
they seek out from head to toe."*

*"And then I savour the subtle
longing in their eyes
and from my outward charms
they imagine the concealed beauties.
Thus this onrush of desire
surrounds me.
It makes me happy, it thrills me."*

(DIRECTED TO MARCELLO.)
*"And you who know, who remember and suffer,
do you seek refuge from me so?
I know well: your anguish
you do not wish to reveal,
but you feel yourself dying."*

As a reaction to critics who had attributed the success of 'Cavalleria Rusticana' to its highly dramatic plot rather than to its music, Mascagni deliberately sought a slight, straightforward story for his next opera and thus l'Amico Fritz came into being. The plot here is simple enough: Fritz Kobus is a wealthy landowner and confirmed bachelor. His friend, the rabbi David, an enthusiastic matchmaker, succeeds in manoeuvring the situation so as to get Fritz to fall in love with and marry Suzel, the daughter of the steward to his estate.

The opera succeeded in living up to the composer's expectations, thanks to the soft chamber music quality of the score. Much care is given to atmosphere and intimacy rather than action. Starting with the prelude, the woodwind and strings are pre-eminent and this continues throughout the work, with the full orchestra being used only occasionally. The general mood could be described as being tender, idyllic and pastoral.

In order to achieve this, Mascagni has used music that is soft and limpid, full of pastel tints and delicate shades, almost impressionistic in character. The off-stage chorus writing, in which two Alsace folk songs are used, is also in keeping with the chamber-like personal touch prevalent in the work, as is its most celebrated piece, the cherry orchard scene. Here, a sensuous cantilena develops into an intimately tender duet, full of gentle, romantic music.

The picture shows a scene in Fritz's house in the first act. He is united with his friends as his birthday celebration dinner is in progress. Caterina, the house governess, introduces Suzel who brings flowers, and Fritz invites her to join the party. As the rabbi David enters, Fritz offers him wine...

L'Amico Fritz Music **Pietro Mascagni** • Libretto **Nicola Daspuro**

First Performance **31ˢᵗ October 1891, at the Teatro Costanzi, Rome**

FRITZ
"Ecco un bicchier di vino."   *"Here's a glass of wine."*

(DAVID SITS DOWN AND DRINKS.)

FEDERICO
"Un brindisi chi fa?"   *"Who'll propose a toast?"*

DAVID
(TO SUZEL.)
"Tu pur, bimba, sei qua?"   *"You're here too, child?"*

(ASIDE)
"Come la bricconcella   "How grown-up and lovely
S'è fatta grande e bella!"   the little scamp has become!"

(THE SWEET SOUND OF A VIOLIN
COMES FROM THE TERRACE.)

HANEZÒ
"Chi mai sarà?"   *"Who can that be?"*

"Lo zingaro!"

"Ah, questi è Beppe!"

"Udite il violino."

"Perchè piangi, perchè?"

"Mi commuove la musica...
Scusatemi."

"Di che?...
Se commuove anche me!"

FRITZ
"The gypsy!"

DAVID
"Oh, that is Beppe!"

FEDERICO
"Listen to the violin."

FRITZ
(LOOKING AT SUZEL.)
"Why are you weeping, why?"

SUZEL
"The music affects me...
Forgive me."

FRITZ
"What for?...
It affects me too!"

The plot of this, Donizetti's 41st opera, is based on the common human-relations problem experienced by two people who are very fond of each other, yet are unable to find a way to communicate and express their feelings. The poor and timid Nemorino loves Adina, a rich and capricious landowner. At one point, he overhears her reading the tale of Tristan and Isolde to her harvesters and the idea of a love potion comes to him, but where could he obtain it? At that moment, a platoon of soldiers rides in. The sergeant, brash and handsome in his military uniform, immediately makes passes at the girl. She appears to respond, leaving Nemorino in a state of anguish.

L'Elisir d'Amore

Music **Gaetano Donizetti**
Libretto **Felice Romani**
First Performance **12ᵗʰ May 1832, at the Teatro Canobbiana, Milan**

Now (as the picture shows) Dulcamara arrives in his gilded cart. He is an unscrupulous quack, selling cheap Bordeaux wine as a love elixir. Remembering the Tristan and Isolde story, Nemorino buys a bottle. The wine does help him overcome his shyness and he takes his chance. However, he is unsuccessful, as he is no match for the aggressive and arrogant sergeant. Desperate, he tries to buy another bottle and finding he has no more money, enlists in the army so that the bounty cash would enable him to do so.

When Adina discovers what Nemorino has done she understands that his love for her is genuine and realises she loves him too. She immediately buys back the enlistment papers. To cap our hero's good fortune, he is told he has just inherited a large sum of money from a rich uncle. Thus the opera ends in general gaiety. Even the sergeant, an out-and-out womaniser, is consoled by the fact that there will be many others to seduce, while Dulcamara, the small-time swindler, having turned both fortune and matchmaker, leaves to the acclaim of all.

The opera, brimming with both wit and emotion as well as engaging music, is the composer's earliest work to have kept a permanent place in the repertory since its highly successful première...

DULCAMARA

"Udite,udite, o rustici;
Attenti, non fiatate.
Io già suppongo e immagino
Che al par di me sappiate
Ch'io sono quel gran medico,
Dottore enciclopedico,
Chiamato Ducamara,
La cui virtù preclara,
E i portenti infiniti
Son noti all'Universo
E...e...e in altri siti.
Benefattor degl'uomini,
Riparator de'mali,
In pochi giorni sgombero,
Io spazzo gli spedali,
E la salute a vendere
Per tutto il mondo io vo.
Compratela, compratela,
Per poco io ve la do.
È questo l'odontalgico
Mirabile liquore
Dei topi e delle cimici
Possente distruttore.
I cui certificati
Autentici, bollati,
Toccar, vedere e leggere
A ciaschedun farò.
Per questo mio specifico,
Simpatico, prolifico,
Un uom settuagenario,
E valetudinario,
Nonno di dieci bamboli
Ancora diventò,
Di dieci o venti bamboli
Fin nonno diventò.
Per questo 'tocca e sana'
In breve settimana
Più d'un'afflitta vedova
Di piangere cessò."

DULCAMARA

"Listen, listen, country folk;
attention, hold your breath.
I presume and imagine
you know as well as I do
that I'm that great medic,
encyclopaedic doctor,
called Dulcamara,
whose illustrious power,
and innumerable marvels
are known throughout the Universe
and...and...and in other places.
Benefactor of mankind,
mender of ills,
in a few days I can clear,
I can empty the hospitals,
by selling good health
throughout all the world I go.
Buy some, buy some,
I'll let you have it cheaply.
This is a cure for toothache,
a miraculous liquor;
of mice and bedbugs
a powerful destroyer;
certificates of which
authentic and sealed,
I'll allow each of you
to touch, see and read.
With this specific of mine,
pleasant and prolific,
a septuagenarian
valetudinarian,
became the grandfather
of ten children;
he even became the grandfather
of ten or twenty children!
With this panacea
in a brief week
many an afflicted widow
has stopped weeping."

Il viaggio a Reims

Music **Gioachino Rossini** • Libretto **Luigi Balocchi**

First Performance **19ᵗʰ June 1825, at the Théâtre-Italien, Paris**

Il viaggio a Reims, Rossini's last Italian opera, was composed with the objective of having the première as part of the celebrations honouring the coronation of King Charles X of France. In keeping with the special nature of the work, the composer instilled some of his most impressive music into its nine numbers. Also, the piece was written for no less than ten leading singers and included a short ballet sequence for approximately forty dancers.

The opera was also intended to fortify Rossini's standing in France. This it succeeded in achieving, as the presentations turned out to be prodigiously successful. Unfortunately, the composer didn't intend the work to survive the special occasion it had been written for. He allowed only four performances and adapted much of the music for his third French opera, 'Le Comte Ory', premièred three years later. As a consequence, the original score was lost and it was not until the late 1970's that piece by piece, its parts were rediscovered and reassembled. Thus a masterpiece was reborn.

The plot is simple. It concerns the interrelationships between a group of dignitaries staying at the hotel of the Golden Lily en route to the coronation of Charles X at Reims.

Musically, there is much to admire. In the third number, a stylish sextet is suddenly interrupted by a magical harp accompanied aria for soprano. Later, in the sixth number, there is a superb patter aria for bass in which the possessions each traveller would be taking with him are listed. There follows a stunning fourteen-voice 'Gran Pezzo Concertato' in number seven. In this eight-minute piece of highly elaborate vocal writing, all ten principals and four others sing intermittently and together. A slow opening section is followed by a fast second part and then a cabaletta, which concludes with a powerful Rossinian crescendo.

When the group learns that lack of transport will prevent them concluding their journey, they decide to make the best of staying on and a lavish dinner is prepared. A short ballet introduces the ninth and final number. Then, each dignitary sings a song or anthem of his country, the others joining in as chorus each time. Germany, Poland, Russia, Spain, England, France and the Tyrol are represented. In a fitting climax the lead soprano, a Roman poetess, delivers, in a second harp accompanied aria, a haunting melody to honour the new King, a theme taken up by the others as the opera ends...

(IN THE PICTURE, THE GERMAN BARON TROMBONOK PROPOSES A TOAST PRIOR TO THE SINGING OF THE NATIONAL ANTHEMS OR SONGS.)

BARON

"Ora, secondo gli usi,
I brindisi facciamo, – Ecco la lista
Che di far m'imponeste
Con decente simmetrica armonia,
E spero che ad ognun ben grata sia."

"Now, in accordance with custom,
let's drink a toast. – Here's the list
you wished me to draw up
with proper symmetrical harmony,
and I hope that it will well please all."

(HE READS THE NOTE.)

"Inno tedesco – Tocca a me."

"The German anthem – that's my turn."

"Or che regna fra le genti
La più placida armonia,
Dell' Europa sempre fia
Il destin felice appien."

"Now that the most peaceful harmony
reigns among peoples,
may the destiny of Europe
always be thoroughly happy."

BARON, OTHERS AND CHORUS

"Viva, viva l'armonia
Ch'è sorgente d'ogni ben."

"Live, long live harmony,
which is the source of all that's good."

BARON

"Altro da dir avrei; ma son già stracco;"

"I'd have more to say, but I'm already exhausted;"

(TO THE MARQUISE.)

"A voi, bella Marchesa, in stil polacco."

"Your turn, fair Marquise, in Polish style."

Alexandre Dumas's celebrated novel about the tragic love story of a consumptive Parisian courtesan has inspired many works of art, of which Verdi's masterpiece is probably the most endearing. Having become acquainted with the play during a stay in Paris, Verdi decided to write an opera on the subject. Starting in the autumn of 1852, composition was rapid and the work was premièred within five months. The story of a beautiful love that withstands all attempts of exploitation and corruption had inspired the composer to write some of his most beautiful music. In spite of this the first night proved a failure, possibly because the singers turned out to be vocally inadequate to the demands of the score. It was not until the following year, with a superior cast, and after the composer had revised the second and third acts, that the opera proved a complete triumph.

Apart from the excellent story and superb music, La Traviata is renowned as being a warhorse in the soprano repertory, requiring a singer who can excel in the first act coloratura and yet be intensely dramatic, particularly in the third act, when the heroine is dying of consumption. All these factors have ensured that the work has attained a permanent position among the elite in the repertoire.

The illustration depicts the opening scene in the house of Violetta Valéry, a young Parisian courtesan. A party is in progress. Alfredo Germont, in love with the girl and wanting her to abandon her wanton profession, proposes a toast...

La Traviata Music **Giuseppe Verdi** • Libretto **Francesco Maria Piave**

First Performance **6ᵗʰ March 1853, at the Teatro La Fenice, Venice**

Alfredo

"Libiamo ne' lieti calici,
Che la bellezza infiora;
E la fuggevol ora
S'innebrii a voluttà.
Libiam ne' dolci fremiti
Che suscita l'amore,"

"Let us drink from merry cups
that with beauty are adorned,
and the fleeting hour
will be replete with sensual pleasure.
Let us drink in the sweet excitement
arising out of love;"

(Indicating Violetta.)

"Poichè quell'occhio al core
Onnopitente va.
Libiamo, amore, amor fra i calici
Più caldi baci avrà."

"Since those eyes
go irresistibly to the heart.
Let us drink, love, for within the cup
are the warmest kisses of love."

Manon, Massenet's most successful opera, was composed between 1882 and 1883, some twenty-six years after Daniel Auber had first put the Abbe Prevost's tale to music, and about six years before Giacomo Puccini had started upon his version of the story.

The opera is graced by much beautiful music. Also, throughout the work, the composer shows a great feeling for human sentiment and passion. There are scenes of great intimacy that contrast strongly with others that depict the worldly life of the social salons and gaming tables of the time. Interestingly, the spoken word is used in places to enhance the dramatic effect. This is particularly telling in the second act, where Des Grieux tells Manon he wishes to marry her and also in the final scene, where in a short passage, starting with 'Nous reparlerons du passé,' Manon nostalgically recalls the past. Indeed, the opera is full of marvellous things and it would indeed be almost impossible to single anything out as being particularly special.

The opera was immediately successful and today, with Bizet's 'Carmen' and Gounod's 'Faust', it is one of the three major French operatic works in the international repertory.

The collage depicts the lovers' apartment in the second act. Des Grieux has asserted he intends to marry Manon and has written to his father about her. However, she has been pressured to leave him and resolves to join the high society life that she finds irresistible. Des Grieux has just gone out to post the letter and temporarily alone, she contemplates with sadness the intimacy of the relationship she is about to lose...

Manon

Music **Jules Massenet** • Libretto **Henri Meilhac and Philippe Gille**

First Performance **19th January 1884, at the Opéra-Comique, Paris**

The title part, in particular, is treated with much love, being adorned with a string of heartfelt solos. Yet, Des Grieux's tenor aria, 'Ah! Fuyez, douce image', which is full of nostalgic passion, is as splendid as anything sung by the soprano. Moreover, there are a number of memorable duets between the lovers, the final one, when Manon dies, being particularly inspired and deeply felt. The other main characters are also well treated and the opera contains much splendid choral work.

In the plot, the heroine is torn between her feelings for Des Grieux on the one hand, and the glitter of society sleaze on the other. Unhappily, she is ultimately unable to resist her attraction towards the latter and the opera proceeds fatally towards its tragic conclusion. Clearly, as shown by the painstaking care lavished on the score, Massenet was much taken by the subject, which was very close to his heart. This is further shown by the fact that ten years later he wrote 'Le portrait de Manon', a one-act sequel to the story.

Manon

"Adieu, notre petite table,
Qui nous réunit si souvent!..
Adieu, adieu, notre petite table,
Si grande pour nous cependant!...
On tient, c'est inimaginable...
Si peu de place...en se serrant...
Adieu, notre petite table!
Un même verre était le nôtre,
Chacun de nous, quand il buvait
Y cherchait les lèvres de l' autre...
Ah! Pauvre ami, comme il m'aimait!...
Adieu, notre petite table, adieu!..."

"Farewell, our little table,
which brought us together so often!...
Farewell, farewell, our little table,
that seemed so large just for us!...
One takes up, unbelievably...
so little space...when one's embracing...
Farewell, our little table.
We used the same glass,
the two of us, and when we drank,
each tried to find the other's lips...
Ah! My poor friend, how he loved me!
Farewell, our little table, farewell!..."

(Hearing Des Grieux returning.)

"C'est lui!
Que ma pâleur ne me trahisse pas!"

"It's he!
My pallor mustn't betray me!"

Mireille

Music **Charles Gounod** • Libretto **Michel Carré**

First Performance **19ᵗʰ March 1864, at the Théâtre Lyrique, Paris**

Composed in the space of two years, Gounod's ninth opera proved a failure at its première. The arduous soprano part, five-act format, absence of spoken dialogue and tragic ending were not well received by audiences accustomed to simple comic operas. Revisions intended to please his critics, including a happy ending, were only partly successful until a three-act revival in 1889 enabled it to attain a permanent position in the French repertoire. The revised ending continued to be generally used until 1939 when the original version at last proved successful. Happily, this five-act structure, which Gounod had first composed, is still the one used today.

The plot is based on a true story. The wealthy Mireille loves the poor Vincent. Her father forbids the union and plans for her to marry Ourrias, a local cowherd, who Mireille rebuffs. In a fit of jealous rage, Ourrias strikes Vincent with his trident and believing he has committed murder attempts to flee by crossing the river Rhône. Meanwhile, Vincent is rescued and taken to a sanctuary in order to recover. When Mireille hears of this, fearing the worst, she undertakes a perilous pilgrimage to the sanctuary, in which she has to cross the Crau Desert. Arriving utterly exhausted, she dies in Vincent's arms.

Gounod has poured much affection into this work. The Act I love duet and the Chanson de Magali (also a duet) in Act II, and briefly reprised in the fourth act, are examples of music of great beauty. Also in the second act, Mireille's 'A toi, mon âme', is charming in its simplicity. On the other hand, Ourrias' aria in which he boasts about his manly exploits is so suitably brash and full of brutish swagger that one is made to wonder whether it might have inspired Bizet's toreador song in Carmen! In a different mood completely is Mireille's aria 'Hélas! à vos pieds me voilà', where a stunning clarinet melody accompanies her as she vainly begs for pity and understanding from her father.
Lastly, in Act IV, her Crau desert aria skilfully conveys despair and then resolution and finally hope. Only the Act III Rhône scene, where Vincent is attacked and Ourrias drowns in his attempt to escape, seems to lack the appropriate drama needed to communicate the supernatural aspect of the situation and is the one weakness in what is otherwise a very fine and underrated work.

The collage depicts two closely related scenes in the third act. Vincent has just been struck by Ourrias. Taven, a gypsy, has heard his groans and quickly tends to his wounds. She curses the fleeing Ourrias, who has meanwhile summoned the ferryman to take him across the river. The boat sinks beneath the waves as the ghostly boatman reminds Ourrias of his crime...

"Un homme est couché la...
Le front baigné de sang,
Glacé!...Dieu tout-puissant!
Je reconnais ses traits dans l'ombre!...
C'est Vincent!"

"Et lui, le meurtrier, le traître,
Qui fuit là-bas comme un bandit,
J'ai su le reconnaître!...
Sois maudit, Ourrias!
Maudit! Troi fois maudit!"

"Saints du ciel!
L'eau se gonfle et mugit...
Et ton bateau s'arrête!
Traître! Tu répondras de mes jours
Sur la tête et sur ton salut éternel!..."

"Ourrias, ta colère est vaine!
Mon bateau porte un poids maudit!
Songe à Vincent...frappé par toi!"

"Qui te l'a dit?"

"Le Dieu vengeur dont la main nous entraine!"

TAVEN
"A man is lying there...
his brow bathed in blood,
and icy!...God almighty!
I recognise his features in the darkness!...
It's Vincent!"

(STRAIGHTENING UP HERSELF ANGRILY.)

"And he, the murderer, the traitor,
who flees down there like a gangster,
indeed I have been able to recognise!...
Be accursed, Ourrias!
Accursed! Three times accursed!"

(SHORTLY AFTERWARDS...)

OURRIAS
"Heavenly saints!
The water swells and roars...
and your boat stops!
Traitor! You shall answer for my life
with your head and your eternal salvation!..."

BOATMAN
"Ourrias, your anger is useless!
My boat carries an accursed load!
Think of Vincent...struck down by you!"

OURRIAS
"Who told you?"

BOATMAN
"The vengeful God in whose hands we are!"

(OURRIAS SCREAMS IN FRIGHT; THE BOAT SINKS.)

T chaikovsky's last opera, written as a companion piece to be premièred with the 'Nutcracker' ballet, took the composer just five months to complete. Although receiving a favourable reaction from the audience, the critics mostly disliked the work, but both generally preferred it to the ballet – as did Tchaikovsky himself. Posterity has ruled otherwise in no uncertain manner!

The story centres round a typical sweet but tormented heroine, in this case suffering from blindness. In order to protect her from the distress of knowing the truth, but probably also unconsciously to jealously keep her closer to himself, her father, King René of Provence, has misguidedly kept her ignorant of her handicap. She is confined to the castle and to the forbidden garden where no stranger may enter upon pain of death. A Moorish physician, Ibn Hakia, is called to help. He informs the King that a remedy is possible, but only if his daughter knows of her impediment and wishes to be cured. Presently, Count Vaudémont, a Burgundian knight, accompanied by Robert, his friend and suzerain Duke, strays unwittingly into Iolanta's forbidden garden. He sees the girl and captivated by her innocent beauty, talks to her. Realising the travellers are tired she offers them wine to restore their strength. During the conversation Vaudémont discovers she is blind and tells her about the gift of sight. The couple fall in love, but King René, on arriving, is immediately shocked and angry when he learns of Iolanta's newly acquired knowledge. Fortunately, at the doctor's instigation, he devises a stratagem to cure his daughter. Vaudémont shall die for having entered the garden unless the physician can make her see. The powerful combination of fear and love work the miracle, and the act concludes with general rejoicing.

"Vot, rytsari, vino...
Yevo atets moy l'ubit..."

IOLANTA
"Here is some wine, sir, knights...
it's what my father likes..."

(VAUDÉMONT TAKES A GOBLET AND LOOKS INTENTLY AT IOLANTA.)

VAUDÉMONT
(TO HIMSELF.)
"Surely this maiden, alone, wouldn't destroy me?"
(RESOLUTELY.)
"So be it!
I'm happy to accept death from these hands!"
(HE DRINKS.)

"Neuzheli min'a ano saboy pagubit?"

"Puskay!
Iz etikh ruk ya smert' primu s atraday!"

(IOLANTA CONTINUES TO HOLD OUT THE TRAY, EXPECTING ROBERT TO TAKE THE OTHER GOBLET.)

IOLANTA
"Where is your friend?
I was glad of his company..."

"A gde zhe drug tvoy?
Yemu byla ya rada..."

"Moy drug ushol, no on virn'otsa..."

VAUDÉMONT
"My friend has left, but he will return..."

Iolanta

Music **Pyotr Ilyich Tchaikovsky** • Libretto **Modest Tchaikovsky**

First Performance **6ᵗʰ December 1892, at the Mariinsky Theatre, St. Petersburg**

The opera suffers from a mediocre libretto with little dramatic action, although the composer does make the most of the few opportunities provided. Also, the one-act format is a handicap for a ninety-five minute work. The arias are not particularly memorable but the orchestral writing has many fine moments. Examples are the haunting opening, and later, the love duet, which builds up to an opulent crescendo to end the scene. Generally, evocative orchestral nuances, particularly with the woodwind, are used to good effect and the opera can be appreciated from an intimate and lyrical viewpoint, if not from a dramatic one.

The picture depicts the garden scene. Iolanta is offering wine to her unexpected visitors. Being blind, she fails to realise that Robert, the Duke of Burgundy has departed, leaving Vaudémont alone with her...

Having taken up residence in Paris in 1887, Luigi Cherubini was able to transform himself from being a rather mediocre opera composer into a far more accomplished and exciting one. His first French effort, 'Demophoon', was staged in 1788 and possibly due to being handicapped by a poor libretto, was a failure, but his second, 'Lodoïska', composed a year later, proved to be a great success. Elisa, written during the height of the French revolution, was likewise successful when it was premièred in 1894.
Indeed, this proved to be a very good time for the composer, who had married a French girl earlier in the same year. His relationship with France was now truly set, for two reasons rather than one!

Like Lodoïska, Elisa is a 'rescue' opera, a genre very popular at the time. However, unlike its predecessor, there is no villain here. In Elisa, the hero is rescued from the elements, that is, the awesome power of natural forces. The plot is simple. Florindo, believing his beloved Elisa has forsaken him seeks solitude by going on a dangerous alpine journey. His object is to die amongst the snows. Elisa, who is in fact still faithful to him, gets to know about this and helped by Savoyard mountain guides, goes searching for him. Happily, although overcome by an avalanche, he is found just in time and rescued. The lovers are reunited and the opera ends in general celebration.

One is naturally led to ask why the opera is such a rarity and why it's not performed more often. In fact, the composer is responsible for several very fine operas written during his stay in France, yet only 'Medea', or 'Medée' in the original French, is well known and that is primarily due to the great soprano, Maria Callas, who made the role her own. A reason is surely the dilemma one would experience with the libretto, many parts of which are written in the Savoyard dialect of the time, a language that presents great difficulty to translate. The original Italian translation has been lost and only parts of it appear still to exist. Thus great problems would have to be overcome by anyone wishing to stage the work. It is unfortunate that such an interesting opera has sunk into an oblivion it certainly does not deserve.

The picture represents the St. Bernard pass at the beginning of the second act. The hospice is seen in the distance. In the foreground, a group of Savoyard travellers can be seen carrying rucksacks, together with their guide. They have a tambourine and some triangles. Some are seated on the ice and are eating and drinking...

Elisa

Music **Luigi Cherubini** • Libretto **Jaques-Antoine de Reveroni de St.Cyr**

First Performance **13ᵗʰ December 1794, at the Théâtre Feydeau, Paris**

The work must have been very close to the composer's heart, for much love has been put into it. There are splendid solos for both tenor in Act I and soprano in Act II, the former being dramatic and full of desperate heartfelt declamation, whilst the latter is also deeply felt, but in a lyrical manner that is inwardly reflective and romantic.
There are fine trios and duets, that between tenor and bass in the first act being deeply moving. Also, the chorus is utilised very well and plays an important part in the opera. To cap it all, the orchestration is light and very skilfully used, without a single dull moment in this romantic work.

"Che dalla Tarantaise
È lungo il cammino fino a Parigi.
Beviamo. Ah! Che letizia! Che felicità.
Andare a vedere una bella città!"

"Che Stai a far? Bevi anche tu!
Viva la Francia! Viva la vita!
Viva la Francia e la libertà!"

TRAVELLERS
"The walk from the Tarantaise
to Paris is long.
Let's drink. Ah! What delight! What happiness
to go and see a beautiful city."

A SAVOYARD
(POURING THE GUIDE A DRINK.)
"What are you doing? Come, drink!
Hooray for France! Hooray for life!
Hooray for France and freedom!"

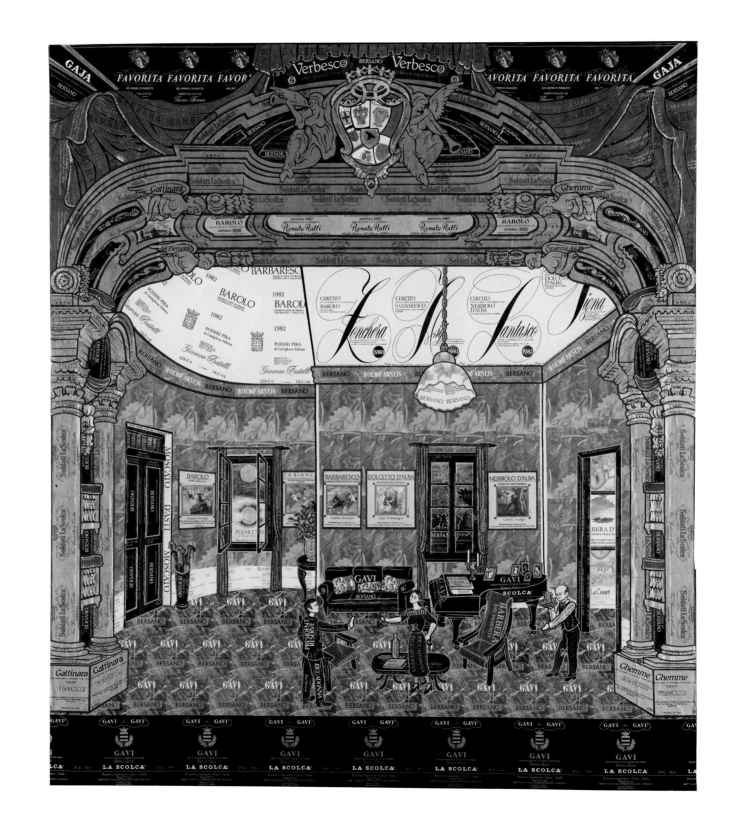

Wolf-Ferrari, born of a German father and Italian mother, composed thirteen complete operas of which 'Susanna's Secret' is the fourth. Although he studied in Munich and spent little of his adult life in Italy, his operas are essentially Italian in style and mostly composed to Italian libretti. Yet all his earlier works, including this one, received their premières in the German language in Germany, where his compositions have enjoyed their greatest success.

Il segreto di Susanna
Music **Ermanno Wolf-Ferrari** • Libretto **Enrico Golisciani**

First Performance **4ᵗʰ December 1909, at the Hoftheater, Munich**

The composer has been particularly good at portraying eighteenth century satirical comedy and four of his best works, 'I Quattro Rusteghi', 'Le Donne Curiose', 'Il Campiello' and 'La Vedova Scaltra', all after plays by Goldoni, bear testimony to this. Susanna's secret is not a Goldonian opera buffa but a light, sparkling comedy, nevertheless. The plot is simple. A young wife has a smoking habit kept secret from her husband. However, the odour of tobacco smoke in the house arouses his jealousy in suspecting she receives a secret lover during his absence. Fortunately all ends well when the truth is discovered and he even promises to try to take up the habit in order to keep her company!

The opera starts with a brief, witty overture and although unpretentious, contains much fine music in its single act. The love duet is particularly beautiful, while the quarrel that follows it is tainted with comedy. Fine use of Debussy-like images is made in order to conjure up the allusion to tobacco smoke. These are then skilfully ingrained within a lovely aria for soprano in which the joys of smoking are expressed. The work ends with the couple reconciled and walking hand in hand into the bedroom; truly a fitting conclusion to this charming little piece!

Wine is not consumed in the opera. However there is a negative reference towards drinking which the artist has used to his advantage in the collage. In the scene, Count Gil is telling his wife he has no vices...other than her!...

"Come sapete...
...a fondo
la scienza d'ingraziarvi!"

"No, cara, vi rispondo:
non so che idolatrarvi.
Vizi non ho: nè gioco,
nè vin, nè fumo-"

"Guai!"

"Ah, me ne duol non poco!"

"E quanto a donne il sai,
non ne amo nè desidero
che una, e me ne vanto.
Mio tutto ti considero
non mia metà soltanto."

SUSANNA
"How you know....
...well
the art of paying compliments!"

COUNT GIL
"No dear, I answer you:
I know only to idolize you.
I have no vices : I don't gamble,
or drink wine, or smoke-"

(TO HIMSELF.)
"Alas !"

SUSANNA
(TO HERSELF.)
"Ah, I'm very sorry about that!"

COUNT GIL
"And regarding women, you know,
I do not love nor desire
but one, and I'm proud of it.
I consider you my all
not my half alone."

Victor Hugo's play, 'Le Roi S'Amuse', had been banned in Paris after only a single performance. The plot, concerning the licentious exploits of Francois I of France, had been too much for the authorities to accept, even in the French capital, which was relatively liberal-minded at the time. When Verdi had decided, with much enthusiasm, to write an opera on Hugo's story, his librettist found himself facing the same difficulties. He had to modify the libretto several times in order to satisfy both the composer on the one hand and the censors on the other. Eventually, a compromise acceptable to both parties was obtained by replacing the French King and his court by an unnamed Duke in the Italian city of Mantova in Lombardy.

Rigoletto
Music **Giuseppe Verdi** • Libretto **Francesco Maria Piave**

First Performance **11ᵗʰ March 1851, at the teatro La Fenice, Venice**

The opera, with its deeply heartfelt Baritone title role, fine soprano part and two splendid tenor arias, was a brilliant success from the start and has survived with hardly any modification to the present day.

The plot revolves around the seduction, by the libertine Duke, of the ingenuous Gilda, his court jester's daughter. Her father, fully aware of the Duke's reputation and his daughter's innocent vulnerability, attempts to exact revenge by having the Duke murdered, with disastrous consequences.

The scene depicted takes place just prior to the assassination attempt. Sparafucile, the hired killer, is in a tavern with the Duke, who orders a room and some wine and then expresses his libertine feelings towards women in one of the most celebrated tenor arias in the operatic repertoire. As Rigoletto and Gilda arrive and look in through a window, Maddalena, the sister of Sparafucile, enters the room and the Duke immediately makes amorous advances towards her...

"Una stanza e del vino..."

"La donna è mobile qual piuma al vento,
Muta d'accento e di pensiero.
Sempre un amabile leggiadro viso,
In pianto e riso, è menzoniero.
È sempre misero chi a lei s'affida,
Chi le confida mal cauto il core.
Pur mai non sentesi felice appieno,
Chi sul quel seno non liba amore!
La donna è mobil, qual piuma al vento,
Muta d'accento e di pensier!"

"Un dì se ben rammentomi,
O bella, t'incontrai...
Mi piacque di te chiedere,
E intesi che qui stai.
Or sappi che d'allora
Sol te quest'alma adora."

THE DUKE OF MANTUA

"A room and some wine..."

"Woman is fickle as a feather in the wind,
changeable of word and of thought.
An amiable pretty face,
in tears or in laughter, is always deceitful.
Ever wretched is he who trusts her,
who rashly confides her his heart.
Yet he never knows complete happiness
who on that bosom does not taste love!
Woman is fickle as a feather in the wind,
changeable of word and of thought!"

(TO MADDALENA WHO HAS JUST ENTERED.)

"If I remember rightly,
oh beautiful one, I once met you...
I was pleased to inquire after you,
And learnt that you live here.
Know now that since then
this heart adores only you."

Don Giovanni

Music **Wolfgang Amadeus Mozart** • Libretto **Lorenzo Da Ponte**

First Performance **29ᵗʰ October 1787, at the Nationaltheater, Prague**

Don Giovanni, Mozart's 18th opera, was almost certainly inspired by that of Giuseppe Gazzaniga on the same subject, staged in February 1787. Aided by Da Ponte's superb libretto, Mozart was able to completely overshadow the previous work with his own, which was premièred just eight months later. The opera proved such a success with the Bohemian audience that Vienna prepared for its own staging with a different cast in the following year. Mozart made a number of changes to suit the whims and limitations of the new singers, with the result that two versions of the opera exist. Most modern performances consist of a particular blend of both.

The basic plot of the opera embodies a simple moral. That is, that crime will get its just deserts in the end. It is divine, and not human, retribution which strikes Don Giovanni down, punishing him for his libertine exploits and the murder he has committed, both carried out without compassion or fear of God. At the beginning of the drama he kills the Commendatore who gives his life to defend his daughter's honour. At the end he is engulfed by flames as, unrepentant, he is dragged down to hell.

In this, Mozart follows Gazzaniga. However, whereas the Italian composer goes no further, Mozart embellishes the plot by expanding the middle section of the work. Thanks to Da Ponte's libretto, intrigue, much of it comical, is introduced. The serious roles of Donna Anna, Don Ottavio and the Commendatore are balanced by the buffo ones of Leporello, Zerlina and Masetto. It takes the composer's genius to fuse the tragic and comic elements into a sublime musical whole and it is this that makes the opera one of the great masterpieces in the repertoire.

The picture illustrates the start of the final scene. Don Giovanni is being served by Leporello, while having supper in his villa. A band is playing music while he eats and drinks...

DON GIOVANNI
(EATING.)

"Ah, che piatto saporito!"

"Ah, what a tasty dish!"

LEPORELLO
(ASIDE.)

"Ah, che barbaro appetito!
Che bocconi da gigante!
Mi par proprio di svenir."

"Ah, what a ravenous appetite!
What gigantic mouthfuls!
I feel really faint with hunger."

DON GIOVANNI
(ASIDE.)

"Nel veder i miei bocconi
Gli par proprio di svenir.

"While seeing my mouthfuls
he feels really faint with hunger.
(ALOUD.)

Piatto!"

Take it away!"

LEPORELLO

"Servo!

"Yes sir!

(THE MUSICIANS CHANGE THE MUSIC.)

Evvivano i 'Litiganti'!"

Long live the 'Litiganti'!"
(REFERRING TO ANOTHER OPERA OF THIS NAME, BY GIUSEPPE SARTI.)

DON GIOVANNI

"Versa il vino,
Eccellente Marzimino."

"Pour the wine,
excellent Marzimino."

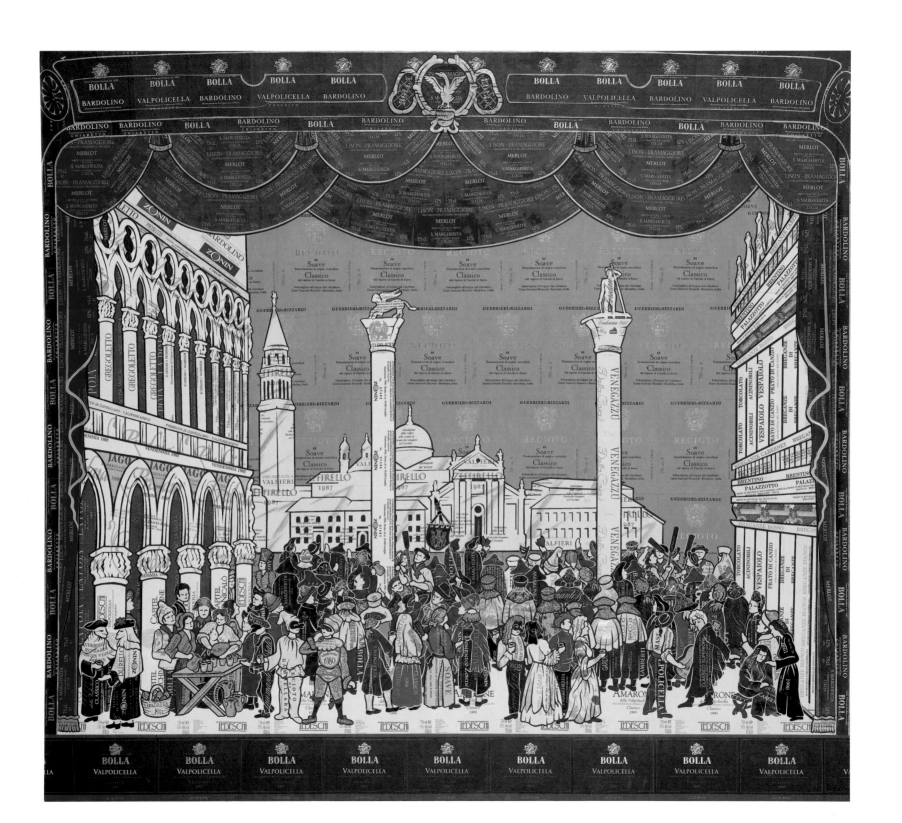

Although this work received its première in the spring of 1876, the composer and librettist carried out a number of revisions to the work, the final version not being produced until 1880.

The opera relates a complex story of intrigue and deception set in seventeenth century Venice. The ballad singer, Gioconda, loves Enzo, an exiled Genoese Prince who, however, is the lover of Laura, the wife of Alvise Badoero, head of the state inquisition.
At the same time, one of its spies, the evil Barnaba, is courting her, but she spurns his advances. In revenge, he accuses her mother of witchcraft. He also knows about the clandestine love affair and denounces it to his masters. At the end of a complicated series of events, Gioconda nobly decides to sacrifice herself in order to get Barnaba to allow the lovers to escape. She promises to give herself to him in return for their freedom and then kills herself as soon as she knows they are safe.

La Gioconda Music **Amilcare Ponchielli** • Libretto **Tobia Gorrio (Arrigo Boito)**

First Performance **8ᵗʰ April 1876, at Teatro alla Scala, Milana**

The disjointed plot is hardly characteristic of Boito's later librettos, written under his real name, for operas by Verdi. However, although musically uneven, the opera has many highlights worth noting. Particularly impressive are the arias 'Voce di Donna' for Gioconda's mother and Barnaba's 'O Monumento' in the first act, Enzo's 'Cielo e Mar' and Laura's 'Stella del Marinar' in Act II, and Gioconda's 'Suicidio', in which she contemplates suicide, in the fourth act. There are also a number of fine, dramatic duets and there is a conspicuous role for the chorus. The work follows the French Grand opera style with the 'Dance of the Hours' ballet sequence, in the middle of Act III. This is often performed as a concert piece and is probably the most celebrated part of the entire work.

The illustration is a composite arrangement of two crowd scenes, both in the first act. People are bearing aloft the winner of the boat race. The victory emblem, a green banner, can be seen...

PEOPLE

"Gloria a chi vince!
Polso di cerro!
Occhio di lince!
Remo di ferro!
Gagliardo cor!
Gloria a chi vince
il pallio verde!"

"Glory to the winner!
Wrist of oak!
Eye of a lynx!
Oar of iron!
Stout of heart!
Glory to he who wins
the green banner!"

(BARNABA, THE SPY, HAS JUST DENOUNCED LAURA, ALVISE'S WIFE, FOR UNFAITHFULNESS. THE ACCUSING LETTER HAS BEEN POSTED INTO THE LION'S MOUTH. HE CAN BE SEEN ON THE RIGHT HAND SIDE OF THE COLLAGE, CARRYING A GUITAR. THE TOWNSFOLK HAVE NOW RETURNED AS A PROCESSION OF MASKERS ENTERS THE SQUARE AND A GAY BACCHANAL TAKES PLACE. GIOCONDA IS COMFORTING HER BLIND MOTHER (LA CIECA), WHO HAS JUST BEEN SPARED FROM BEING ARRESTED AS A WITCH. THEY CAN BE SEEN IN THE FAR RIGHT HAND CORNER OF THE PICTURE.)

PEOPLE

"Carneval! Baccanal!
Carneval! Baccanal!
Gaia turba popolana,
su, danzate la furlana, la furlana!"

"Carnival! Revelry!
Carnival! Revelry!
Merry throng of people
come, dance the furlana, the furlana!"

Attila

Music **Giuseppe Verdi** • Libretto **Temistocle Solera and Francesco Maria Piave**

First Performance **17ᵗʰ March 1846, at the Teatro La Fenice, Venice**

The subject of Attila, taken from Zacharias Werner's 1808 play, captured Verdi's imagination and stimulated him to plan his ninth opera. As a result of their recent triumph with 'Ernani' he engaged Francesco Maria Piave as librettist and discussions took place as to the structure of the work. However, as plans were proceeding, another venture with Piave, 'I due Foscari' was premièred with only moderate success while 'Giovanna D'Arco', composed to Temistocle Solera's libretto, proved to be a triumph. All this, added to the fact that in Attila Verdi had French grand opera in mind and Solera was a master of that genre, Piave was dropped and the services of the Spaniard assumed instead. Unfortunately, with the libretto almost completed, Solera followed his soprano wife to Spain following the singer's fiasco in a Donizetti opera in Milan. At this point Verdi recalled Piave who obligingly completed the libretto and also modified parts of it to better suit the composer's requirements.

The score was completed in a mere six months in spite of the fact that Verdi had become seriously ill at the time. The première was only reasonably successful, but the work soon attained great popularity. It is probable that Rome's resistance to the spread of Attila's conquests was seen as a parallel to Italy's insurrection to Austrian domination, a rebellion that was very much bubbling beneath the surface at the time.

The plot centres round Attila's attempted conquest of Italy and the revenge of Odabella, whose family had been slaughtered by the Huns. At the end of the opera, as the Romans attack the Huns' camp, she gains retribution by stabbing Attila to death.

Musically, the opera is rich in choral work, much of it of a martial nature. Some solo pieces, such as Odabella's 'Allor che I forti corrono' in the prologue and Ezio's Act II 'Dagli immortali vertici', also suggest a call to arms. On the other hand, there is no shortage of lyrical pieces throughout the work. The arias sung by Odabella in act I, Ezio in Act II and Foresto in Act III are good examples.

The picture shows Attila's camp near the end of the second act. Attila is about to take wine but Odabella stops him, disclosing it has been poisoned. (An apparently friendly act, but done to gain his confidence and favour, so she can be truly avenged by killing him herself at a later opportunity...)

"Si rannodi la danza ed il giuoco...
Sia per tutti festivo tal giorno,
Porgi, Uldino, la conca ospital."

"Perché tremi? S'imbianca il tuo volto."

"Libo a te, gran Wodano, che invoco!"

"Re, ti ferma!...È veleno!..."

"Che ascolto!"

"Chi'l temprava?"

"Oh, momento fatal!"

"Io!"

"Foresto!"

ATTILA
"Let dance and sport be resumed...
let this be a festive day for all,
Uldino, hand me the cup of hospitality."

FORESTO
(QUIETLY TO ODABELLA.)
"Why do you tremble? Your face is pale."

ATTILA
(RECEIVING THE CUP FROM ULDINO.)
"I drink to thee, great Odin, whom I invoke!"

ODABELLA
(RESTRAINING HIM.)
"O King, hold! It's poison!..."

CORO
"What do I hear?"

ATTILA
(WITH FURY.)
"Who has tampered with it?"

ODABELLA
(ASIDE.)
"Oh fatal moment!"

FORESTO
(ADVANCING FIRMLY.)
"I!"

ATTILA
(RECOGNISING HIM.)
"Foresto!"

La Cena delle Beffe

Music **Umberto Giordano** • Libretto **Sem Benelli**

First Performance **20ᵗʰ December 1924, at Teatro alla Scala, Milan**

La Cena delle Beffe, 'the mockery supper' and not 'the jester's supper', as it is often incorrectly referred to in English, is the last of Giordano's fourteen (including one incomplete) operas. Although considered a 'verismo' piece, the complex and highly unlikely story hardly lends itself to the genre. Also, the strong, declamatory lines of the two leading antagonists are interspersed with a number of set pieces in the older traditional style. It is interesting to note that the composer completely abandoned verismo in his last opera, 'Il Re'.

Set in Florence at the time of Lorenzo il Magnifico, the gruesome plot relates the macabre revenge of Giannetto Malespini against two brothers, Neri and Gabriello Chiaramantesi. These, envious and angered by his love and relationship with the beautiful Ginevra, had captured him, bound him in a sack and immersed him in the river Arno before branding him. Subsequently, to the frustration of Gabriello as well as the anger of Giannetto, Ginevra had become Neri's lover. The opera opens at the home of Tornaquinci, a nobleman who is acting as peacemaker and who has arranged a conciliatory supper for the enemies. He is unaware that the real motive behind this meal, ordered by Lorenzo de Medici is to enable Giannetto to embark on a complicated sequence of events, which will end by his exacting terrible revenge on the brothers. The opera concludes with Neri mistakenly thinking Giannetto is in bed with Ginevra and becoming insane when realising he has stabbed and murdered his own brother instead of his enemy.

In the picture, the supper is over and Giannetto has just put his plan for revenge into action. He has dared Neri, who has over-indulged in drink, to show himself in the most disreputable district of Florence where the 'real tough guys' hang about. Neri, who always boasts about his strength and courage, has immediately accepted and asked for his armour and weapons. He orders Ginevra to leave, but before setting off on his dangerous mission, asks for wine. The men look on as Neri drinks and pours scorn over the rulers of Florence...

NERI
(TO THE SERVANT.)

"Datemi bere, qua; vo' prima bere!"

"Give me a drink, here; I want to drink first!"

TORNAQUINCI

"A tutti date bere!"

"Give drinks to all!"

(THE SERVANTS POUR THE WINE.)

NERI

"Bevo alla barba di chi non ha debiti."

"I drink to the beard of who has no debts."

GIANNETTO
(INTERRUPTING HIM.)

"Certo di non offendere i presenti!"

"Certainly not to offend anyone present!"

NERI

"Bevo alla barba di chi signoreggia
questa terra di vili:
femminette, mercanti ladri
e santi solamente in agonia!"

"I drink to the beard of who rules
this country of cowards:
harlots, thieving merchants
and saints only in the throes of death!"

GIANNETTO

"Che il giusto Dio ti dia!"

"May God forgive you!"

NERI

"A te!
Bevo esaltando i capri e gli asini
che Lorenzo Magnifico pastura,
aiutato dai suoi prodi compagni,
pappatori, beoni e tavernieri...
Chi non beve con me, peste lo colga!"

"Here's to you!
I drink in praise of the goats and asses
that Lorenzo the Magnificent has pasturing,
helped by his valiant companions,
pimps, boozers and tavern keepers...
A plague on he who won't drink with me!"

(GIANNETTO, FEIGNING, QUICKLY DRINKS
TO THE TOAST...)

Francesca da Rimini Music **Riccardo Zandonai** • Libretto **Tito Ricordi**

First Performance   **19th February 1914, at the Teatro Regio, Torino**

The tragic love story of Francesca da Rimini was first brought to prominence by the supreme Italian poet, Dante, in the fifth canto of the 'Inferno' component of the 'Divine Comedy'. Since then, a number of authors have been inspired by the event and it is from Gabriele D'Annunzio's play, premièred in 1901, that the opera has been constructed.

Although based on fact, it is probable that the story has been embellished through the ages, resulting in the present belief that Francesca was tricked into marrying the lame and brutal Gianciotto while believing her spouse to be his handsome younger brother, Paolo. Naturally, the two became lovers until betrayed by the devious and evil youngest brother, Malatestino. Francesca and Paolo were both murdered by the vengeful Gianciotto, as indeed happens at the end of Zandonai's composition.

Clearly, D'Annunzio's play was the stuff from which grand opera is made and the publisher, Tito Ricordi, was quick to realise this. With D'Annunzio's help, he wrote the libretto himself, trimming the five-act play into four acts. Unfortunately, in doing so, a number of important details in the plot were removed with the result that the significance of some of the action is unclear in parts of the libretto.

However, Zandonai's music is highly inspired and evocative with a medieval flavour brought about by the utilisation of several ancient instruments in the score. Leitmotifs are used to depict moods as well as characters. The violent sounds of the battle scene and the disturbed music in the meeting between Gianciotto and Malatestino contrast strongly with the soft harmonious world of the ladies. This is typified by the duet between Francesca and Samaritana and the women's chorus, both in Act I and also the Francesca-Biancofiore duet in Act IV. Also, the love scene is aptly passionate, being brought to a sudden close by the tragic ending. It is not surprising that a story which inspired Ambroise Thomas, Tchaikovsky and Rachmaninov, should have stimulated Zandonai to compose his masterpiece, reaching musical heights which he was never again able to attain.

The collage scene is taken from the second act. Gianciotto and his men have just beaten off an attack by the Ghibelline faction on his Guelph stronghold. Francesca orders wine to quench the thirst of the battle weary men...

FRANCESCA
"Gran sete voi dovete avere."

"You must be very thirsty."

GIANCIOTTO
"Si, ho gran sete."

"Yes, I'm very thirsty."

FRANCESCA
"Smaragdi, porta il vino."

"Smaragdi, bring the wine."

(THE SLAVE COMES FORWARD WITH A FLASK AND GOBLET.)

GIANCIOTTO
(WITH JOYFUL SURPRISE.)
"E come, donna, aveste voi pensiero
Della mia sete?
Cara donna mia!"

"And why, my lady, have you thought
of my thirst?
My dear wife!"

(FRANCESCA POURS THE WINE AND HANDS THE GOBLET TO HER HUSBAND. PAOLO STANDS ASIDE, IN SILENCE.)

FRANCESCA
"Ecco, bevete..."

"Here, drink..."

GIANCIOTTO
"Prima bevete, in grazia, un sorso."

"You drink first, I beg you, a sip."

(FRANCESCA TOUCHES HER LIPS TO THE GOBLET.)
"È dolce cosa rivedere la vostra faccia,
Dopo la battaglia, e da voi avere offerta
Una coppa di vin possente,
E beverla d'un fiato!"

"It is sweet to see your face again,
after the battle, and to have you offer
a cup of powerful wine,
and drink it in one gulp!"

(HE EMPTIES THE GOBLET.)
"Così, tutto si rallegra il cuore."

"This cheers up all my heart."

Since Rossini objected to supernatural elements in his operas, his librettist greatly altered Perrault's fairy tale in order to make the story acceptable to the composer. In the first place, he dispensed with the fairy godmother, replacing her with the Prince's tutor, Alidoro. Disguised as a beggar, he is testing the ground for the Prince and realising that Cinderella is the right girl for his master, proceeds to scheme on her behalf. Secondly, Cinderella has a clumsily brutal stepfather, Don Magnifico, rather than the traditional stepmother. Naturally he is made to look ridiculous and the need for a Basso Buffo role must have strongly influenced this decision. Thirdly, the Prince's choice must be based on qualities more noble than mere beauty.

Thus, he disguises himself by changing roles with his attendant Dandini in order to gage the real feelings of the girls seeking to win him. It is here that Cinderella emerges totally triumphant.

However, the most important difference between Perault's fairy tale and Rossini's opera lies in the character of the protagonist herself. This Cinderella – Angelina (little Angel) is her real name – is no passive recipient to her fate. She is good and virtuous but no pushover. This is seen towards the beginning of the opera in the way her stepsisters fail to keep her quiet when she sings the aria 'Una volta c'era un Re', in which she almost predicts her royal destiny. Later, she puts up a strong, albeit losing battle against her stepfather in her desire to join her sisters at the ball.

Then, during this, when she meets the prince, who is disguised as Dandini, she tells him that wealth doesn't interest her but what she seeks is respect, love and kindness. Finally, on leaving, she gives the prince one of a pair of bracelets inviting him to look for and find her as the girl wearing the other one.

This is not an accidentally dropped slipper, but a challenge to the Prince, who she still thinks is Dandini; he must seek her out if he is really interested in her! Clearly then, our Cinderella is a strong willed lady with both feet firmly on the ground, a far cry to what Perrault had envisaged in his fairy tale. Even when she pardons her family at the end she does it with an air of confidence, since for her, forgiveness is the sweetest possible revenge!

As usual with Rossini, the opera was composed in a rush. The libretto took twenty-two days and the music just twenty-four! It has no overture of its own, Rossini having borrowed one from a previous work, 'la Gazetta'. Nevertheless, after a shaky start the work gained great fame, rivalling and even surpassing that of 'Il Barbiere di Siviglia'. However, with the birth of Verismo at the end of the Century, it became increasing difficult to find suitable interpreters. The coloratura mezzo had become a rarity. Also its fairy tale origins cannot have done the opera any good. Thus it lost popularity for a very long time. Now, with plenty of good Rossini-style singers about, the work has at last regained much of its former prestige.

La Cenerentola

Music **Gioacchino Rossini**
Libretto **Giacopo Ferretti**
First Performance **25ᵗʰ January 1817, at the Teatro Valle, Rome**

The scene shown occurs towards the end of the first act. It shows Dandini disguised as the prince and the courtiers offering Don Magnifico the status of Castle Vintner in recognition for his prodigious wine tasting and drinking talents. Don Magnifico accepts and immediately proclaims an edict forbidding the use of water to dilute wine...

COURTIERS

"Conciossiacosacché
Trenta botti già gustò,
E bevuto ha già per tre
E finor non barcollò;
È piaciuto a Sua Maestà
Nominarlo cantinier:
Intendente dei bicchier
Con estesa autorità,
Presidente al vendemmiar,
Direttor dell' evoè;
Onde tutti intorno a te
Ci affolliamo qui a ballar."

"Inasmuch as
he has sampled thirty barrels
and already drunk for three
and so far hasn't staggered;
His Majesty has been pleased
to appoint him vintner:
superintendent of the wine glasses
with extensive authority,
president at the grape harvest,
director of the Bacchic revels;
whence all around you
we throng here to dance."

"Intendente? Direttor?
Presidente? Cantinier?
Grazie, grazie! Che piacer!
Che girandola ho nel cor!
Si venga a scrivere quel che dettiamo."

"Seimila copie poi ne vogliamo."

"Già pronti a scrivere
Tutti siam qui."

"Noi Don Magnifico...Questo in maiuscole.
Bestie! Maiuscole! Bravi! così.
Noi Don Magnifico,
Duca e Barone
Dell'antichissimo
Montefiascone;
Grand'intendente,
Gran presidente,
Con gli altri titoli,
Con venti et cetera,
In splenitudine
D'autorità,
Riceva l'ordine
Chi leggerà:
Di più non mescere
Per anni quindici
Nel vino amabile
D'acqua una gocciola,
Alias capietur et strangulatur.
Perché et cetera, laonde et cetera,
Nell'anno et cetera, Barone et cetera."

"Barone et cetera,
È fatto già."

DON MAGNIFICO

"Superintendent? Director?
President? Butler?
Thank you, thank you! What a pleasure!
My heart is in a whirl!
Come write what we dictate."

(THE COURTIERS SIT AROUND THE TABLES AND WRITE.)

" Then we want six thousand copies."

COURTIERS

"We're all here now
and ready to write."

DON MAGNIFICO
(OBSERVING HOW THEY WRITE.)

"We, Don Magnifico...In capital letters.
Dolts! Capitals! Well done! That's it.
We Don Magnifico,
Duke and Baron
of age-old
Montefiascone;
grand superintendent,
grand president,
with the other titles,
with twenty et cetera,
in full power
of authority,
will receive the order
they who will read:
to no longer mix
for fifteen years
a drop of water
with sweet wine,
else they will be seized and strangulated.
because et cetera, therefore et cetera,
in the year et cetera, Baron et cetera."

COURTIERS

"Baron et cetera,
That's it – it's done."

The Cenci Music **Giorgio Battistelli** • Libretto **Giorgio Battistelli and Nick Ward**

First Performance **11ᵗʰ July 1997, at the Almeida Theatre, London**

The tragic story of the sixteen-year old girl, beheaded for having participated in the murder of a brutal and licentious father who had raped her repeatedly, has captured the imagination of many painters, writers and musicians.

Count Francesco Cenci, the heir to a huge fortune, had previously been imprisoned three times for savage acts of debauchery, but had been released on each occasion by Pope Clement VIII on receiving generous gifts from the condemned man. At home, he expected his daughter, Beatrice, to submit to rape as a duty to her father. Eventually the girl and her stepmother connived in his murder, but on being discovered, were both executed without pity. Clearly the death had deprived the corrupt pontiff of a major source of income, and it seems likely that this led to the refusal of a pardon more than any sense of principle or scandal on his part.

Posterity has vindicated Beatrice in no uncertain manner. The young girl is considered a heroine and also as a martyr to the cause of freedom by the Roman people and her name is revered to this day. At least five operas have been written on this sixteenth century subject, four of them in the twentieth century. The best-known ones are by Alberto Ginastera, premièred on 10th September 1971 in the U.S.A., and by Bertold Goldschmidt. The latter, written for the 1951 Festival of Britain competition, was one of four operas to win a prize but had to wait until 16th April 1988 to receive its first performance, at a concert in the Queen Elizabeth Hall, London. The work, although modern, does not abandon operatic tradition and contains set pieces and passages that are richly melodic.

Very recently, the young Italian composer, Giorgio Battistelli, has written an eighty-minute melodrama on the story. The work consists of music and the spoken word and is supplemented with sections of film and highlighted by a number of strange stage and electronic effects. Although the music is extremely modern it is pervaded with an inherent melodic vein, which betrays the composer's nationality. The libretto is taken from Antonin Artaud's 1935 account of the tragedy, of which it is a shortened translated version. The work was commissioned by the British Arts Council and was written for the Almeira Opera.

The collage represents the fourth of eleven scenes. Beatrice is confronted by her lustful father. She tries to show respect, while at the same time spurning his advances. He asks for wine, which she serves him. As his craving increases she runs out. Alone, he asserts that she will not escape his clutches...

COUNT FRANCESCO CENCI
(EXCITED.)
"Beatrice!"

BEATRICE
(EMOTIONAL.)
"Father!
Leave me, ungodly one...
I can never forget you are my father...
But disappear...
and I may forgive you."

COUNT FRANCESCO CENCI
"Your father is thirsty, Beatrice.
Will you not give your father
something to drink?"

(BEATRICE POURS HIM A LARGE GLASS OF WINE.
HE TOUCHES HER HAIR. BEATRICE REACTS VIOLENTLY.)

"Ah! Viper!
I shall weave a spell that will make you
sweet and submissive."

(BEATRICE LEAVES IN PANIC.)

"Let her go. Let her go.
The spell is working.
From now on she won't escape me."

L'Incoronazione di Poppea

Music **Claudio Monteverdi**
Libretto **Giovanni Francesco Busenello**
First Performance **Carnival of 1643, at the Teatro SS. Giovanni e Paolo, Venice**

The oldest surviving complete operatic work, Euridice, composed by Jacopo Peri, was first performed in 1600 and it appears that the artistic genre had just been discovered around that time. Monteverdi's first example, Orfeo, was premièred in 1607. It was written in the general style prevalent then, namely a text declamation to notes that were accompanied by fairly simple supporting chords. Now, in 1642, he had used a new musical language that interpreted and dramatised the nature of his characters, their feelings, their speech and their movements. Monteverdi had embarked on this style in his previous opera 'Il ritorno di Ulisse in Patria', but in 'Poppea' he put far more emphasis on the aria as opposed to the recitative. Also, it is probably no coincidence that he was now dealing with real people who had definitely existed and not, as previously, with some cardboard deity from mythology or semi-legendary hero out of an ancient poem.

In the opera, all the main characters are treated in an unsympathetic, negative manner. It should be remembered that the underlying theme, a courtesan becoming an Empress, is an insult to moral values as well as to Rome and its people. Clearly, the plot could not be sustained realistically with positive, virtuous characters. In the event, Monteverdi and his librettist make the story not only credible, but also acceptable.
Indeed, 'L'Incoronazione di Poppea' is a far cry from what the same composer had written thirty-five years before and points the way towards future operatic composition.

Unfortunately, the original autographed manuscript has been lost and modern performances are based on two existent versions, (one in Naples and the other in Venice), both containing revisions by the composer's contemporaries, particularly Francesco Cavalli. The Neapolitan version is probably the older and closer to Monteverdi's first edition.

The plot is complex. Put simply, the Emperor Nero wishes to leave his wife Octavia and marry Ottone's lover Poppea. In order to achieve this he has to eliminate, either by execution or exile, all those who stand in his way...

The collage scene takes place in the third act. Ottone, with the help of Drusilla, who loves him, has failed in his attempt to murder Poppea. They and Octavia, who instigated the deed, have been banished and Nero fulfils his marriage promise...

NERONE

"Hoggi come promisi
Mia sposa tu sarai."

"Today, as I promised
you shall be my bride."

POPPEA

"Si caro dì veder non spero mai."

"I didn't dare to hope for such a happy day."

NERONE

"Per il nome di Giove e per il mio,
Hoggi sarai ti giuro
Di Roma imperatrice.
In parola regal te n'assicuro."

"In the names of Jupiter and myself,
I swear that today you shall become
Empress of Rome.
I assure you by my royal word."

POPPEA

"Idolo del cor mio, gionta è pur l'hora,
Che del mio ben godrò,"

"Idol of my heart, the hour has come
that I shall enjoy my love."

NERONE AND POPPEA

"Ne più s'interporrà noia o dimora.
Cor nel petto non ho,
Me'l rubasti sì, sì,
Dal sen me lo rapì,
De' tuo' begli occhi il lucido sereno,
Per te, ben mio, non ho più core in seno.
Stringimi fra le braccia innamorate,
Chi mi trafisse ohimè!
Non interrotte havrai l'hore beate.
Se son perduto in te,
In te mi cercarò,
In te mi trovarò,
E tornerò a riperdermi, ben mio,
Che sempre in te perduto esser voglio io."

"May no bother or distance interpose.
I have my heart no more.
You stole it, yes, indeed!.
You stole it from my breast
with the clear light of your lovely eyes.
My love, for you, I've lost my heart.
Clasp me in the loving arms
that have vanquished me, alas!
You will have uninterrupted blissful hours.
I'm lost in you,
I will seek myself in you,
I will find myself in you,
and I shall lose myself again, my love
for in you I wish to be lost forever."

Il Campanello

Music **Gaetano Donizetti**
Libretto **Gaetano Donizetti (Adapted from the French vaudeville 'La Sonnette de Nuit'.)**
First Performance **1ˢᵗ June 1836, at the Teatro Nuovo, Naples.**

Il Campanello (The Night Bell), is Donizetti's 53rd opera. It is a comedy about the first wedding night of an old pharmacist and his young bride. Enrico, the girl's ex-boyfriend, a bounder who has continually let her down in the past, having been spurned, is intent on revenge. Since the law requires a chemist to answer his bell at any hour, he has decided to ruin the couple's first night together. He is able to intrude on three separate occasions by masquerading as different patients, who urgently need the chemist's assistance.
He first appears as a French dandy. This part is sung with unusual piano accompaniment to a farcical mixture of Italian and broken French. He then appears as a singer who has lost his voice when due to appear in the production of a new opera by Donizetti (Il Campanello of course!). Lastly, he presents himself as an old man who requires a prescription of comically endless length. The wedding night is indeed wrecked but the young man gets his just deserts the following morning when the virtuous bride yet again rejects his advances.

The opera is extremely endearing, being packed with humour, accompanied by an endless array of good tunes, particularly for the baritone and bass voices.

The scene shown in the collage depicts the wedding reception at the beginning of the opera. The action takes place near Naples and Vesuvius can be seen in the background. The artist has added a group of his own, on the left-hand side of the picture. Here, the enraged Enrico is being restrained while the couple and their friends are toasting the wedding...

"Evviva Don Annibale!
Evviva Serafina!
Vogliam danzare e bevere
Insino a domattina."

"Pistacchio è un Esculapio,
La sposa è una Ciprigna;
Fia a così bella coppia
La sorte ognor benigna.
Ei fra speziali domina,
Ella fra le bellezze;
Amore e Imen preparano
Torrenti di dolcezze."

"Vogliam fra lieti brindisi,
Vogliam danzare e bevere
Insino a domattina:
Evviva Don Annibale!
Evviva Serafina!
Viva,viva!"

RELATIVES AND WEDDING GUESTS
"Hurrah for Don Annibale!
Hurrah for Serafina!
We want to dance and drink
until tomorrow morning."

"Pistacchio is an Aesculapius,
the bride is a Venus;
may fate be always kind
to such a handsome pair.
He the greatest chemist,
she the fairest beauty;
may the gods of love and marriage
bestow sweet joys a' plenty."

"We want to dance and drink
with happy toasts between,
until tomorrow morning;
Hurrah to Don Annibale!
Hurrah to Serafina!
Hurrah, hurrah!"

Così Fan Tutte

Music **Wolfgang Amadeus Mozart** • Libretto **Lorenzo Da Ponte**

First Performance **26ᵗʰ January 1790, at the Burgtheater, Vienna**

Mozart's last Da Ponte opera and his nineteenth, was written on the commission of the Emperor Joseph II. Composition was rapid, the work being completed in about one month. The theme, that of a lover testing the constancy of his betrothed by masquerading in disguise, was a well-known one and the Viennese public took to the opera with much enthusiasm. The plot, set in Naples, concerns two young military officers, Ferrando and Guglielmo, who are bragging about the fidelity of their respective fiancées, Dorabella and Fiordiligi. Their more realistic friend Don Alfonso lays a wager that given the appropriate circumstances, the girls will prove no less fickle than other women. The bet is accepted and the fun begins. The young men pretend they have received a call to arms and depart, later to return, disguised as Albanian nobility. Now Da Ponte doubles the constancy test, as each woos the other's fiancée. The two women show resolute steadfastness at first, but egged on by their maid, Despina (who is in cahoots with Don Alfonso), eventually succumb. The charade is revealed as a mock wedding is about to take place between the girls and the Albanians. Fortunately, in the end the young ladies, a little less virtuous, are reunited with their original lovers. Naturally, Don Alfonso has won his wager.

The farcical and frivolous plot is accompanied by some of the composer's most engaging music. There are serious passages of great lyrical beauty, but the comic element surfaces repeatedly throughout the work. Among the former, the Act I trio, 'Soave sia il vento' and Fiordiligi's Act II solo, 'Per pietà, ben mio, perdona' are memorable, while the latter include Despina's 'In uomini, in soldati' in Act I and the girls' second act duet 'Prenderò quell brunettino'. Notable pieces in which both elements are to be found are the quintet 'Di scrivermi ogni giorno ...' and the Albanians' feigned suicide scene, both in the first act. The finale to the opera is superb, starting with a lyrical duet 'Idol mio, se questo è vero', sung by the two ladies. This is then expanded into a quartet as the young men join in and then a quintet, thanks to the arrival of Despina. Lastly, as in his previous opera, 'Don Giovanni', Mozart concludes with an ensemble singing a moral, in this case one that calls for the need to accept and forgive the fragility and waywardness of human nature.

The collage is a medley of different parts of the mock wedding scene between the girls and the Albanians and that just preceding it in which Don Alfonso has won his bet. Wine is served and a toast is proposed. Despina enters, disguised as a notary...

FERRANDO E GUGLIELMO
"Tocca e bevi!" — *"Clink and drink!"*

FIORDILIGI E DORABELLA
"Bevi e tocca!" — *"Drink and clink!"*

FIORDILIGI, DORABELLA FERRANDO
"E nel tuo, nel mio bicchiero
Si sommerga ogni pensiero.
E non resti più memoria
Del passato ai nostri cor."

"And in your glass and in mine
may all thoughts be submerged.
And may no memory of the past
remain in our hearts."

(SOON AFTERWARDS...)

DESPINA
(DISGUISED AS A NOTARY.)
"Per contratto da me fatto
Si congiunge in matrimonio
Fiordiligi con Sempronio
E con Tizio Dorabella
Sua legittima sorella.
Quelle, dame ferraresi,
Questi, nobili Albanesi,..."

"By contract prepared by myself
Let there be joined in marriage
Fiordiligi with 'Harry'
and with 'Tom', Dorabella
her legitimate sister.
Those, ladies from Ferrara;
these, Albanian nobles,..."

(JUST BEFORE THIS SCENE, DON ALFONSO HAS CLAIMED VICTORY OVER HIS WAGER.)

DON ALFONSO
"Tutti accusan le donne ed io le scuso
Se mille volte al dì cangiano amore,
Altri un vizio lo chiama, ed altri un uso.
L'amante che si trova alfin deluso,
Non condanni l'altrui, ma il proprio errore.
Già che giovani, vecchie, e belle, e brutte,
Ripetete con me: così fan tutte."

"All accuse women and I excuse them
if they change their love a thousand times a day,
some call it a vice and others the done thing.
The lover who finds himself at length deluded,
should not condemn others, but his own error.
Since women young, old, pretty and ugly ...
Repeat with me: thus do they all."

FERRANDO, GUGLIELMO, DON ALFONSO
"Così fan tutte." — *"Thus do they all."*

Leoncavallo, who wrote his own libretto, is reported to have taken the story of this opera from a real life event. Many years before, his magistrate father had judged a case involving a 'Delitto d'onore', a crime of honour. In this case the crime had been one of passion resulting from a love triangle consisting of two men, and the wife of one of them.

The opera, vividly depicting the rough way of life of the lower classes in Calabria, southern Italy, in the mid-nineteenth century, is an excellent example of verismo. Furthermore, the idea of a play within a play, with the acted and real life dramas being identical is very telling, particularly as this goes not only for the plot but also for the music and words. Indeed, when in the harlequinade the jealous Canio overhears Nedda's fateful words, "Until tonight and then I shall be yours for ever", it is for the second time within a few hours. His reaction is "My God, those very same words", and immediately events that cannot be controlled are set into motion. The play-acting, and the real life drama become increasingly interwoven – the latter inexorably and tragically taking over completely by the end of the opera.

I Pagliacci

Music **Ruggero Leoncavallo**
Libretto **Ruggero Leoncavallo**
First Performance **21ˢᵗ May 1982, at the Teatro Dal Verme, Milan**

The work is full of admirable music, initiated by Tonio's melodious prologue, then Nedda's aria in which she envies the birds their freedom, the pretty play-acting tunes, Canio's two heartfelt arias and finally the increasingly violent declamation leading to the double murder at the end. The final words "La commedia e finita" (The play is over), provide a chilling ending to a story which shows verismo at its most vehement and brutal.

The picture represents a scene in the first act. Canio has just announced his spectacle for 11 p.m. that evening. The villagers invite him to go and drink with them at a nearby tavern. He accepts the offer...

"Di', con noi vuoi bevere
un buon bicchiere sulla crocevia?
Di', vuoi tu?"

VILLAGER
"Say, do you want to drink
a good glass with us at the crossroads?
Say, do you?"

"Con piacere."

CANIO
"With pleasure."

"Aspettatemi, anch'io ci sto!"

BEPPE
"Wait for me, I'll also accept!"

"Di', Tonio, vieni via?"

CANIO
"Say, Tonio, are you coming?"

"Io netto il somarello. Precedetemi."

TONIO
"I'll groom the donkey. You go ahead."

VILLAGER
(LAUGHING.)
"Watch out, Pagliaccio, he wants to stay
to woo Nedda."

"Bada, Pagliaccio, ei solo vuol restare
per far la corte a Nedda."

CANIO
(SMILING SARCASTICALLY AND FROWNING.)
"Oh! Oh! You think so?"
(HALF SERIOUS, HALF IRONIC.)
"Such a game, believe me,
better not be played
with me, my friends;
and I speak to Tonio,
and a bit to all of you!
The stage and real life
are not the same thing..."

"Eh! Eh! Vi pare?"

"Un tal gioco credetemi,
È meglio non giocarlo
Con me, miei cari;
E a Tonio,
E un poco a tutti or parlo!
Il teatro e la vita
Non son la stessa cosa..."

(HE CONTINUES AND REMINDS THE VILLAGERS THAT ON THE STAGE PLAY A LOVER STEALS HIS WIFE AND HE, PAGLIACCIO, EVEN GETS A BEATING FOR IT, BUT WARNS THAT THINGS WOULD TURN OUT VERY DIFFERENTLY IF THIS SHOULD HAPPEN IN REAL LIFE.)

Giovanni Gallurese

Music **Italo Montemezzi** • Libretto **Francesco D'Angelantonio**

First Performance **28**th **Junuary 1905, at the Teatro Vittorio Emanuele, Turin**

Giovanni Gallurese, Montemezzi's second opera, was composed originally as a one-act piece for a competition sponsored by Sonsogno, the Italian publishing house. When it failed to win it was revised and converted into a three-act work and this proved much more successful when it received its première under the baton of the conductor Tullio Serafin. Apart from its popular acclaim, it was supported by the publisher Ricordi and served as a springboard towards future commissions for the composer. Unfortunately it failed to become established in the operatic repertory.

The plot and setting of the work fit well into the 'verismo' genre. On the other hand, although the second act contains a song in the Sardinian dialect, the opera is hardly verismo in the musical sense, being lyrical and inward looking in character. Montemezzi's mature style, as in his best known opera, 'L'Amore dei tre Re', is already evident in this earlier work, which features a move towards the union of Italian traditional values with Wagnerian elements in the music. This is typified by the love duet in Act I when the colourful orchestral flow continuously sustains the vocal line in a skilful manner.

The scene is set in seventeenth century Sardinia. Giovanni Gallurese, a bandit, is fighting the island's tyrannical Spanish rulers. During the course of the action, he saves Maria from a masked kidnapper who is in fact a Spaniard, Rivegas. The couple fall in love, but Gallurese dares not expose himself, an unfortunate decision since Maria believes it was he who had tried to seize her. Later, the bandit and his men attack the Spaniards, defeat them and capture Rivegas, who reveals to Maria the identity of her saviour. The girl instantly repulses Gallurese but then, unable to live without him, returns to him, an action that enrages the Spaniard. Having been magnanimously set free by his captor, he treacherously murders him. Gallurese dies in Maria's arms as his men kill Rivegas in revenge.

The picture shows Rivegas drinking with some friends and bragging about his having saved Maria from abduction by Gallurese, in fact the complete opposite of the truth. However, unseen by the Spaniard, Gallurese has arrived and overhears this arrogant inversion of the facts. Boiling over with anger he starts to intervene, but is restrained by his friend Bastiano, who sorts out the matter on his behalf. In the meantime women are climbing up the steps towards the church where a mass commemorating the patron saint, Anthony, is about to begin...

(IN THE INTERESTS OF SIMPLICITY, THE LINES OF RIVEGAS, GALLURESE AND BASTIANO ARE PRESENTED 'EN BLOC', WHEREAS THEY ARE IN FACT INTERSPERSED IN THE TEXT.)

RIVEGAS

"E l'ultima, ascoltate;
quel briccon aveva osato di rapir Maria..."

"Listen to the latest;
that rogue had dared to abduct Maria..."
(MANY OH!S OF SURPRISED INDIGNATION.)

"Sì, di rapir la vaga montanina,
fra le belle osilesi la piu bella.
La ragazza a quel selvaggio
fu da me strappata, e ridonata al padre!"

"Yes, to kidnap the charming mountain lass,
the loveliest amongst the beautiful Osilo girls.
I wrested the girl from that savage,
and returned her to her father!"

GIOVANNI

"Che ascolto?! È mostruoso! Infame!
Strappata a me? Sfrontato! Disonesto.
Per l'inferno, lo uccido!..."

"What do I hear?! It's monstrous! Infamous!
Wrested from me? Shameless, dishonest man!
Hell, I'll kill him!..."
(MAKES TO DASH INTO THE INN,
BUT BASTIANO STOPS HIM.)

BASTIANO

"No! Dissennato! Ti perdi! Debb'io smentirlo."

"No! Madman! You'll be lost! I must expose his lie."

(BASTIANO ENTERS THE INN AND BURSTS INTO
A RESOUNDING LAUGH. THERE IS GENERAL SURPRISE.)

"Ebben, voi gli credete? Ah! ah! ah! ah!
E col vin fole bevete a sazietà!
Cantastorie, fanfarone, mentitore, gran buffone!"

"Well, you believe him? Ha! ha! ha! ha!
You drink wine with fables to overflowing!
Storyteller, braggart, liar, great buffoon!"

(POINTING TO RIVEGAS WITH A VIOLENT GESTURE.)

"Egli tentò rapir la montanina
che un ignoto salvò! L'eroe...fuggì!"

"He tried do abduct the mountain lass
whom an unknown person saved!
That hero...fled!"

(A CHORUS OF LAUGHTER AND EXCLAMATIONS IS RAISED.)

T he opera is based on a Giovanni Verga play of 1883. This interested Mascagni to the point of asking a friend to write a libretto. In the event, two librettists were utilised and the composer completed his score in the early part of 1889. The work was submitted to the second one-act opera competition organised by the Italian publisher Sonsogno, and captured one of three prizes. Premièred in Rome a year later it became an instant success and within two years had been performed with much acclaim in many theatres abroad. This realistic drama, involving ordinary lower class people, captured the public imagination and led the way to the 'Verismo' style of opera. Yet no future attempt by any composer was able to better Mascagni's forerunner in its raw and violent passion.

Cavalleria Rusticana Music **Pietro Mascagni**

Libretto **Giovanni Targioni-Tozzetti and Guido Menasci** • First Performance **17ᵗʰ May 1890, at the Teatro Costanzi, Rome**

The plot involves betrayal and revenge. The scene is set in Sicily on Easter Sunday. Turiddu is having an affair with his former love, Lola, who is now married. His present girl, Santuzza, quarrels with him over this, and her jealousy is aroused to fury as the argument becomes more and more heated.

At the climax she wishes him an evil Easter, as he throws her to the ground. In despair she discloses the betrayal to Lola's husband, with tragic consequences.

The opera abounds with ear-catching, tuneful melodies and impassioned singing. It contains a beautiful Easter hymn, a number of fine arias (including a splendid drinking song depicted in the collage), fiery duets and excellent choral work. Moreover, a number of interesting effects help to intensify the action. For example, the prelude is suddenly cut short by a 'Siciliana' with which Turiddu serenades his mistress, only to be dramatically taken up again with increased tragic power. Similarly, later, Turiddu's quarrel with Santuzza is frozen as Lola appears singing a ditty to her lover. This has the effect of inflaming Santuzza, and the dispute resumes with ferocious intensity to proceed towards its fatal conclusion. Again, at the point when Alfio has been told of his wife's infidelity and has sworn revenge, the action is halted by an intermezzo that merely serves to heighten the tension in one's expectation of what is to follow. At the end of the opera, the dramatic news of Turiddu's death is delivered by a screaming woman offstage.

The fashion of verismo led Leoncavallo to write the equally successful 'Pagliacci' two years later. The two works were paired and became an inseparable double bill, a position they still hold. Significantly, neither composer was able to repeat such success again...

"Viva il vino spumeggiante
Nel bicchiere scintillante
Come il riso dell'amante
Mite infonde il giubilo!
Viva il vino ch'è sincero,
Che ci allieta ogni pensiero,
E che affoga l'umor nero
Nell'ebbrezza tenera."

TURIDDU

"Here's to sparkling wine
in the glittering glass
which awakens joy
like the laughter of one's lover!
Here's to wine that is honest,
that cheers up every thought
and drowns every sombre feeling
in sweet abandon."

Fidelio

Music **Ludwig van Beethoven** • Libretto **Joseph Sonnleithner and Georg Treitschke**

Original version **'Leonore' 20th November 1805, at the Theater an der Wien, Vienna**
Final version **'Fidelio' 23rd May 1814, at the Kärntnertortheater, Vienna**

Although Beethoven, interested in composing an opera, was always on the lookout for a good libretto, Fidelio is, in fact, the only one he ever wrote. On the other hand, ballet and incidental stage music had already formed a considerable part of his output.
A clue to an explanation for this apparent paradox lies in fact that he could write symphonies, concertos, instrumental and chamber music as he liked, whereas the completion of his one opera took ten years to achieve. During this time the work was revised twice and a total of four overtures were created in order to arrive at the definitive one. Clearly, the writer of orchestral music was not at home in the operatic medium. Nevertheless, his musical experience and genius saw to it that he finally did complete the work to his satisfaction.

Two Cherubini operas had left a deep impression on Beethoven. They were 'Lodoïska' and 'Les Deux Journées'. Both featured heroic action in the face of oppressive tyranny.
The ideals fundamental to those works were close to Beethoven's heart and the intention of composing something on the same lines was an obvious outcome. His personal situation also played a part. The concept of a wife totally devoted to her man appealed to him particularly as he had just experienced an unhappy love affair with Josephine von Brunswick.
This and his deafness, which was isolating him increasingly from the world, enabled him to associate vividly with the innocent Florestan languishing in prison in his opera.

The plot of Fidelio is based on real life. A few years previously in France, during the reign of terror, a woman had disguised herself to free her politically imprisoned husband from jail. Beethoven had come across a libretto based on this event. A German version was prepared and an opera was composed, being completed in about 18 months.
This three-act version proved a failure. There was too much repetition in the first act and overall it was loosely constructed and too long. The composer revised it by changing the overture, removing some of the repetition and cutting it down to two acts. The response was better but Beethoven himself, unsatisfied, withdrew it. Eight years later, Treitschke carried out a thorough revision, in collaboration with the composer. A new, shorter overture was composed and nearly every scene was modified. The opera was tightened up, some parts were removed and more emphasis was placed on ensembles. At last Beethoven had arrived at the opera we know today. It proved an immediate and lasting success.
Indeed, the fundamental plot of the opera, the triumph of conjugal love and revolutionary idealism over despotism and oppression was so much in tune with the composer's inner feelings that its eventual successful achievement had always been a certainty.
Beethoven had taken ten years to get it right but had positively succeeded in the end!

The opera is set in Spain in the outskirts of Seville. The collage depicts the gaoler's quarters in the first act. Leonore, disguised as Fidelio has just returned, carrying heavy chains from the blacksmith. The gaoler, Rocco, praises him for his industry.
He believes Fidelio is helping him with such zeal because he has aspirations towards his daughter, Marzelline...

ROCCO
"Gut! Du bist ein kluger Junge! Ich kann gar nicht begreifen, wie du deine Rechnung mochst."
"Good! You're a smart lad! I cannot understand how you make up your bill."

LEONORE / FIDELIO
"Ich tue was ich kann."
"I do what I can."

ROCCO
"Sei versichert, dein Lohn wird nicht ausbleiben."
"Rest assured, you will get your reward."

LEONORE / FIDELIO
"O glaubt nicht, dass ich meine Schuldigkeit nur des Lohnes wegen...ich..."
"Oh do not believe that I do my duty just for some reward...I..."

ROCCO
"Still! Meinst du, ich könne dir nicht ins Herz sehen?"
"Hush! Do you think I cannot see into your heart?"

MARZELLINE
"Mir ist so Wunderbar, Es engst das Herz mir ein; Er liebt mich, es ist klar. Ich werde glücklich sein."
"It's so wonderful, my heart is bursting; he loves me, that is clear. I shall be happy."

Cervantes' masterpiece has not been short of operatic interpretations, of which the best-known are probably those by Massenet (1908-9) and Henze (1976). The Paisiello work, premièred in 1769, is based on a musical play on the subject staged in Vienna some fifty years before. The librettist, Lorenzi, with whom Paisiello was to have a lasting partnership, modified the script to suit the opera's intended audience. He achieved this by having a couple of male Neapolitan comic characters clumsily court and eventually win over two of the ladies (a duchess and a countess), in the action. In addition to the mad but transcendently heroic Quixote and the buffo Sancho Panza, three serving girls, one of whom masquerades as Dulcinea, made up the cast.

Don Chisciotte   Music **Giovanni Paisiello** • Libretto **Giovanni Battista Lorenzi**

First Performance **Summer of 1769, at the Teatro dei Fiorentini, Naples**

The libretto, naturally in Italian, has Neapolitan dialect thrown in, used on and off by the two comic suitors and the serving girls. Written for the Naples audience of the time, it is old fashioned by today's standards, but nevertheless not without interest. The whole thing is a farce in which the ladies make fun of their suitors, and in particular, conspire to render Quixote and Panza more and more ridiculous at every turn.

The music is simple, light and lyrical. An example is the scene between the countess and Don Quixote towards the end of the second act. Beautiful solos for soprano and then tenor lead up to a lovely duet, showing the composer at his best. On the other hand, the music accompanying the entrance of the Countess and Carmosina, disguised as an enchantress and Dulcinea respectively, is appropriately pompous and affected, clearly illustrating the artificial and ironic nature of the scene.

The opera ends with general rejoicing as the two couples declare their love while Quixote and Panza move on to new adventures.

The picture represents the final scene of the first act. Don Quixote and his squire have been invited to an open-air banquet. The knight-errant refuses to wash his hands, while Sancho rapidly sits at the table and starts to eat...

SANCHO
"Signori miei, mi onorino:
Si servino: si prendano
Un bocconcin con me"

"Ladies and Gentlemen, do me the honour:
serve yourselves: take
a small bite with me."

CARMOSINA AND CARDOLELLA
"Buon pro',
vecchio affamato!"

"Good for you,
old starver!"

DUCHESS AND COUNTESS
"Evviva, evviva Sancho!"

"Cheers, cheers, to Sancho!"

QUIXOTE
"Evviva il bestialissimo
Scudiero incivilissimo."

"Cheers for the most beastly
and uncivil of squires."

SANCHO
"Cos'è? cos'è di grazia?
I piatti si raffreddano:
I vini si riscaldano,
Ed io l'errato corrigo facevo.
Che cos'è?"

"What is it? Pardon, what is it?
The dishes are getting cold:
the wines are becoming warm,
and I was correcting this error.
What's the matter?"

Carmen

Music **Georges Bizet** • Libretto **H.Meilhac e L.Halévy**

First Performance **3ʳᵈ March 1875, at the Opéra-Comique, Paris**

Carmen is Bizet's last opera. The composer, having taken two years to write his masterpiece, tragically died at the age of thirty-six and never knew how popular it would become.

The plot, taken from Prosper Mérimée's novel, was very ably modified by Bizet's librettists in a number of ways, most of which had the purpose of making the work more presentable to the Parisian audience. Even so, many spectators and most of critics found a number of things hard to digest. Carmen's provocative sexual nature, the disorderly and unruly behaviour of the squabbling, cigarette smoking women's chorus and the murder of Carmen on stage are clear examples of what a bourgeois society did not appreciate.
The opera was therefore generally condemned as being immoral and although it ran for nearly fifty performances, it wasn't re-staged in Paris until 1883, a gap of eight years.
Carmen did, however, fare rather better abroad. In particular, it did much to accelerate the development of the 'Verismo' school in Italy where it was widely acclaimed.
Also, many celebrated composers, including Brahms, Tchaikovsky and Wagner praised the work very highly. Unfortunately Bizet became ill shortly after the première and failed to recover fully. It is possible that the unfavourable reception to his opera contributed in part to his death.

The story is well known. Carmen, a gypsy, seduces Don José, a hitherto virtuous soldier and causes him to abandon the chaste Michaela and desert his regiment. She drags him into increased degeneracy and lawlessness and then drops him for the more exciting Escamillo, a bullfighter. The opera ends with José, desperate, murdering her and then giving himself up to the authorities.

The composition has a fine libretto and boasts Bizet's most complex and tuneful music with more than a hint of Spanish flavour where Carmen herself is involved.
Much of the work is quintessentially French, however; Don Jose's 'flower song', Michaela's aria and the music embracing the smugglers, El Dancairo and El Remendado are good examples of this. The orchestral palette of the opera is extremely rich, the action is highly dramatic and well presented and the whole work leaves a memorable impression.
It is not difficult to understand why Carmen has remained one of the most popular and most performed operas in the repertoire.

The picture depicts the start of the second act. The scene takes place at the tavern of Lillas Pastia. A group of soldiers is drinking. Some gypsies are strumming guitars while others dance. Carmen begins to sing, then together with her friends, Frasquita and Mercédès, joins the dance. Presently Escamillo, fresh from a bullfighting success in Granada, arrives on the scene...

CARMEN

"Les Bohémiens a tour de bras
De leurs instruments faisaient rage,
Et cet éblouissant tapage,
Ensorcelait les zingaras!
Sous le rhythme de la chanson,
Ardentes, folles, enfiévrées,
Elles se laissaient, enivrées,
Emporter par le tourbillon!
Tralalala!"

"The gypsies, with all their strength
drove their instruments to fury,
and this dazzling din
bewitched the gypsy women!
Beneath the rhythm of the song
ardent, crazy, feverish,
they let themselves go, inebriated,
transported by the giddy round!
Tralalala!"

(CARMEN DANCES.)

(PRESENTLY, ZUNIGA, JOSE'S LIEUTENANT, NOTICES THE APPROACH OF A TORCHLIGHT PARADE.)

ZUNIGA

"Une promenade aux flambeaux!
C'est le vainqueur des courses de Grenade.
Voulez -vous avec nous boire, mon camarade?
A vos succès anciens, à vos succès nouveaux!"

"A procession with torches!
It's the victor of the bullfights in Granada.
Will you drink with us, my friend?
To your old triumphs, to your new triumphs!"

(ESCAMILLO ENTERS.)

ESCAMILLO

"Votre toast, je peux vous le rendre,
Señors, señors, car avec les soldats,
Oui, les Toréros peuvent s'entendre,
Pour plaisirs ils ont les combats!"

"I can return your toast,
sirs, sirs, because with soldiers,
yes, bullfighters have an understanding,
their pleasure lies in fighting!"

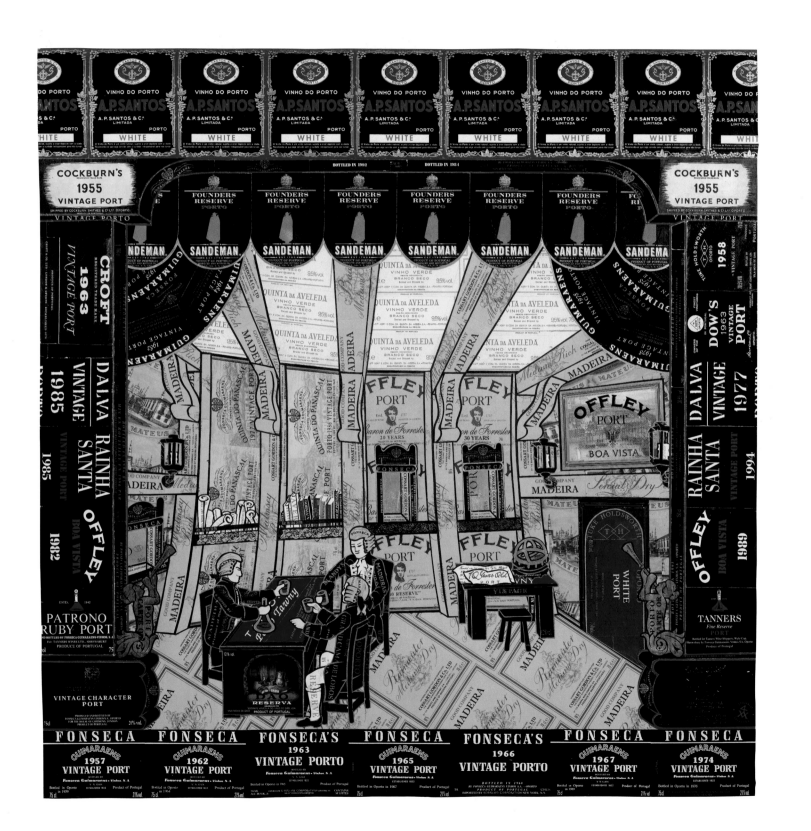

Billy Budd

Music **Benjamin Britten** • Libretto **E.M. Forster and Eric Crozier**

First Performance **1ˢᵗ December 1951, at the Royal Opera House, Covent Garden, London**

Billy Budd is Britten's sixth opera, having been commissioned by the Great Britain Arts Council for the 1951 Festival. The libretto underwent several drafts before satisfying the composer and was eventually completed by the end of 1949. Composition was started in the summer of the following year, but although Britten had conceived a two-act work, the opera was premièred at the end of 1951 in a four-act format. However, increasingly dissatisfied and feeling that the work needed a greater continuity to maintain its dramatic impetus, the composer reverted to his original concept and in 1969 altered the opera into its presently accepted two-act version.

Although being unusual in not having female roles, the opera is one of Britten's very best. The opulent orchestration and excellent libretto combine to portray the action aboard a British warship in Nelson's time very vividly, both musically and dramatically.

The plot concerns the trial and execution of Billy Budd, a good and enthusiastic but simple-minded seaman, for having struck and accidentally killed the ship's master-at-arms. This evil officer had first victimised him repeatedly without good reason and then falsely accused him of planning mutiny and treason. The captain's role, in putting duty above compassion in spite of being aware of the facts, forms a poignant part of the story.

The picture portrays the beginning of the second scene in Act I (or, the start of Act II in the four-act version). The captain invites his two senior officers into his cabin to take wine with him...

CAPTAIN VERE
  "Boy!"
(THE BOY ENTERS.)
  *"My compliments to Mr Redburn and
  Mr Flint, and will they take a glass of wine
  with me."*
(THE BOY GOES OUT.)

(A LITTLE LATER.)

(THE BOY OPENS THE DOOR TO ADMIT THE
FIRST LIEUTENANT AND THE SAILING MASTER.)

BOY
  (SPEAKING.)
  "Mr, Redburn and Mr. Flint, sir."
(THE BOY SETS A BOTTLE AND GLASSES ON THE
TABLE AND GOES OUT.)

CAPTAIN VERE
  *"Gentlemen, I am glad to see you.
  Be seated."*
(THEY SIT.)
  "Gentlemen, the King!"

MR. REDBURN AND MR. FLINT
  "The King!"

ALL
  "God bless Him!"
(THEY DRINK.)

The composition of Musorgsky's opera on Pushkin's historical tragedy was initiated in 1868 and completed in just fourteen months. During this process, the twenty-four original scenes were drastically reduced. Several, especially those in which the main protagonist didn't feature, were eliminated. Others were fused while some material was invented. The resulting seven tableaux were finished by the end of 1869 and submitted to the Imperial Theatres' directorate where the work was rejected, mainly on the grounds of it having no major female role. Musorgsky immediately revised and expanded the opera, making a number of adjustments. Of particular importance was the incorporation of a new third act, set in Poland, which provided the hitherto missing leading female part. Again the Imperial Theatres committee rejected the work but then happily changed its mind and the première took place, with great success, in early 1874.

The chorus is elevated to being a major character in the action, the interplay between Boris' tormented mind and his subjugated people being an important part of the drama.

It is therefore because of its dramatic impact that Boris Godunov, quintessentially the most Russian of all the Russian operas, has now gained a permanent place in the operatic repertory.

The picture represents the second scene in the first act, set in an inn near the Lithuanian border. Two monks, Varlaam and Missail enter, followed by the disguised Grigory, the pretender to the throne. Wine is ordered, but Grigory refuses to drink...

Boris Godunov

Music **Modest Musorgsky**
Libretto **Modest Musorgsky**
First Performance **27th January 1874,
at the Mariinsky Theatre, St. Petersburg**

After Musorgsky's death, the opera disappeared from the stage. Rimsky-Korsakov believed this was due to the fact that the work was flawed, particularly because of an orchestration which was, in his opinion, bland and uninspired. Thus, he re-orchestrated the opera and made a number of other alterations. His version, first produced on 28th November 1896, revived the work and held the stage for seventy years, after which Musorgsky's definitive version began making a comeback. Nowadays, the latter is commonly performed while the Rimsky-Korsakov version, in spite of its more sumptuous orchestral palette, is rarely seen.

Musically, Musorgsky's opera gets its strength from its dramatic quality rather than its musical beauty. The story of Boris, who, suspected of having murdered the Tsarevich and then becoming ruler seven years later on the death of the Tsar, is tailor-made for powerful drama and Musorgsky makes full use of the opportunities offered. There is no deeper portrayal of a main protagonist in any other opera. Boris's address to his people in the prologue, his Act II soliloquy, his interview with Shiusky and the subsequent clock scene, and finally his dying address to his son involve a profound analysis of this dominating, intimidating and yet wretched individual. The orchestration is simple but eloquently powerful, being directly linked into the dramatic action rather than an opulent background to it.

*"Vot vam, otsy moi,
peite na zdorove."*

INNKEEPER
(PLACING THE WINE ON THE TABLE.)
*"Here for you, reverent fathers,
drink to your good health."*

*"Spasibo, khozyayushka,
bog tebya blagoslovi!"*

MISAIL AND VARLAAM
*"Thank you, landlady
may God bless you!"*
(THEY POUR THE WINE AND DRINK,
EXCEPT FOR GRIGORY.)

(LATER.)

*"Odnako, brat: kogda ya pyu,
tak trezvykh ne lyublyu.*

Ino delo pyanstvo,

*ino delo chvanstvo;
khochesh zhit kak my,
milosti prosim!
Nyet ?!
Tak ubiraisya, provalivai!"*

VARLAAM
*"Yet, brother: when I drink,
I don't like sober men.*
(HE DRINKS.)
Drunkenness is one thing,
(HE DRINKS.)
*pride is another;
if you wish to live with us,
you're welcome!
If not ?!
Then go, get out!"*

GRIGORY
*"Drink but keep your thoughts
to yourself father Varlaam!..."*

*"Pyei, da pro sebya razumei,
otets Varlaam!..."*

A university Professor of chemistry by profession, Borodin spent most of his time at the St. Petersburg medical academy where he taught and carried out research. Untrained from a musical point of view, he regarded composition as a relaxing pastime to be carried out whenever his professional duties allowed. Consequently it comes as no surprise that his only opera took eighteen years to compose and was left unfinished when he died, unexpectedly, at the early age of fifty-three.

Prince Igor

Music **Alexander Borodin** • Libretto **Alexander Borodin**

First Performance **23rd December 1890, at the Mariinsky Theatre, St. Petersburg**

The story of Prince Igor, a Russian leader, who unites his fragmented people against the barbaric Polovtsian tribes who had laid the country to waste, greatly appealed to Borodin as he saw a similar need for unity in nineteenth century Russia. Composition started in 1869 but after one year, a four-year break followed until a resumption took place in 1874. Thirteen years of intermittent composition failed to complete the opera, which was finished jointly by Glazunov and Rimsky-Korsakov. Glazunov wrote the overture, filled in several gaps and reconstructed the third act while Rimsky-Korsakov edited the work and then orchestrated it. The première followed quickly and turned out to be a great success.

The libretto, written in stages by Borodin himself, is weak dramatically. Fortunately Borodin's music and Rimsky-Korsakov's orchestration are truly inspired. The solo and choral writing is excellent and the quality of the music lyrical yet enthralling with an extraordinary richness of colour and evocative images. The splendid Polvtsian dances are particularly famous and are often performed as a concert piece. Consequently, a rather unsatisfactory libretto is compensated by a superb score. Prince Igor is not a connoisseur's opera but remains immensely popular with the general public nevertheless.

It has long been asserted that in completing the work, Glazunov and Rimsky-Korsakov had not respected Borodin's intentions sufficiently. Other performing versions have been written, supposedly more faithful to the composer. However they have failed to dislodge the original version from the repertoire.

The collage represents the first scene in Act I. Prince Igor has left to fight the Polovtsians. In his absence his brother in law Prince Vladimir Galitzky is celebrating in his palace. Two gudok-playing jesters, Skula and Yeroshka, perform for him while the wine flows...

"Ne to, chto u knyazya Volodimira!
On-to, otets nash narod zhaleet,
Glyadi: bochku vykatil."

"Chto u knyazya da Volodimira,
Volodimira svet Yaroslavicha
Sobiralsya knyazhoi narod,
Da chto knyazhoi narod vse gorky pyanitsa."

"Gorky pyanitsa vse knyazhoi narod."

"Stonom stonet knyazhoi narod:
Da propilisya my, okayannye,
Za tvoe li zdorove knyazhe,
Vse my propili, knyaz, ty kormilets nash,
Otets batyushka, knyaz."

S K U L A

(She's) "Unlike Prince Vladimir
who is a real father to us, caring for his people
Look: he has presented us with a barrel of wine!"

(THE PRINCE'S SERVANTS BRING THE BARREL.
THE PEOPLE GATHER AROUND THE CASK;
THE GUDOK PLAYERS PLAY.)

(ROBUSTLY, FULL OF COMICAL SELF-IMPORTANCE.)
"At the palace of Prince Vladimir,
Prince Vladimir Yaroslavich,
all his courtiers have gathered.
Fine princely men they were indeed.
all dead drunk."

P E O P L E
"The princely courtiers were drunkards."

Y E R O S H K A :
"The Prince's courtiers were groaning:
Oh, dear me, we drank too much:
to the health of our Prince,
we've drunk too much to the Prince,
our benefactor, our father, our Prince."

Operas for Oceania

Voss - Richard Meale | 151

Richard Meale's first opera relates the attempt by Voss, a German explorer, to be the first man to go right through the outback and thus cross the Australian continent. In order to finance his expedition, he obtains the support of Bonner, a rich merchant, and it is at a party held at the latter's house that he meets Laura, his host's niece. A powerful attraction forms between them and they immediately fall in love. This bond is maintained after Voss has set out on his expedition and although Laura remains behind in Sydney, the two are able to communicate spiritually. It is upon this relationship, with the two main characters many miles apart, rather than the journey itself, that the opera is based.

Voss
Music **Richard Meale** • Libretto **David Malouf**

First Performance 1ˢᵗ **March 1986, at the Adelaide Festival, Australia**

Clearly, the adaptation of such a complex idea, taken from a novel by Patrick White, was not an easy undertaking. Although the opera took six years to compose, the time was well spent. Malouf's libretto is skilfully executed and has deservedly received much praise, while Meale has incorporated a number of unusual features into the music. Mainly an avant-garde composer at the time, he utilised a much more lyrical style to fit the period of the piece. In particular, he borrowed three quadrilles written by William Ellard for the party scene. Also, a piano is used here, making the setting more realistic. Only when the expedition meets disaster does the music become dissonant and distorted, and therefore more in Meale's usual style.

The picture shows the opening party scene at Bonner's house. Laura is seated in the garden, while Voss proclaims his exploratory ambitions. The other guests mock him...

VOSS
(WITH HIS ARMS OUTSTRETCHED.)
"I will cross this country from one side to the other.
I mean to know it with my heart.
It is mine by right of vision!"

(AS THE LIGHTS COME UP, DANCE MUSIC BEGINS:
QUADRILLE, 'LA SYDNEY', BY WILLIAM ELLARD.)

GUESTS
"Have you seen such a scarecrow?
Voss, he's called.
Some sort of German.
Means to cross the country looking for gold,
looking for an inland sea."

Wine in Opera

Wines of Africa and the Middle East

The wines of Israel

Wine production in Israel dates from very ancient times. It is written in the biblical book of Genesis, that Noah's first action after the great flood was to plant a vine and subsequently become inebriated with the wine produced! Also, writings from 1800 B.C. suggest that at that time wine was more common than water and used for a variety of different purposes. Later, during the Roman occupation, the wines of Judea were much appreciated and exported all over the empire, including Britain. Subsequently, the Crusaders, on arriving in the Holy Land, found vines already planted in a number of places, including near Bethlehem and Nazareth. During this period vines were destroyed and replanted as Moslems and Christians vied for domination.

In more recent times, in 1882, Edmund de Rothschild re-established wine production in Palestine. Zionist settlers took up the art well before the foundation of the state of Israel, thanks to the Baron's teaching and advice. Then, when the vineyards were destroyed by the Phylloxera Vastatrix insect, they were replanted by grafting them onto aphid resistant American root stocks.

Since 1948, when Israel was formed, the wine industry has continued to develop. In 1957 the Israel Wine Institute was formed. This organisation selected and adapted the best grape varieties to the most appropriate climates and soils, a formula already partially used by Rothschild in 1882 when he had chosen varieties from the Rhône Valley and the Midi in France, which had been considered to enjoy an equivalent climate at the time.

Nowadays, wine production in Israel can be divided into five basic regions, as follows:

(a) Northern Israel, including Galilee, Caanan-Meron, Nazareth-Cana, Naftali, Tabor and the Golan Heights.
(b) Upper central Israel, or Shomron, including Mount Carmel and Sharon.
(c) Shimshon, the lower coastal area between the Judean mountains and the plains around, Tel-Aviv, including Adulam, Latroun and Dan.
(d) Harey Yehuda, the Judean hills, including Jerusalem, Bethlehem, Hebron and Beth-El.
(e) The Negev southern desert country, including Beersheva and Ramat Arad.

Generally, the wines produced at high altitude are better than those made in the coastal areas, which tend to suffer from low acidity. Clearly, due to the hot sun and lack of summer rain, irrigation is an essential necessity and is consequently applied.

Most wine making is carried out by collective farming practices. Nevertheless there are a number of private owners. More modern wineries have improved the quality of their product by introducing the latest cellar techniques such as strict temperature control and new oak barrels. Also a greater number of varieties are now being used, and with much success. All kinds of wines are produced, including sweet and sparkling types. The latter are made using Chardonnay. Approximately 10% of the vintage is exported, including Kosher wine, principally to the U.S.A.

Israeli wines tend to be sold as varietal products, but some bear the district name on the label instead. ❧

Principal wines and grape varieties of Israel

REDS AND ROSÉS
Carignan, Alicante, Grenache, Cabernet Sauvignon, Merlot, Colombard.

WHITES
Muscat, Sémillon, Clairette, Sauvignon Blanc, Ugni Blanc, Riesling, Chardonnay, Dobuki (An indigenous variety).

The wines of Lebanon

Principal grape varieties of Lebanon

REDS AND ROSÉS
  Cabernet Sauvignon, Cinsault, Syrah, Carignan, Alicante.

WHITES
  Sauvignon Blanc, Obaideh, Meroué.

Viticulture in this part of the world is extremely ancient, dating from far before Roman times. Later, in the middle ages, the wines, much sought after by Europe, were widely traded by the Venetians. Nowadays, in spite of intermittent wars, the Christian population has continued to produce wine, much of it of good quality. In the Bekaa valley, cool nights ensure a reasonably late ripening in September. Here, the noble Bordeaux grapes, Cabernet Sauvignon and Sauvignon Blanc, the latter blended with local varieties, turn out rich and powerful products with good lasting potential.

The wines of Lebanon and the North African countries that follow are marketed as 'red' or 'white' wine, together with the producer's name. 🏃

The wines of North Africa

Viticulture over the whole North African continent is an ancient tradition. Wall and pottery paintings are evidence that wine consumption was an upper class cult in ancient Egypt. Wine production continued to prosper during Phoenician and Roman times. Then, in the early Middle Ages, Arab rule took over and the industry ceased to operate. It was not until the nineteenth and early twentieth centuries when French authority was established in Algeria, Morocco and Tunisia, that wine making was restored in those countries. At present, hardly any wine is produced in Egypt.

Algeria's potential for good viticulture was soon noted by French wine producers. Thus, when phylloxera caused havoc in Europe in the 1880's and many growers abandoned their vineyards and established themselves there, they expanded an already growing industry. Unfortunately, when the country was granted independence in 1962, the loss of French technical skills led to a crisis, particularly since exports of wine for blending purposes to France fell rapidly due to a surplus in Europe. At present, the situation is rather unclear. Although vineyards are being run down and no new vines appear to have been planted recently, a drive to boost exports by a quality increase, made possible by the country's good growing conditions, has taken place.

Algeria has seven designated regions. The mild winters and hot, dry summers favour red wine production, which accounts for about 60% of the total output. Whites take up about 30% and rosés 10%. The red wines are generally concentrated with a high alcohol content, but are not without interest. On the other hand, the whites tend to be soft and smooth with an agreeable degree of fruit. The rosés are excellent and well worth trying. Algeria is an important producer of wine bottle corks.

In Morocco, wine production has declined since independence in 1962. At present, in a mainly state controlled industry, there are two basic vine-growing regions. Due to the very hot weather early ripening is a problem. Consequently, reds, which account for approximately 85% of the total output, tend to be powerful but lack finesse, whereas whites, (a mere 5%), are prone to oxidation. A recent quality drive has improved some reds, which are now reasonably smooth. Also, an attempt to make better whites by introducing Chardonnay and Chenin Blanc has taken place. However, the most interesting Moroccan wine is probably 'Vin Gris', a pale rosé type made from the Cinsault grape.
This accounts for about 10% of the country's total production. Morocco is, like Algeria, a producer of wine corks.

Tunisia, a French protectorate until 1953, has similar problems to Morocco. Oxidation due to premature grape ripening is even more of a problem and reds tend to oxidise as well as whites. However, the country has gone some way towards overcoming this by using varieties that have a greater tolerance to the weather conditions. Some good, full-bodied reds are now made using Cabernet Sauvignon and even Pinot Noir and Mourvèdre grapes. Rosés are attractive and light, but must be dunk young due to the usual tendency to oxidise. Whites are decidedly inferior, but some interesting sweet wines are produced from the Muscat grape, which is also used to make some of the better dry products. Most wines are produced in two regions, at Nābul and Cap Bon.

Principal grape varieties of North Africa

REDS AND ROSÉS
Cabernet Sauvignon, Mourvèdre, Carignan, Cinsault, Alicante, Grenache, Pinot Noir, Syrah, Merlot, Morrastel, Nocera.

WHITES
Clairette, Ugni Blanc, Aligoté, Farrana, Macabeo, Ximénez, Chardonnay, Chenin Blanc, Muscat d'Alexandrie, Frontignan, Terracina, Beldi, Sauvignon Blanc, Sémillon Blanc.

ROSÉS
Cinsault, Alicante, Grenache.

The wines of South Africa

Principal wines and grape varieties of South Africa

REDS

Pinot Noir, Hermitage, Pinotage, Cabernet Sauvignon, Cabernet Franc, Merlot, Shiraz, Gamay, Carignan, Zinfandel, Pontac, South African 'Port' from Tinta Barroca grapes.

WHITES

Chenin Blanc (called Steen), Sémillon, Cape Riesling, Rhine Riesling, Sauvignon Blanc, Chardonnay, Gewürztraminer, Colombard, Clairette Blanche, Ugni Blanc, Bukettraube, Muscat of Alexandria (called Hanepoot), Chenel (a cross between Chenin Blanc and Ugni Blanc), White Muscadel, South African 'Sherry' from Palomino and Pedro Luis grapes.

ROSÉS

Pinot Noir, Hermitage.

The origin of wine production in South Africa can be traced back to 1657 when Jan van Riebeck set up the first Dutch colony there. He had brought Rhine Valley vine cuttings with him and two years later the first wine had been made. However, it was the second Dutch governor, Simon van der Stel, who put South Africa on the map as a major wine producing country. In 1684 he planted what turned out to be country's finest vineyard, the Groot Constantia, and in recognition of his efforts the major town in the area, Stellenbosch, was named after him. The final important historical date is 1688, when French Huguenots, fleeing from religious persecution, settled in what is now known as the Franschhoek Valley and greatly expanded the industry.

The foundations were now complete. Winemaking flourished and increased in fame. By the early nineteenth century, South Africa was competing internationally at the highest level. In particular, the dessert wine produced at the Constantia estate was proving a serious rival to the very best Sauternes that Bordeaux could make. This boom came to a sudden and tragic halt in 1885 when phylloxera devastated the vines. Unfortunately, they were not replanted until over thirty years later.

In spite of its glorious winemaking history, South Africa is traditionally a country of spirit drinking people. In 1973, in an effort to revive the industry, the government introduced strict controls on wine production, designating fourteen areas that could bear the 'Wine of Origin' title, a system similar to that in France. Other measures were taken to control and improve quality. For example, the go-ahead was given to plant many top level European grape varieties. The result of all this has been a marked general improvement in the wines and an increase in home consumption that is showing no signs of slowing down. Foreign demand and exports are also going up.

The wine producing regions of South Africa encompass the whole of the Cape peninsula. Around the coast this is mainly centred round the towns of Stellenbosch, Paarl and Wellington. Although the most famous vineyard of all, the Groot Constantia, is now used as a government controlled experimental station and museum, its locality is a region in its own right, in which some fine red, white and sweet wines are made. Indeed, partly due to a large variance in the soils, most regions tend not to specialise. However, Stellenbosch leans towards the making of table wines; whites in the west where the ground is inclined to be light and sandy, and reds on the granite soils in the areas at the feet of the Simonsberg and Stellenbosch Mountains. On the other hand, Paarl is the centre of the dessert and fortified wine industry. The Port and Sherry wines made here are excellent and at their best are second in the world only to Portugal and Spain respectively. Areas further inland, such as Klein Karoo, suffer from a hotter and drier climate, partly compensated by good irrigation techniques. Estates in these localities mainly specialize in the production of sweet wines. Other regions of interest are Robertson, situated due east of Paarl, Mossel Bay, a promising new area lying on the Indian Ocean east of the Cape, Walker Bay, north west of the Cape and Elgin, mid-way between Walker Bay and Stellenbosch. Other regions, where wine is produced in large quantities, mainly for bulk sale, are Worcester, Olifantsriver and Orange River.

In South Africa, wines are generally named by the grape variety they are made from. An interesting case is Pinotage, a red wine produced from a blend of Pinot and Hermitage (a variety of Cinsaut) grapes.

Wines of America

The wines of the U.S.A.

Principal wines and grape varieties of the U.S.A.

REDS AND ROSÉS

Concord, Catawba, (American Hybrids); Baco Noir, Marshall Foch, De Chaunac, Chancellor, Chelois, (French American Hybrids); Cabernet Sauvignon, Cabernet Franc, Merlot, Pinot Noir.

WHITES

Niagara, Delaware, Catawba, (American Hybrids); Aurora, Seyval Blanc, Cayuga GW3, Melody, Vidal Blanc, (French American Hybrids); Chardonnay, Riesling, Sémillon Blanc, Sauvignon Blanc, Chenin Blanc, Pinot Blanc, Pinot Gris, Gewürztraminer, Müller Thurgau.

Although native vines grew wild all over the country, the early European settlers found the resultant wine unsuitable to their taste. From 1619 onwards many attempts to plant varieties from Europe were made, but all ended in failure due to phylloxera and fungal diseases. Undaunted, the venture continued for 150 years, when French, German, Italian and Spanish know-how strove for a positive outcome—but in vain; the vines just died. California didn't appear to encounter the fungal problems, a fact not known to the rest of the country. There, wine making developed steadily and the state proceeded to dominate American wine production, a position still very much in evidence today.

Regarding the other states, a hybrid (the 'Alexander') was discovered by chance in Pennsylvania. It was found to be disease resistant and to produce an acceptable product. Further hybrids were sought out and at last, in the early nineteenth century, wine production on a commercial scale was undertaken successfully. As the years passed, new and better hybrids were discovered. Also, European vines were grafted onto American phylloxera-resistant stock. Wine production thus continued to expand.

In 1919, the prohibition laws wrecked the industry and even when these were repealed in 1934, conditions were such that a quick recovery was impossible. A depressed market and excesses caused by a reaction against prohibition were the cause.
There was no incentive to take risks on a population whose palate had become accustomed to stronger alcoholic drinks than wine. Then, with the advent of the Second World War, any resurgence was further postponed.

After the war some progress took place. However, it wasn't until about 1970 when the industry finally really took off.
Naturally California led the way, but other states soon followed. The planting of more European vines, the advances in viticultural techniques and laws to help new small-scale growers and producers initiated a huge expansion that is still under way.

The state of Washington on the north-west coast is the second largest producer of wines made from European grapes in the U.S.A. In quantity it lies far behind California but in quality the difference is not so great. Most of the vineyards lie on the eastern side, in the Columbia and Yakima valleys. Rigorous continental weather conditions make irrigation essential during the summer and south facing slopes are just as vital in the winter.
However, these circumstances impart an intensity of flavour to the wines that enable them, at their best, to rival those of California. Particularly successful are Riesling, Sémillon Blanc and Merlot while Chardonnay, Sauvignon Blanc, Chenin Blanc, Cabernet and Pinot Noir give results that are good rather than brilliant.

In Oregon, just south of Washington, most vineyards are grown on the western side. Here, the climate is far less rigorous but very wet. Although most rain falls during the late autumn, winter and early spring, it can cause severe problems at harvest time in late-ripening years. The most notable vine growing distinct is the Willamette valley although other areas of note are found further south. As in Washington, European grape varieties are used. Although Pinot Noir and Pinot Gris are particularly successful, other varieties such as Chardonnay and Riesling are also commonly found.

Other up and coming wine producing states are Texas and Idaho, both of which also use European varieties. Texas has been particularly successful with Chenin Blanc, Sauvignon Blanc, Chardonnay and Cabernet Sauvignon. Michigan uses both hybrid and European grapes, while the states of Maryland, Pennsylvania and West Virginia, all of which suffer from summer humidity, tend to plant the more resistant hybrids rather than European strains. These, being susceptible to damp induced rot, make them more difficult to manage. An exception is Virginia, where recently Chardonnay, Merlot and Cabernet have been produced successfully and where European grapes now outnumber the hybrid varieties in spite of the humidity problems.

Most other American states make some wine regardless of climatic problems of one kind or another. It will be very interesting to discover what surprises the future will have in store. 🖎

The wines of California

Principal wines and grape varieties of California

REDS AND ROSÉS

Cabernet (Franc and Sauvignon), Cabernet Sauvignon, Zinfandel, Barbera, Syrah, Pinot Noir, Merlot, Petite Sirah, Sangiovese, Sangiovese-Cabernet Sauvignon, Carignan, Gamay, Grenache, Alicante Bouschet, Mourvèdre, Petit Verdot, Carnelian, Carmine, Centurion, Ruby Cabernet, Charbono.

WHITES

Chardonnay, Sauvignon Blanc, Riesling, Pinot Blanc, Chenin Blanc, Gewürztraminer, Sémillon, Sauvignon-Sémillon, Muscat Blanc a Petit Grains, Colombard, Viognier, Malvasia Bianca, Emerald Riesling, Flora, Symphony.

Many producers sell 'Proprietary' Red wines. These are always Cabernet blends, often with some Merlot. Other particular names worth mentioning are:
- *Dominus (Napa Valley) – Cabernets / Merlot / Petit Verdot.*
- *Fumé Blanc (Napa Valley) – Sauvignon Blanc.*
- *Old Patch Red (Alexander Valley) – Carignan / Petite Sirah / Zinfandel / Alicante Bouschet.*
- *Old Telegram (California) – Mourvèdre.*
- *Orion Old Vines (California) – Syrah.*

According to records, the Spanish 'Conquistadores' introduced wine making to the New World in 1524. A Franciscan monk, Father Junipero Serra, planted the first vines in California over two hundred years later, in 1769. Subsequently other members of various orders introduced plantations in a score of missions along the Pacific coast, the vines bearing what was later named the 'Mission' grape due to its religious connection.

In 1850, the missions were secularised and settlers took up the activity, a change that resulted in the introduction of several European varieties. The gold rush brought much prosperity to the wine makers who were encouraged by legislation to increase the number and size of their plantations. This expansion was shattered in 1870 by the Phylloxera epidemic and then again, when the industry had overcome this disaster, by the prohibition laws of 1920.

It took thirty years for recovery to take place. However, when it did, a spate of new European varieties were introduced, substituting most of the old. The modern surge in successful wine production was about to take place...

California now produces about 80% of all wine in the U.S.A. This is an awesome situation when one considers that the area planted with vines has increased three-fold in the last twenty years. The state's vine growing districts can be classified, for convenience, into four basic regions, or from a scientific point of view, five different climatic zones. These regions are the northern coast, the central coast due south of San Francisco bay, the southern coast and the centre valleys near Stockton and Sacramento. The climatic areas vary from I which is the coolest, having temperatures resembling those of Northern Europe, up to V which resembles the south of Spain and even North Africa.

The most important centres of wine production in California are in the North Coastal region. This lies north of San Francisco and includes, among others, the Napa Valley, the Sonoma Valley, the Russian River Valley, Mendocino, Los Carneros and the Anderson Valley. Of these, by far the most important is the Napa Valley, which dominates the state's top quality production.

The valley consists of a strip some 30 km long and 8 km wide running between the towns of Calistoga to the north and Napa in the south. The climatic zone is the coolest but the valley temperature increases northward. The best soil, a quick draining gravel bearing loam, is found on the lower slopes of the surrounding hills. This area is also less prone to late frosts in the spring than is the valley floor, the soil being a less suitable, heavier clay variety.

A particular sub-area that deserves mention is the Rutherford Bench. This runs due east of the St. Helena highway between the towns of Rutherford and Oakville, and produces some of very best in quality. The dominating grapes are the red Cabernet Sauvignon and the white Chardonnay but many top class wines are made using other varieties. The Sonoma and Russian River Valley also boast a number of first-rate producers as does the Mendocino. However, the wines in these areas are less uniform and their character varies widely with the winemaker. The whole of the northern district produces some excellent 'champenois' sparkling wines. The Napa Valley and the Anderson Valley deserve particular mention in this respect.

The centre coast includes areas just south of San Francisco bay. These are the Santa Cruz Mountains, the Santa Clara Valley, the Livermore Valley and Monterey County. The region extends southwards for nearly three hundred kilometres to include areas around Paso Robles, Santa Maria and Santa Barbara. Here also, the climate is favourable being at its worst in zone III. The region produces many notable and at times surprising blends, a Gamay Beajolais and some very good sparkling wines. Livermore is well known for its sweet wines similar to Sauternes and also produces a number of aperitif wines. Other wines worth mentioning are a powerful Zinfandel and an Italian Nebbiolo made at Paso Robles and the Sauvignon Blanc, Merlot and Pinot Noir of the Santa Ynez Valley.

The southern coast centres around Los Angeles where the first Californian plantations were started. Here the climate is hotter, being in zones IV and V. White wines based on Chardonnay, Pinot Blanc and Chenin Blanc dominate production.

The central region, including the San Joaquin and Sacramento Valleys, Lodi and El Dorado, produce 80% of all California wines. Unfortunately the climatic zone is mainly V and grapes naturally gain a high level of sugar with virtually no acidity. This would result in wines seriously lacking in body. Fortunately, modern technology and know-how has changed what was formerly a watery produce into light but pleasant wines. In achieving this, temperature control has been an important factor but the introduction of new, more suitable grape varieties, by crossing the best of the old, has also played a part. Emerald Riesling, Ruby Cabernet, Carmine, Centurion and Carnelian, among others, have helped transform the region and encouraged further research aiming to do even better in future.

As in Germany, wines tend to be named by the grape variety they contain. By law, any wine named by a grape variety must contain at least 75% of that grape. 🐾

The wines of New York and New England

Principal wines and grape varieties of New York and New England

REDS

Concord, Catawba, Baco Noir, Marshall Foch, Chancellor, Chelois, De Chavnac, Seibel, Landot Noir, Isabella, Cabernet Sauvignon, Cabernet Franc, Merlot, Pinot Noir, Gamay.

WHITES

Niagara, Delaware, Catawba, Aurora, Seyval Blanc, Cayuga GW3, Vidal Blanc, Duchess, Moore's Diamond, Elvira, Chardonnay, Riesling, Sauvignon Blanc, Gewürztraminer.

ROSÉS

Cabernet Sauvignon, Belle View Blush.

Although the New York climate, with its harsh winters, early thaws, short growing season and wet autumns makes vine growing a hazardous business, the state is by far the biggest wine producer in the U.S.A. after California.

A great diversity of grapes is used, including American hybrids, French-American hybrids and internationally familiar European, mainly French, varieties. However, due to the climatic conditions most of the wine made is white, even if more recently some growers are producing reds as well. The vineyards are located in four main areas, all of which show a moderation of the unfavourable climate due to the presence of water in the guise of ocean or lake. These are as follows:

(a) The Finger Lakes near Ontario, which specialises in making sparkling wine, mainly of a very sweet nature. American hybrids are traditionally used, as these suit the weather conditions best. However, helped by modern technology, they are slowly being replaced by French-American hybrids and even some European varieties. These do not suffer from a tendency towards foxy odours produced by the American grapes.

(b) The Hudson River valley tends to use not only French-American hybrids but also European varieties, particularly Chardonnay. Proportionally more reds are made here than around the finger lakes.

(c) Long Island. The two forks on the eastern end of the Island are very promising areas. The very proximity of the Atlantic Ocean has a strong moderating influence on both the hottest and coldest temperatures, making the growing season nearly a month longer than in any other area. Here reds as well as whites are made and Cabernet, Pinot Noir, Chardonnay and Sauvignon Blanc have all been produced with good results.

(d) Lake Erie has the largest grape growing area in the New York State but is the smallest wine producing region as most grapes are used as fruit and non-alcoholic juice.

New England has two viticultural areas. These are the western Connecticut Highlands and South Eastern New England. The inland climate is quite severe whereas coastal regions enjoy more moderate conditions due to the presence of the Atlantic Ocean.

Most wineries appear to be found in Connecticut and Rhode Island, where wines are made from French-American hybrids as well as the standard European varieties. The situation is similar in Massachusetts where, in addition, Mead wine and a Brut Champagne style sparkling wine are also made. New Hampshire makes very little wine and this appears to be based on hybrid varieties while Maine and Vermont specialise in fruit 'wines'.

Blueberries, raspberries, strawberries, peaches, cherries and pears are utilised as well as grapes. Oak ageing is sometimes used for normal wine.

Most states produce both reds and whites, although the latter appear to predominate. Rhode Island not only makes rosé from Cabernet grapes but also produces a sweet wine resembling Port. Both red and white styles can be found. ❧

The wines of Canada

Although wine making had been going on in Canada for at least three centuries, a successful industry was only initiated in the early nineteenth century, thanks to a German settler, Johann Schiller. One hundred years later, the prohibition laws, in contrast to those of the U.S.A., boosted wine production at the expense of the spirits industry.

Canadian wine mostly comes from four provinces. These are Ontario, by far the most important, with vineyards in the Niagara Falls area, British Columbia, Nova Scotia and Quebec. Traditionally, Canadian wine has been mainly of the sweet, reinforced type, akin to port and sherry. However, the late 1970's saw a shift towards dry table wines, which nowadays account for over 90% of the total production.

Ontario, with its climate tempered by the Great Lakes, produces successful red wines as well as whites. Elsewhere whites tend to dominate, often made from German as well as French grapes. As in the U.S.A., French-American hybrids are also used, mainly because of their resistance to the extremely harsh winters. At times this is done with considerable success.

An interesting curiosity, thanks to the sub-zero temperatures in the late-autumns, is the production of 'Ice-Wine', akin to the German 'Eiswein'. The constant excellent quality of this product has led Canada to now produce more than Germany, an impressive achievement. As with the U.S.A., most wine is sold with varietal labels. 🍷

Principal wines and grape varieties of Canada

REDS
Pinot Noir, Cabernet Sauvignon, Cabernet Franc, Gamay, Merlot, Baco Noir, Maréchal Foch, Chancellor.

WHITES
Chardonnay, Riesling, Gewürztraminer, Ehrenfelser, Bacchus, Pinot Blanc, Seyval Blanc, Vidal, Ice-Wine.

The wines of Argentina

Principal wines and grape varieties of Argentina

REDS

Malbec, Cabernet Sauvignon, Merlot, Syrah, Pinot Noir, Sangiovese, Barbera, Nebbiolo, Lambrusco, Bonarda, Tempranilla.

WHITES

Criolla Grande, Cereza (both native grapes), Chenin Blanc, Sémillon, Moscatel, Ugni Blanc, Pedro Giménez, Pinot Blanc, Tokay Friulano, Riesling, Sylvaner.

ROSÉS

Criolla Grande, Cereza.

Principal wines and grape varieties of Uraguay

REDS

Tannat, Cabernet Sauvignon, Cabernet Franc, Merlot.

WHITES

Sauvignon Blanc, Pinot Blanc, Chardonnay, Riesling, Gewürztraminer.

Argentina's first vineyards were planted by settlers in the sixteenth century, both secular pioneers and religious orders playing their part. Later, new varieties were brought from France, Italy, Spain and other European countries.

The wine producing regions lie along the Andean foothills. Most important is Mendoza, which accounts for about 70% of the total production. Further north, San Juan can claim another 20%. Most of the rest is shared between La Rioja, Catamarca and Salta in the north and Rio Negro and Neuquen, which lie to the south.

Until recently, Argentina was fifth in wine production worldwide. Yet little was exported since the Argentines are avid wine drinkers and kept most to themselves. However, a drop in home wine consumption and a continuous improvement in quality is ensuring that an ever-increasing quantity of wine is finding its way abroad. More and more is now being made on an industrial scale using modern equipment and sophisticated techniques.

On the whole, red wines tend to be more successful than whites, all the main French varieties being now used. Malbec is particularly good here, and is showing far better than it does in France. Surprisingly a broad cross section of Italian and other European varieties are also utilised, sometimes in the most unexpected blends. White wines have improved since the introduction of noble French grapes at the expense of traditional native ones. These, however, still account for over half the total production. The wines are sold under varietal names.

The wines of Uruguay

Uruguay has a relatively short viticulture history, wine making having been introduced by Basque settlers as late as the end of the nineteenth century. As with Argentina, a flourishing home market has meant that the country has begun to export its wine only in recent years. The reasons for the change are similar to those for Argentina.

The major vine growing areas are Canelones (the most important), Colonia, Soriano and San Jose de Mayo. All are on the southern side of the country near Montevideo, on the same latitude as Mendoza and Santiago and quite close to Buenos Aires.

Traditionally, the main variety used was the Tannat grape, imported by settlers from the Madiran area in France. Now, a switch towards other French varieties is taking place as the drive for better quality and increased exports gains momentum. As with Argentina, varietal labels are used.

The wines of Brazil

Wine production here was initiated, but with only limited success, by Portuguese settlers in the sixteenth century. Further attempts, by Jesuits in the seventeenth century and a new wave of immigrants, one hundred years later, failed to consolidate the industry. It was only in the late nineteenth century that Italian settlers finally succeeded where the others had failed.

The major area of production is in the Rio Grande do Sol province. This lies in the most southern part of the country by the Uruguayan border, at latitude only slightly north of Mendoza and Santiago. The rainfall is high, but the climate, although humid, is relatively mild – a positive asset.

In the past, American vines have been grown as well as Italian varieties. More recently, the U.S.A. has contributed studies aiming at improving quality by the planting of clones of French varieties that do well in the soil and climatic conditions.

At present Brazil exports a considerable quantity of wine to the United States but only a trickle finds its way to Europe. However, this small quantity is on the increase as quality standards continue to improve. As in other South American countries, wines are marketed as varietal products. ⁂

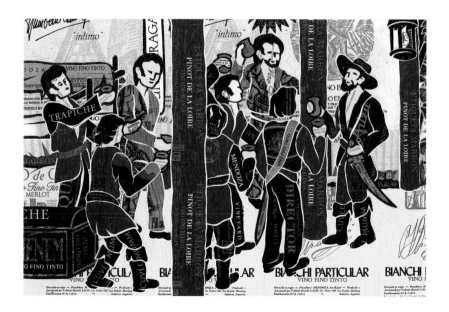

The wines of Chile

Although only third in the quantity produced, Chile is the most important wine making nation in South America. As with neighbouring countries, the first vineyards were planted by settlers (in this case, Spanish), in the sixteenth century. However, the importance of the noble French varieties was recognised about one hundred and fifty years ago. In 1857 the main Bordeaux vines were imported from France. This proved to be fortunate for the world wine industry because Chile escaped the great phylloxera epidemic that was to follow. Consequently, devastated European vineyards were replanted with Chilean vines that had originated from France in the first place!

The Bordeaux varieties do especially well around Santiago, particularly in the Maipo Valley, which produces the best wine in Chile. This area is no more than 240 km west of Mendoza in Argentina, with just the Andes Mountains separating them. Chile possesses essentially three main growing areas. That described above, in the centre, produces excellent table wine. The arid northern region, lying between the Choapa River and the Atacama Desert turns out strong reinforced wines in the style of Port and Madeira. The wetter southern region lies between the rivers Maule and Bio-Bio. Here, the high-yield low-in-alcohol products are used for local consumption.

It should be noted that Chile's drier wine areas are heavily irrigated, thanks to a network of canals and streams, many of which are of Inca origin. What are still needed are better cellar conditions with modern oak barrels rather than the indigenous beech ones still mainly used. Certainly, Chile enjoys natural advantages over pretty well every other wine producing country. The absence of both mildew and phylloxera avoids costly measures such as repeated spraying and the grafting of vines onto special disease-resistant stock.

Already an important wine exporter, Chile has the potential to do even better. How much, only the future will tell. ⁂

Principal wines and grape varieties of Brazil

REDS
Cabernet Sauvignon, Cabernet Franc, Merlot, Pinot Noir, Zinfandel, Barbera, Bonarda.

WHITES
Chardonnay, Sémillon Blanc, Pinot Blanc, Gewürztraminer, Moscato, Trebbiano.

ROSÉS
Cabernet Sauvignon, Merlot.

Principal wines and grape varieties of Chile

REDS
Cabernet Sauvignon, Merlot, Pinot Noir, Syrah, Carignan, Cot (Malbec), Pais.

WHITES
Chardonnay, Sauvignon Gris, Sauvignon Blanc, Sémillon, Chasselas, Moscatel Alejandria, Tocai Friulano, Riesling, Torontel.

Wines of Asia

The wines of China

Vines were brought to China from Persia (now Iran) and Uzbekistan during the Han dynasty in about 130 B.C. It follows that wine was being made there some 2000 years ago. Since then a number of scattered references exist. During the T'ang Dynasty, in the seventh century, wine appeared to be quite popular and quantities were imported from Uzbekistan. In the eleventh century, under the Chu Dynasty, wine-making throughout China increased. Later, Marco Polo, reported finding an abundance of vines in the Chan-Si province and much more recently, in the seventeenth century, a number of large vineyards were planted under the rule of the Emperor K'anghi with vines brought from Turkestan. At the end of the nineteenth century well over one hundred different vine varieties, including the still popular Welschriesling, were imported from Europe and the first wineries were established almost immediately.

Clearly, although of ancient origin, wine has not captured the imagination of the Chinese as it has with western civilisations, beer and stronger alcoholic drinks based on rice being much preferred. Consequently, vineyards are to be found in a relatively small number of places. Most important is the Shandong peninsula. Other locations are to be found north of the Yangtse and near the Liao rivers. Finally, the Sinkiang province (Xinjiang) in the very north west of the country has vineyards that produce almost no wine. The extremely low temperatures in the winter require very hardy, cold-resistant rootstocks. Then, intense summer heat causes the grapes to completely dry up on the vines. As a result, only a small quantity of very sweet dessert wine can be made, the bulk of the produce being sold as raisin grapes.

China has been fortunate not to have been affected by the great world-wide phylloxera epidemic. However there are other serious problems which still need to be overcome. Although the soils are suitable for vine growing, not only does the inland climate suffer from the continental extremes mentioned above but also the Monsoon rains bring humidity and consequential fungal problems in areas near the coast.

Fortunately, the Chinese are at last appearing to show a greater interest in wine and encouraged by the West, are taking the first steps towards expanding their production. New vineyards are being projected in the Shandong province in addition to the established ones in the Qingdao and Yantai districts. The new vines are being planted in granite / limestone soils on south facing hill slopes with good water drainage. First results are promising, with wines showing more interest than the rather bland products of the past. It is indeed possible that the Shandong peninsula, thanks to the south-facing slopes of the Dazashen Mountains with their favourable climate and suitable soil, could become a major wine-producing region in the future.

At present grapes include both traditional and western varieties, the latter being more common in the newer, recently planted vineyards. All types of dry wine are made, including rosé. In addition, sweet and sparkling products can be found. Bottles tend to be labelled simply as 'Chinese Red Wine' or some similar name. A white wine of note is called 'Dynasty'. More recently, with the introduction of the French noble varieties, some wines have been sold as varietal products. ❧

Principal wines and grape varieties of China

REDS AND ROSÉS
- *European Varieties: Cabernet Sauvignon, Cabernet Franc, Merlot, Pinot Noir, Carignan, Gamay, Saperavi, Muscat de Hambourg.*
- *Traditional Variety: Beichun.*

WHITES
- *European Varieties: Welschriesling, Muscat de Hambourg, Sauvignon Blanc, Rkatsiteli, Chardonnay, Sylvaner, Muscat à Petits Grains, Sémillon, Chenin Blanc, Gewürztraminer, Marsanne.*
- *Traditional Varieties: Dragon's Eye (Long Yan), Cock's Heart.*

The wines of Japan

Principal grape varieties used

REDS AND ROSÉS
  *Campbell's Early, Cabernet Sauvignon,
  Cabernet Franc, Merlot.*

WHITES
  *Koshu, Delaware, Muscat Bailey,
  Sémillon, Chardonnay, Riesling,
  Müller Thurgau, Zweigelt.*

It is probable that wine was being made in Japan over one hundred years before the birth of Christ, the vine having been introduced from Persia at that time. However, the earliest references to wine making in Japan date from the eighth century when it was consumed at the court of Nara. It appears that Buddhist missionaries were responsible for viticulture at the time.

Later, in 1186, the white Koshu grape was selected as being the indigenous one best suited to the local climatic conditions.

Then, in the fifteenth and sixteenth centuries, Europeans introduced red wine to the country. However, in the seventeenth century, western ideals and practices, including wine making, were rejected. It was not until the late nineteenth century that the first steps to turn wine production into a commercial enterprise were taken. Even then progress has been extremely slow. It can be concluded that although interest has been shown, the Japanese have resisted the temptation to produce wine on a large scale for over one thousand years.

The reason for this is not difficult to understand. Trapped between the world's greatest land-mass, Asia, on one side and the largest Ocean, the Pacific, on the other, Japan suffers from extreme weather conditions ill-suited to wine making.

Siberian winter winds, spring monsoons and summer typhoons make viticulture an arduous occupation. To make matters worse, further monsoons in the autumn can easily wreck the harvest.

An acid soil that suffers from poor drainage completes a depressing picture, which fully explains the reluctance of the Japanese to expand the industry. At present, vineyards are to be found in carefully chosen areas possessing less extreme weather.

The Kōfu valley in the province of Yamanashi, the Niigata plain, the provinces of Yamagata and Nagano, and the vicinity of Osaka are examples, producing between them about half the nation's total output. In fact, nearly all the provinces produce some wine, even if small quantities and in scattered localities.

Recently a number of American and European varieties have been introduced with some success. At best, Japanese wines are light and pleasant. The huge rainfall makes for low sugar levels and can result in watery products. The law allows the addition of sugar and the blending of the home produce with imported wine.

Most is white but there are some reds. Although modern technology is leading to improvements, there is still a long way to go. 🎐

The Tanazukuri Vine System

The monsoon climate with its summer rains makes grape rotting a serious problem. In an attempt to minimise this, the Tanazukuri system of cultivation is used.

A similar method, known as Tendone is utilised in southern Italy and some other countries, particularly in places where the combination of heat and humidity create a rotting problem. However a more expedient reason exists for this type of pergola, particularly in the western world, and that is one of quick profit where quantity is placed above quality.

Vines are trained vertically to a height of about seven feet and then made to stretch their branches horizontally on wire supports. This results in the grape bunches hanging below the leaves and therefore having a greater exposure to circulating air. Also, in Japan, a minimum amount of land is used, leaving a greater amount free for the cultivation of other crops.

However, this giant vine pergola has its own drawbacks. The blanket of leaves hides the sun from the grapes. This and the extremely huge crop of fruit from each plant results in an exceedingly low sugar content and a consequently diluted product. In order to make up for this, Japanese law allows for Chaptalization, that is the addition of substantial amounts of sugar to the musts.

In addition, the blending with imported foreign wines is permitted so as to help boost the alcohol content of the product. 🐝

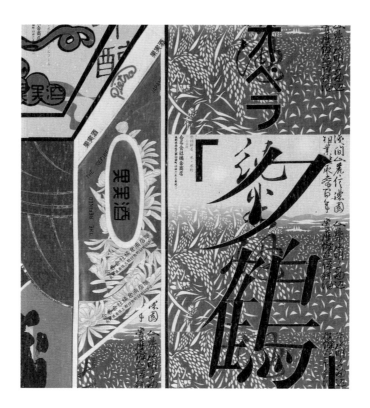

Wines of Europe

The wines of Europe

Pride of place must go to France, which has traditionally produced top class wines with great regularity. The regions of Bordeaux, Bourgogne and Champagne are in a class of their own in their field and boast no peers. In Bordeaux, Pomerol, Pauillac, Margaux, Graves and St. Émilion have wines in the very top bracket while St. Julien and St. Estèphe are not far behind. Moreover one should not forget Bourg, Blaye and Bergerac.
Reds are dominant but whites are also very good. In particular, the dessert wine Sauternes has no equal throughout the world.
Reds again dominate in Bourgogne with Vosne-Romanée, Nuits St-Georges and Beaune but then Montrachet and Chablis are the very best whites, the former having no equal. Champagne is justly celebrated for its dry sparkling wines, which, at their best have no rivals anywhere. Naturally one can find first class wines in other regions. The Rhône Valley is also well known for red, Hermitage, Côte Rôtie, Châteaneuf-du-Pape and Gigondas being particularly well known, but white and rosé can be very good as well.

The Loire Valley and Alsace pride themselves particularly for their whites, while in Provence and Corsica all types are made, but the rosés are of particular importance. Other regions of note are Languedoc and Roussillon, the south west, Savoie and the Jura. Finally, the countless corners producing Vins de Pays should not be forgotten and are worth investigating.

Italy is the largest wine producer in the world and boasts a greater diversity of styles than any other country. Here, Piemonte and Toscana reign supreme. In Piemonte the very best Barolos and Barbarescos are not far behind the top French red wines while in Toscana the finest Brunellos and a few Cabernets are in a similar position. Also the best Chianti can be surprisingly good. In addition, Piemonte produces the world's best Vermouth and also some very good sparkling wines while Toscana's Vin Santo dessert wine deserves consideration. Not far behind comes Veneto where the dry Amarone and sweet Recioto wines, at their best, border on the fantastic. Also the red Valpolicella and white Soave made here can be very good. In the far north, in the Trentino-Alto Adige and Friuli- Venezia Giulia, white wines dominate, while in Lombardia and Valle d'Aosta reds come more into play. In the centre, in Emilia-Romagna, Marche and Abruzzo, both reds and whites deserve some consideration, while around Rome and in Umbria the latter are far more prominent. In the south, in Campania, Puglia and Sicilia all kinds, including sweet wines merit attention. The same is true of the island of Sardegna, which should not be forgotten.

Germany produces wines of a sweeter nature and generally lower alcoholic content than France and Italy. Here the Rheingau deserves special recognition as being the world's best producer of Riesling wine. Other regions specialising in whites are Mosel, the Saar, the Ruwer, the Nahe, the Rheinpfalz, Rheinhessen and Baden. Franken also produces white wines but of different grape varieties and of a drier nature than the other regions. Ahr, in the extreme north west and Württemberg in the far south east are at opposite ends of the country, yet have the common exceptional distinction of producing considerably more red than white.

Of particular interest throughout Germany is the production of the Beerenauslese and Trockenbeerenauslese dessert wines. These golden coloured super-sweet products are in a class of their own and possess a huge ageing potential.

Austria produces mainly interesting white wines, similar in style to those of Germany and of a considerably higher standard than is generally supposed. The main regions, all on the eastern side of the country, are the Wachau, Wien, the Weinviertel and Burgenland. The latter is on the Hungarian border and its best wines show some similarity to those of its neighbour, being sweet. Switzerland makes a small amount of very good white wines, the most noted region being that around Lausanne.

In Spain the best-known regions are Rioja and Andalusia. The former is well known for its reds although whites are also made, while the latter is justly famous for its aperitif and dessert wines, Sherry, Málaga and Montilla. Catalonia produces all types including some very good sparkling 'Cava' wines. The Duero is less well known but boasts Spain's finest red, the Vega Sicilia Unico, which at its best is as fine as the top French products. Other regions worth investigating are Galicia, which produces both reds and whites, Rueda, where good white wines are made and Valencia, where dark full-bodied reds are predominant.

Portugal, like Spain, is famous for its dessert wines. Port is produced in the alto Douro, while Madeira comes from the Island of that name. Other regions deserving recognition are Bairrada, which specialises in good red wine (although some sparkling white is also made), Minho and Dão, which are renowned for fresh Vinho Verde and solid Vinho Maduro respectively. The former can be red or white while the latter is always red.

In central Europe, Hungary has an ancient tradition of wine making. Although the reds can be good the country's characteristic product lies in its white wines. The main regions are Tokaji, the north shore of Lake Balaton and the Plain of the Danube.

The best, Tokaji, produces wines not unlike the German 'Auslese' but the Nation's pride lies in its sweet, dessert wines. These, also, are similar to those of Germany. In addition, a super concentrated type called 'Essencia', with a supposed ageing potential of up to two hundred years is made! The best wines of Romania, Slovakia and the Czech Republic are white but some promising reds can also be found.
Conversely, Bulgaria specialises in reds that are ever increasing in quality, while some nice whites are made. Former Yugoslavia produces both whites and reds, although the whites of Slovenia and Croatia are probably the best known.

Russia, Moldova, Ukraina and Georgia are the major wine producing countries in Eastern Europe. Great strides in planting new varieties and in new techniques are being made with promising results. Both reds and whites are made in all these countries. Of particular interest in the former Soviet Union, however, is the production of a variety of dessert wines.

After Italy, Greece and its islands are the most important Mediterranean producers. All types are made, although some regions tend to specialise. The major areas and their better-known wine types are as follows: Attiki (red and white), the Peloponnisos (red and white), Makedonia (red), Thessalia (red), Ipiros (white), Sterea Ellas (red), Kriti or Crete (red), the Ionian Islands (white is best but also red) and the Aegean Islands (all types, but dessert wines are best known). Cyprus and Malta produce both reds and whites, but the sweet red Commendaria of Cyprus is the most characteristic and interesting product. Turkey makes small quantities of all kinds of wine.

Finally, a few countries in the north west of Europe make some wine. These are Luxembourg, Belgium, England, and to a very small extent, the Netherlands. The varieties used tend to be of German origin and the wines produced are therefore predominantly white. ❧

 Opera **Falstaff** - see page 47

The wines of England

There are at present about 430, mainly small, vineyards in England, Wales and the Channel Islands. These cover about 1000 hectares and represent a revived industry. Although most are to be found in the south, particularly in Kent and Sussex, many are scattered elsewhere, including some northern counties. One even lies in Durham, being the most northerly in the world!

It is generally accepted that the Romans introduced the grapevine to Britain and there is chronicled evidence of vineyard cultivation in Saxon England. This intensified during the Norman period but the Black Death and later, the dissolution of the monasteries by Henry VIII, devastated the industry as a commercial enterprise. Only a few county estates retained their vines, a situation that continued right up to the middle of the twentieth century. Then, shortly after the Second World War, a renaissance took place. Experiments were carried out to investigate which varieties best suited the English climate. More recently, an increasing number of growers have been attracted to the industry, which is still expanding.

By far the great bulk of what is produced is white, using mainly German but also a number of French varieties, there being, it seems, no indigenous British grape. Some rosés and a few reds are also made. As cellar techniques become more sophisticated, new styles are being attempted. Champagne method sparkling wines and sweet dessert wines are examples of what might be produced in greater quantities in the future. Naturally, the unpredictability of the weather is a prime drawback. Good vintages are few and far between, a handicap in any case, but particularly where growth and innovation are concerned.

Wines are sold as 'English Table Wine', the label bearing the producer's name and sometimes the grape variety used.

Principal wines and grape varieties of England

Reds and Rosés

Pinot Noir, Triomphe d'Alsace.

Whites

Müller Thurgau, Seyval Blanc, Reichensteiner, Bacchus, Schönburger, Madeleine, Huxelrebe, Chardonnay.

British wine

Principal British wines

RED WINES
British Ruby style wine.

WHITE WINES
British white wine, British fortified wine.

British wine shouldn't be confused with English wine. The latter is produced from grapes grown and freshly picked in English and Welsh vineyards. British wine is made in bulk, in far larger plants than English wineries, using grape must concentrate, imported from various foreign countries, particularly Cyprus, Spain and Italy.

The practice of importing dried grapes in order to make wine in the British Isles is far from new, and has been going on since the mid-seventeenth century. However, once a reliable method of concentrating grape juice had been found, the industry took off in earnest. Highly concentrated must keeps well and is both easy and cheap to transport because of its reduced mass and bulk. The juice is then turned into wine by adding water and then fermenting with an appropriate yeast strain.

This method is used to make a number of products. Ordinary British table wine is a dry product suitable to be taken with food. Although quite common at present, it is a fairly recent addition to the British wine range, having really taken off in the last twenty years. Most of what is made is white. On the other hand, fortified wines, suitable as aperitifs, have been produced traditionally over a much longer period of time. As hinted above, they were originally produced from imported dry grapes, the reconstitution of imported must dating from approximately one hundred years ago. Two kinds of fortified wine are made, a normal type in the style of Sherry and a ruby wine, which is an imitation of Port. ❧

Wines of Belgium

Belgium was a notable producer of wine in the Middle Ages. Then, unable to compete with the best from France, the vineyards were steadily run down, and were finally abandoned in the fifteenth century. They were not replanted until the 1970's.

Nowadays, as lovers of wine, the Belgians are importers rather than producers. However, some, mostly white wines, are made, resembling those of southern Netherlands which lies just across the border. The Belgians have an affinity for French wine and it is therefore no surprise that all three Pinot grapes feature prominently among those used. Wines are sold using varietal labels. ❧

Wines of Luxembourg

Viticulture and wine making in this small country dates from Roman times. During the first part of the twentieth century, the wines were of mediocre standard, being used mainly for blending. Fortunately, well-directed research in the 1930's led to a change of emphasis from quantity to quality, resulting in a marked improvement in the products, which are now, as in Belgium, sold with varietal labels.

Most of the vineyards lie along the West Bank of the Moselle River. Here, morning sunshine and thick forests covering the overlying hilltops, protect the vines from the wind and ensure a reasonable ripening period. This allows for the production of light fruity white wines that have characteristics somewhat between those made in Alsace and the German Moselle. The best soils are a mixture of limestone and clay found at Remich, Grevenmacher and Ebnen. Particularly good sites are those at the villages of Remich, Wintrange, Wellenstein and Ahn.

Although decreasing in proportion, the most planted grape variety is still the Rivaner, a strain of Müller-Thurgau that does not produce particularly interesting wines. Another mediocre indigenous grape used frequently is the Elbling. By far the best products are now obtained from varieties of French and German origin. Although Riesling can produce some fine long ageing wines, the best results are probably those obtained from Auxerrois and Pinot Gris grapes, which appear to thrive in the northern latitude. Pinot Blanc and Gewürztraminer also do well, the latter yielding products that are smooth and aromatic.

A long tradition of sparkling wine, the so-called 'Crémant de Luxembourg', exists. At one time it was much consumed in Germany as 'Sekt', a name the Germans now generally give to any inexpensive bubbly product, often made from French and Italian grapes. The present Crémant de Luxembourg wines are made from Elbling, Pinot Blanc, Riesling and Pinot Noir grapes.

Most of what Luxembourg produces is consumed at home and therefore very little is exported. Consequently, the wines are not as well-known as they deserve to be. ❧

Principal wines and grape varieties of Belgium

REDS
Pinot Noir.

WHITES
Pinot Blanc, Pinot Gris, Müller Thurgau, Auxerrois, Optima, Leopold III, Maréchal Joffre.

ROSÉS
Pinot Noir.

Principal wines and grape varieties of Luxembourg

REDS
Pinot Noir.

WHITES
Rivaner, Elbling, Auxerrois, Pinot Gris, Pinot Blanc, Riesling, Gewürztraminer, Crémant de Luxembourg.

ROSÉS
Pinot Noir, Crémant de Luxembourg.

The wines of The Netherlands

Principal wines and grape varieties of The Netherlands

WHITES
Riesling, Müller-Turgau, Sylvaner, Auxerrois.

Although viticulture is known to have existed here over 600 years ago, very little wine is made due to the fact that the country lies rather too far to the north. Wine production appears to be limited to a handful of producers who all own the small vineyards they operate. These tend to be situated in the most southerly part of the country, next to the borders of Belgium and Germany.

Having re-started in the late 1960's, following a long dormant period, wine making in Holland is still in its infancy. As far as one can make out all the production is white, being medium dry and rather low in alcohol, in a similar style to that of Germany, but also resembling English wines. As expected, mainly German grape varieties are used, the others being French in origin.
Chaptalization, the addition of sugar to the must in order to bring up the alcoholic content of the product, is necessarily practised. Although not on the same level as the best of Germany, the wines are reasonably well made and improving. It is hoped that in the future the industry is able to expand in quantity and fulfil the present promise shown in quality. ❧

The wines of Switzerland

Wine has been produced in Switzerland since the end of the ninth century. There is documented evidence that the Lausanne region was growing vines at around 900 A.D. The Dézaley area is mentioned in sources dating back from 1141 and 1142. During the next fifty years vines in this region were being established as the most important in the country. However it took another two hundred years to organise the commercialisation of the product. Another important event took place in 1536, when the town of Lausanne was given the control of the Dézaley region. This was then fully confirmed in 1548.

Much more recently, in 1913, the Appellation d'Origine titles were bestowed upon some of the finest and most important wines. Others have followed since.

Switzerland is extremely wine conscious, but is unable to produce enough to meet its own needs. Therefore, hardly any is exported. On the other hand, the Swiss are enthusiastic importers of the best wines from France, Italy and Germany.

The major regions of wine production are, in order of importance, Valais, Vaud , Genève and Neuchâtel, all four in the French speaking part of the country.

German speaking regions with important viticulture are Zürich, Schaffhausen, Limmattal, Herrschaft and Graubünden.

Other vineyards worthy of consideration are those around Berne, Fribourg and Jura. Although some interesting reds are made, particularly in Valais, most regions have traditionally produced white wines. The best area, Dézaley, lies between Lausanne and Montreux, in the Vaud canton. More recently, however, particularly in the Italian-speaking canton of Ticino, a number of reds, mostly from the French noble grapes, have been produced with considerable success. ✺

Principal wines and grape varieties of Switzerland

REDS

Blauburgunder, Dôle, Gamay, Goron, Humagne, Klevner, Merlot, Nostrano, Pinot Noir, Rèze, Salvagnin, Schafiser, Twanner, Viti.

WHITES

Amigne, Arvine, Dézaley, Dorin, Ermitage, Fendant, Johannisberg, Malvoisie, Mandement, Paien, Perlan, Riesling-Silvaner, Schafiser, Twanner.

ROSÉ

Oeil de Perdrix.

The wines of Germany

The Romans introduced the vine to Germany two thousand years ago. When the Roman Empire collapsed the monasteries eventually took over wine making as they did in the rest of Europe. This situation was to continue until 1803 when Napoleon's conquest of Germany had the effect of removing the wine trade from the control of the church and making it secular.

Quality control was first introduced over 250 years ago. An important year for this was 1775. It is said that a careless abbot forgot to order the harvesting of grapes. When he realised his error the grapes had rotted on the vines. The peasants, who were then given a free hand to utilise the product as best they could, proceeded to make a far better than ordinary wine from it! This supposedly initiated the custom of Spätlese (late harvesting) which, given the right conditions, produces wines which are richer and fuller on the palate due to the higher sugar content present in the grapes. The Napoleonic era also saw the introduction of Crus. These were finally reclassified and reduced in number in 1971. Also, co-operatives were introduced and developed in the nineteenth century.
They are now well established and play on important part in German wine production and sales. The Association of German Fine Wine Producers (V.D.P.) was established in Trier in 1910 and then modified in 1971. The resulting very strict regulations have given German wines an international reputation for quality. This has been achieved by classifying all wines into eight grades, based on increasing levels of ripeness and hence sweetness.
These are: 1. *Tafelwein*, 2. *Landswein*, 3. *Qualitätswein* (*QbA*), 4. *Kabinett*, 5. *Spätlese*, 6. *Auslese*, 7. *Beerenauslese* and 8. *Trockenbeernauslese*. Eiswein is Germany's most unique and expensive wine, being made from frozen grapes. It is not included in the above classification.

Being situated well to the north of Europe, Germany is hardly a country where one would expect good wine to be produced. Indeed, there are late frosts and frequent autumn rains. Yet there are microclimates and even the Romans chose the best possible for the vineyard location areas.

These are situated along the warmest banks of the Rhine, the Moselle and their tributaries. Mists and fogs around these rivers seem to constitute a means by which they are able, during cold spells, to re-diffuse heat that they had formerly captured from the sun.

The wine growing areas of Germany can be divided into seven basic regions. These are briefly described as follows:

(a) Mosel-Saar-Ruwer
This starts at the Luxembourg border and runs roughly northwards, past the city of Trier, up as far as Koblenz.

(b) Nahe
The region is scattered around the same named river, a tributary that joins the Rhine at Bingen.

(c) Rheingau
This is considered to be Germany's finest wine area. It lies along the north banks of the Rhine and Maine around the city of Wiesbaden.

(d) Rheinpfalz
The biggest wine producing area in Germany. It is also the sunniest and driest of the country, lying along an 80-kilometre stretch running due north of Alsace in France.

(e) Rheinhessen
This lies on the south and west banks of the Rhine around the city of Mainz at which point the river changes its direction and veers westwards. The region is enclosed by the Nahe and the Rheinpfalz to the west and south respectively.

(f) Baden-Württemberg
This is in two separate parts. Württemberg is bordered by the town of Heilbronn in the north and the city of Stuttgart to the south, whilst Baden consists of a long huge stretch of land, starting at Heidelberg in the north and running southwards as far as Basel on the Swiss border.
Although the combined area is massive, the vineyards tend to be scattered about and the region does not produce as much wine as expected.

(g) Franken-Main
This is the most easterly area in German wine production. It is concentrated around the city of Würzburg.

Although wine making in Germany is growing quickly, particularly in the Baden-Württemberg area, its total production is still relatively small, being no more than one seventh of that of France.

Consequently, Germany imports far more wine than she can export. Indeed, her people have both the knowledge and the means of buying fine wine. The main grape varieties used are the Riesling, the Müller-Thurgau, the Sylvaner the Gewürztraminer and the Ruländer. The great majority of the wine produced is white. The valley of the Ahr near Bonn does specialise in red wine. Also some fine red is produced in the Rheinhessen but this represents less than 5% of that region's output. The few reds produced are based on Pinot Noir, Portugieser and Trollinger grapes.

Unlike France and Italy most German wines are named simply after the main grape variety used or the region in which they are made. Further details of named German wines are better explained while dealing with the region in question. ❧

The wines of Baden and Württemberg

The Baden part of this region has a great wine making tradition. In the middle of the last century it was the biggest producer of wine in Germany, that is, until the 1860's, when phylloxera destroyed half the vines there.

Although the actual area of land is huge, the combination of all the necessary factors needed to make good wine is not easy to find and consequently the vineyards are limited to a few localities scattered far and wide. Recently, however, Baden's vineyards have doubled in size and quadrupled in production. This is due to the modernisation techniques introduced by the many co-operatives that handle ninety per cent of the grapes and must produced.

The vineyards of Baden lie in an 130-kilometre strip between the Black Forest in the east and the Rhine valley bordering on Alsace to the west. The best spots lie either on the southern slopes of the forest massif or on two high altitude islands in the Rhine valley, the Kaiserstuhl and the Tuniberg. Here, the soil, a mixture of clay and volcanic outcrop, appears to suit the Pinot Noir (Spätburgunder) and the Silvaner, two grape varieties that do not do well in most other parts of Germany. An area of particular quality is the Ortenau, near Baden-Baden. The granite soil produces fine Riesling wine, a product not generally made in the region.

Although the Müller-Thurgau accounts for about 40% of the vines, it is true to say that no grape variety is dominant here. Each small area has its own preferred vine. The Pinot Noir and Pinot Gris (Ruländer), together account for another third, but pockets rely on, and make very good wine from many other varieties that do not grow well in the region as a whole. Examples of these are the Pinot Blanc (Weissburgunder), the Gewürztraminer, the Traminer, the Gutedel and the Nobling.

As expected the great majority of wine produced is white. The best wines are excellent but are quite unlike those of the more noted Rhine and Moselle vineyards, being less ethereal and more substantial in character. Thus they are not so suited to be drunk alone and are best taken with food. They are very popular in Germany but since they are rarely exported, tend to be overlooked by the outside world.

The small quantity of red wine made from Pinot Noir is often of remarkably good quality. Unfortunately it tends to be sold at a premium price.

Although the region lies more to the south than those of the Rhineland and Moselle, the proximity of both river and forest tend to make the weather conditions more damp and cloudy.

The climate of the Württemberg section is even more difficult and the locality of any vineyard there has to be chosen with great care. Most are found in the Württembergisch Unterland, just to the north of Stuttgart, being situated around the river Neckar and its tributaries. Surprisingly, more red is grown than white, varieties used being the Pinot Noir, the Trollinger, the Limbeger and the Pinot Meunier (Schwartzriesling). With a number of notable exceptions, however, most reds are light-bodied and not very impressive. They are drunk by the local population, who seem to enjoy them. Whites produced in this area are the Müller-Thurgau, the Silvaner, the Traminer and in common with most other parts of Germany, in a class of its own, the Riesling.

As normal in Germany, wines of both sections are sold with varietal labels. ⌇

Principal wines and grape varieties of Baden and Württemberg

REDS
Pinot Noir, Trollinger, Pinot Meunier, Roter Gudentel, Limberger.

WHITES
Müller Thurgau, Kerner, Riesling, Pinot Gris, Pinot Blanc, Traminer, Gewürztraminer, Gudetel, Silvaner, Freisamer, Nobling.

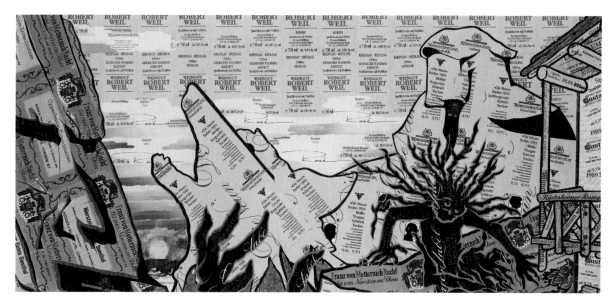

The wines of Franken

Principal wines and grape varieties of Franken

RED AND ROSÉ

Spätburgunder (Pinot Noir).

WHITES

Müller-Thurgau, Silvaner, Bacchus, Kerner, Riesling, Scheurebe, Rieslaner, Perle, Ortega.

In spite of its northerly position and hence a relatively short growing season, wine making in Franken was introduced as long ago as the seventh century A.D. by Christian monks. It is known that in the Middle Ages the Bishops of Würzburg actively encouraged viticulture along the river Main. By the sixteenth century the activity was well established and probably at its height.

Nowadays, the wine growing areas are considerably less than at the peak period. However, the region, being atypical of German wine productions a whole, is a highly interesting one to investigate. The wines produced are much drier and more powerful than those made in the rest of the country, making them more similar to French Burgundy than any other in Germany. As though to emphasise these differences, the product is sold in flask shaped Bocksbeutels rather than the traditional flute shaped bottles. A rare common factor with the rest of Germany is that the great bulk of what is made is white. Red wines account for no more than about 4% of the total. However, their popularity is growing rapidly and Pinot Noir is so much sought after that it commands a considerably higher price than the equivalent whites.

Due to the continental type weather with great temperature fluctuations and bitterly cold winter nights, as well as the short growing season, Riesling, although utilised, does not do well here. Conversely, the Silvaner grape, although susceptible to the large nocturnal temperature drops, does, and is therefore largely used in top-class locations. A late-ripening cross of Silvaner and Riesling called 'Rieslaner' is also grown. Given good weather conditions, it can produce some interesting wines. However, the Müller-Thurgau is the most widely used grape variety, particularly in the less sheltered sites.

The main area of Franken vine growing follows a meandering 'V' shaped tract of the river Main, starting from Volkach in the northeast, going southwards to Frickenhausen and then north-westwards through Würzburg right up to Hammelburg. The vines are on scattered hill-sites facing south. The alkaline limestone soil is a common denominator. As capital of the wine region, Würzburg is unique. The city possesses three fine estates with quality vineyard sites. Wines made here are among the very best in the region.

Franken wines are mostly made by co-operatives and sold either locally or in the rest of Bavaria. Although the vine area has doubled since 1965, the home market has still been able to absorb nearly everything, so very little is exported. It is hoped that the industry will continue to expand with the result that the wines of this region become better known internationally. They certainly deserve to be. In typical German tradition, wines are sold as varietal products, bearing the name of the dominant grape variety on the label. ⚘

The wines of Mosel-Saar-Ruwer

Wine has been made here since Roman times. The ancient city of Trier has been at the centre of wine production administration and several of its institutions still own many of the region's vineyards.

The grape originally used was similar to the Elbling, now used mainly in making sparkling wines. The supremacy of the Riesling was not discovered until relatively recently when its dominance was formally established in 1787, just over two hundred years ago. Since then, its proportion has increased steadily, reaching a remarkable peak of 90% in the 1950's. Unfortunately, with the planting of new vineyards a focus on quantity then set in, resulting in the high yielding but unexciting Müller-Thurgau being used.
The proportion of Riesling is now less than 60%, thus lowering the general standard of the product and consequently the image of the region. This is a fate not deserved by those still striving for and getting the best in quality by still using the noble grape.

The Moselle region of wine production is only the fourth largest in Germany but arguably the best. It is divided into five districts. These are the Zell-Mosel, Bernkastel, Saar, Ruwer and Obermosel & Moseltor. The region follows the Mosel valley, from the border with Luxembourg in the south, through Trier, to the city of Koblenz in the north. The valleys of the Mosel's tributaries, the Saar and the Ruwer, are included in the region.

The Middle Mosel or Bereich Bernkastel produces the finest wines in Germany. The heat retaining soil, consisting of slate, occasionally mixed with clay, and the extremely steep, south-facing river banks cause the Riesling grape to flourish as nowhere else, producing in good years a poetic wine which is fruity and aromatic and also delicately elegant and full of finesse. The best vineyards are to be found at Erden, Piesport, Graach, Wehlen, Zeltingen, Brauneberg, Trittenheim and Bernkastel. The last named, founded in 1291 by the Emperor Frederich Barbarossa, possesses the 'Doctor' vineyard, probably the most famous in the country.

The Saar and Ruwer can also produce excellent wines. Here the soil again consists of slate but the district, being higher in altitude, is cooler and a high quality is more difficult to attain. The wines can be comparable to those of the Middle Mosel in the best years, but these account for no more than one third of the total. Otherwise, incomplete ripening leads to a sharp and inferior product.

The Bereich Zell Mosel (Lower Mosel) produces good wine, even if not in the same class as the foregoing. The Schwarze Katz wine produced at Zell is well known and much appreciated. Other fine wines are made at Neef, Bullay and Winningen.

The chalky soil in the Bereich Obermosel (Upper Mosel) results in a difference in the grape varieties used. Elbling and Ruländer are grown as well as Riesling and Müller-Thurgau. The wines are the least interesting in the Mosel region but at the same time the lowest in price.
The region's wines are marketed as varietal. There are no red wines of note. ✒

Principal wines and grape varieties of Mosel-Saar-Ruwer

WHITES
Riesling, Müller-Thurgau, Elbling, Ruländer.

The wines of Rhinelands & Nahe

Principal wines and grape varieties of Rhinelands & Nahe

REDS

Spätburgunder, Potuguiser.

WHITES

Riesling, Müller-Thurgau, Sylvaner, Kerner, Scheurebe, Ehrenfelser, Bacchus, Faber, Huxelrebe.

ROSÉS

Spätburgunder.

(a) The Rheingau

As with the other Rhine regions, wine production in this area was initiated by the Romans. However, the industry didn't really flourish until the Middle Ages when the church took over its control. River bank forests were uprooted and vines planted in their place. The Riesling was first noted in the fifteenth century, far before the Mosel region had seen it. It took over as the main grape variety in the seventeenth century, replacing Spätburgunder (Pinot Noir), the stocks of which had been brought to the region from Burgundy.

Nowadays Riesling accounts for over 80% of the grapes while Spätburgunder fails to reach even 10%. It is no coincidence, that together with the Mosel, the Rheingau, at its best, produces the best wine in the country.

The region lies between Lorchhausen in the west and Wiesbaden in the east, spreading into the banks of the river Main around Hochheim. Nearly all the plantations are on the northern banks, giving them south-facing slopes. The vines are protected from cold winds by the Taunus Mountains that lie towards the north. Although there are some steep slopes, the land is generally more gently undulating than that in the Mosel. Also, the soil is much more varied in composition, consisting of clay, limestone, loess, slate, sandstone, quartz and gravel. The result is that Rheingau wines tend to have more flavour and complexity and also a longer life than those of the Mosel, which are, on the other hand, more ethereal and delicate.

Towns and villages where the best products are to be found include Hattenheim, Hallgarten, Raventhal, Johannisberg, and on the river Main, Hochheim. Unfortunately, quality does not go with quantity. As in the Mosel, much of the Rheingau production is well below the top level. An important point to remember is that traditional Auslese is sweet and hardly suitable with food. At its best this is a meditation wine, to be enjoyed on its own. Furthermore, modern bias towards dry wine has not favoured it. Even where sweet wine is concerned, Eiswein is easier to make yet more expensive than Auslese, so its production has increased at the expense of the latter.

An interesting point concerns the town of Assmannshausen, the most westerly in the region. Here, only red wine from Spätburgunder is made. The product, the best-known red in Germany, is pleasant but lacks the body and strength of Burgundy's original Pinot Noir. Sweet rosé wines are also produced from the same grape.

(b) The Pfalz (Rheinpfalz or Palatinate)

The Palatinate vies with the Rheinhessen for being the largest wine region in Germany. It is located at the edge of the high lying woods of the Pfalz forest. It also borders the Rheinhessen to the north, the river Rhine in the east and Alsace to the south.

The Pfalz is blessed by early springs, long and warm summers and mild winters. Also, the soil, consisting of volcanic basalt and clay, is both able to trap and hold the heat from the sun and retain water. Unlike the Rheingau, the main grape in the region is the Müller-Thurgau, which accounts for nearly 30% of the total. However, in the Mittelhaardt, the region's best district, which runs from Kallstadt to Ruppertsberg, the Reisling is again by far the principal grape, producing some very good sweetish wine in the true German tradition. Some of the best towns and villages are Deidesheim, Wachenheim, Forst, Bad Dürkheim and Ungstein. Two other promising places, to the north of the Mittelhardt district, are Freinsheim and Herxheim.

As in the Rheingau, although the great bulk of the product, including some dry sparkling wines, is white, some red is made using Spätburgunder and Portuguiser grapes. Again this lacks the complexity and body of the corresponding French products.

The comparatively favourable climatic conditions of the Rheinpfalz results in wines which have more body and a greater alcoholic strength than those from other regions in Germany. Thus the Palatinate has the potential to suit modern dry wine requirements. In fact the region has, with some success, shown a great expansion towards a drier product, which now accounts for as much as 25% of its total wine production.

(c) Rheinhessen

This large region is situated towards the south and west of the Rhine and the east of the Nahe. It also lies due north of the Pfalz.

The region is divided into three districts, the East, the Northwest and the South. The East, the Bereich Nierstein, contains the Rheinterasse, which produces the best wine in the region. As with the Pfalz, although the most common grape variety is the Müller-Thurgau, the best district uses a far higher than normal (in this case 35%) amount of Riesling. This district, which runs from just south of Oppenheim to Nackenheim, has a soil containing red sandstone, slate and clay, which traps the heat from the sun. This, coupled with a mild climate and a dry harvesting season, explains its pre-eminence in the region. The Northwest, or Bereich Bingen, produces some good wines, namely at Bingen itself and at Ingelheim, whose limestone soil encourages the production of some red as well as the standard white. The South, or Bereich Wonnegau, generally makes the least impressive product in the region.
It is particularly from here that Liebfraumilch, a sweetish 'wine for the masses' is produced. This accounts for 50% of all that is made in Germany. The use of high yielding crossings results in wines that are poor both in style and in quality.

The Rheinhessen, possibly due to the variance of the soil (which can consist of clay, limestone, loess, marl, quartz, sandstone, schist and slate), in different areas, uses a higher number of grape varieties than any other Rhine region. As elsewhere in the Rhinelands some sparkling white wine is made.
Also, as mentioned above, some red is made. Its proportion, at 5% is low, but due to an effort intended at meeting present day demands, is increasing.

(d) The Nahe

This region, although not belonging to the Rhine is close by and does have some common features.
The vineyards are situated on the south facing banks of the river and can be divided into three main sections.

The best of these is almost certainly the most southerly, starting at Schlossbockelheim, passing through Niederhausen and Norheim and ending at Bad Münster. Contrary to the region as a whole, the Riesling is the main grape used here, taking full advantage of the excellent volcanic and porphyritic soil. The finest vineyard, the Kupfergrube, produces a wine that is both intense and delicate at the some time. Other vineyards of note in this area are the Hermannsberg and Hermannshöhle. The second section lies just north of Bad Kreuznach, the wine capital of the region. This also boasts many fine vineyards cultivated with the Riesling grape, those at Brückes and Kahlenberg producing exceptional wines. The most northerly section, around the town of Bingen yields products that are more full-bodied than those of the other areas. Although less memorable, they are still well above the national average in quality.

Generally, the wines of this region possess characteristics of those both of the Rheingau and Mosel. It should be noted that although not as renowned as these regions and hence less expensive, the wines of the Nahe, at their best, are their equal in quality. As with the Rhineland a switch toward a drier product is taking place in order to meet present-day demands. In common with other German regions, all Rhine wines are varietal. ✒

The wines of Austria

Principal wines and grape varieties of Austria

REDS

　Zweigelt, Blaufränkisch, Cabernet Sauvignon, Pinot Noir, St. Laurent.

WHITES

　Grüner Veltliner, Müller-Thurgau, Welschriesling, Chardonnay, Weissburgunder (Pinot Blanc), Neuburger, Riesling, Muscat Ottonel, Muskateller, Traminer, Gewürztraminer, Ruländer (Pinot Gris), Sauvignon Blanc, Zierfandler, Rotgipfler.

ROSÉS

　Wildbacher.

Wine production in Austrian territory probably dates from Celtic times, over four centuries before the birth of Christ. It flourished under the Romans in the then provinces of Noricum and Pannonia, suffered a long setback during the barbarian invasions, but eventually experienced a resurgence at the time of the Holy Roman Emperors, thanks to monastic interest and patronage. Viticulture has continued until the present day, gaining ground due to the pre-eminence of Tokay during the Habsburg Empire, but then taking a body-blow as the result of the discovery of illegal additives in 1985. However, this has proved to be a blessing in disguise as the strict new laws that followed have given Austria a sound base on which the industry has greatly improved and can look forward to a future that shows much promise.

It is interesting to compare and contrast wine production in Austria to that in Germany. Many grape varieties are the same as is the overriding tendency toward whites. Also, the styles and labelling customs are very similar. However, some varieties and styles resemble those of the neighbouring Czech Republic, Hungary, Slovakia and Slovenia. Also the wines are generally more full-bodied and stronger in alcohol than those of their German counterparts. This is due partly to warmer summers and also lower yields thanks to the Lenz-Moser 'high culture' vine training system. As in Germany, wines are labelled according to must weight and quality. The scale, in ascending order, is: 1. Tafelwein, 2. Landwein, 3. Qualitätswein and Kabinett, 4. Spätlese, 5. Auslese, 6. Strohwein, Schilfwein, Eiswein and Beerenauslese, 7. Ausbruch, 8. Trockenbeerenauslese. It should be noted that standards are higher than in the German equivalents.

The soil varies in different regions, but generally, Lower Austria is rich in limestone, Burgenland is copious in sand and iron, Styria in volcanic minerals and the Wachau and neighbouring areas in loess. Rainfall is on the low side but quite high in Styria in the south, which however, boasts the greatest amount of sunshine.

The vine growing regions of Austria are divisible into thirteen districts. These all lie on the eastern side of the country and are as follows:

(a) Weinviertel

　This is the largest region. It lies to the north in lower Austria and borders the Czech Republic and Slovakia. It is flat, fertile and dry and produces relatively high yields, resulting in the least interesting of the country's wines. However some good Pinot Blanc and passable reds are made, as is a sparkling wine known as 'Sekt'.

(b) Kremstal, Kamptal and Donauland

　A large region lying in lower Austria, to the west of Wien-viertel. The loess soil results in some superb Grüner Veltliner and Riesling wines. The headquarters of the Lenz-Moser firm of vine training fame is located here, at Rohrendorf.

(c) Wachau

　This is lower Austria's smallest district and lies south of the above. The vineyards lie on the steepest banks of the river Danube and produce some of the finest wines in the country. The Grüner Veltliners and Rieslings are justly famous, having good body, fine aroma and high acidity. The local association has produced its own quality level system. There are three grades, these being 'Steinfeder' (the lightest), 'Federspiel' and 'Smaragd' (the most concentrated).

(d) Carnuntum

　A large district located in lower Austria. It stretches along both east and west of Vienna. Many varieties of wines are made here, the best being the whites produced on the western end, near the Wachau.

(e) Thermenregion

　This is the warmest part of lower Austria. Whites made from Zierfandler and Rotgipfler are particular to this region and full of interest. A variety of reds are also produced.

(f) Vienna

The vines are found on both banks of the Danube. Riesling and Pinot Gris grapes are used to make products with a good longevity, while the Grüner Veltliner and Müller-Thurgau varieties go into the production of wines intended to be drunk young and served in the countless taverns found in Austria's capital. It is appropriate that 'Wine, Women and Song' is the title of one of Johann Strauss' celebrated Viennese waltzes!

(g) Neusiedlersee

The largest Burgenland region on the Hungarian border takes its name from the homonymous lake. Rich soils make for good growing conditions while the lake and surrounding marshes encourages the formation of noble rot. Very good Pinot Blancs, Traminers and Welschrieslings, both dry and sweet, are made. The region specialises in first class characteristic sweet wines. Eiswein is produced, as are two other specialities, Strohwein and Schilfwein. Grapes are dried on straw for the former and on reeds from the lake for the latter. Also some good reds are made from Zweigelt and Cabernet Sauvignon.

(h) Neusiedlersee-Hügelland

A large Burgenland region lying on the opposite (western) side of the lake. The wines produced are very similar to the neighbouring district above. An additional speciality sweet wine, Ruster Ausbruch is produced. At its best it is superb.

(i) Mittelburgenland

A much smaller region, again on the Hungarian border, lying south of the above. The warm climate makes this district an exception in Austrian viticulture, as nearly all the produce is red. Increasingly fine wines are being made using Blaufränkisch, Zweigelt, Pinot Noir, Cabernet Sauvignon and St. Laurent grapes.

(j) Südburgenland

This is the smallest region in Burgenland. Red wine is made from the Blaufränkisch grape while the Welschriesling is used to make whites.

(k) Süd-Oststeiermark

Although large, a relatively little and sparsely planted region is Styria. A variety of white grapes are cultivated here. The most successful is Traminer but the two Pinots, Gewürztraminer, Müller-Thurgau and Welschriesling are commonly found as well.

(l) Südstreiermark

The smallest region but most widely planted area in Styria on the Slovenian border. The vineyards are located on steep south-facing slopes. As expected white grapes are used. The most noted are Sauvignon Blanc and Chardonnay. However, Welschriesling, Pinot Blanc and Muscat are also used. The wines are fresh, full bodied and aromatic with a good level of acidity.

(m) Weststeiermark

The region with the smallest planted area in Styria. As for Mittelburgenland, it is anomalous, but in that its main product is rosé wine made using the Wildbacher grape. ❧

The wines of the Czech Republic

Principal wines and grape varieties of the Czech Republic

REDS

    Pinot Noir, Cabernet Sauvignon, St. Laurent.

WHITES

    Sauvignon Blanc, Riesling, Welschriesling, Gewürztraminer, Traminer, Grüner Veltliner, Silvaner, Pinot Blanc, Pinot Gris.

Wine production in the Czech Republic is over one thousand years old. An introduction of vines from Burgundy during the Renaissance put the country on the map as an important wine centre, but a succession of wars and later, the phylloxera epidemic, continually halted the industry's progress. Now, at last, advances are being made.

Viticulture takes place mainly in two regions, Bohemia and Moravia. The former is found north of Prague, while the latter is located on the eastern side of the country, south of Brno, by the Slovakian border. Moravia is by far the biggest and most important region. In comparison, Bohemia makes a comparatively small amount, being far more renowned for its splendid crystal, extensively used in the manufacture of quality wineglasses.

Grape varieties, cultivation methods, production techniques and wine styles are similar to those of Austria. For example, the Lenz Moser system of vine training is used. Also, as in Austria, the great majority of wine is white.

Unfortunately, very little is exported, and so the wines are hardly known in the West. This is a pity, as the wines, particularly those of Moravia, are reputedly well made and show considerable interest. Labelling is confusing, wines being sold under brand names, without necessarily indicating the grape varieties contained. ❧

The wines of Slovakia

Slovakia produces approximately twice as much wine as the Czech Republic. The vineyards lie along a 600 km-stretch along the southern part of the country, running from Skalica, next to the borders of the Czech Republic and Austria in the west, to Košice, in the south east, on the Hungarian and Russian borders. Most vineyards face a southerly direction and being situated on gentle, low altitude hills, are protected from the wind by higher slopes to the north.

As in the Czech Republic, the great majority of wine is white, which accounts for approximately two thirds of the total production. As in Moravia, some interesting wines are made and modernisation is leading to an improvement in quality. Again, unfortunately, most wines are consumed internally, very little being exported to the West. Wine production here is as much akin to Hungary as Austria, a fact seen in the main varieties utilised. In particular, the Košice area borders with the Tokaji-making part of Hungary and the appropriate grapes are grown.

Wine labelling, as in the Czech Republic, is based on brand names. The grape varieties may, or may not be stated. ⛃

Principal grape varieties of Slovakia

REDS

Pinot Noir, Cabernet Sauvignon, St. Laurent.

WHITES

Sauvignon Blanc, Riesling, Welschriesling, Gewürztraminer, Müller-Thurgau, Grüner Veltliner, Silvaner, Pinot Blanc, Pinot Gris, Irsay Oliver, Leányka, Furmint, Hárslevelú, Muscat Ottonel, Ezerjó.

The wines of Romania

Principal wines and grape varieties of Romania

REDS AND ROSÉS

Cabernet Sauvignon, Merlot, Pinot Noir, Fetească Neagră, Roșioara, Băbeașcă Neagră, Cadarca.

WHITES

Cotnari, Fetească Regală, Fetească Albă, Welschriesling, Sauvignon Blanc, Aligoté, Pinot Gris, Rkatsiteli, Muscat Ottonel, Gewürztraminer, Chardonnay, Tămîioasă, Mustoasă, Majarcă Albă, Galbenă, Plăvaie, Selection Carriere, Furmint.

That Romania is one of the biggest wine producers in Europe might come as a surprise to some, but the fact is that its wine appreciation is so strong that most is used at home and very little finds its way to the West. This is the very opposite to Bulgaria, which makes much less but exports considerably more. It is certainly not a case of the wines being poor. Many show much interest, whether made with indigenous or noble French and German grape varieties, a multitude of both types being utilised.

The continental climate and low rainfall would appear to make good viticulture difficult to achieve. However, a combination of choosing the best sites with the appropriate microclimates, irrigation where necessary, improvement of cellar techniques and a passion for wine culture has enabled the country to surmount these problems.

Wine production in Romania is a very ancient tradition. It was already well established during its Roman occupation as the province of Dacia. It is possible that viticulture existed even before the Greeks colonised part of the country in the seventh century B.C. It has been maintained, uninterrupted throughout the ages, in the face of numerous annexations, including that by the Ottoman Empire. Only the phylloxera epidemic, in the late nineteenth century, was able to temporarily halt it. Although Romania suffered a period of over-planting and overproduction, especially of disease-resistant hybrids, the present situation is happily one of a quality drive with an eye to an increasing export market in the future.

Due to the scattered nature of the wine producing areas, it is not easy to apportion Romanian viticulture into definite regions. However, five important divisions are immediately obvious. These are, Transylvania, situated in the centre of the country north of the Carpathian Mountains, Arad and Banat between the Hungarian and Serbian borders, Moldavia by the Russian border, Dobrudja on the Black Sea and the regions of Muntenia and Oltenia, to the north and west of Bucharest, respectively.

The best Romanian wine is traditionally its white, that from Moldavia being particularly fine. The sweet wine of Cotnari, made with a blend of four grapes, Grasă, Tămîioasă Românească, Fetească Albă and Frîncusă, was particularly famous before the phylloxera epidemic. Unfortunately, unlike the Hungarian Tokaji, it has so far failed to recover its former reputation. Hopefully the future will put this right. As well as many interesting dry table wines Moldavia makes good sweet wine at Huși, and sparkling wines at Iași and Panciu. White wine specialisation is also found at Transylvania, which produces much that is of interest. Other regions with nice whites are Arad, Banat and Dobrudja. Although red wines haven't the same reputation, Romania prides itself as having the largest planted area of Cabernet Sauvignon in Europe outside France. Moldavia, as the country's best region, naturally makes some interesting specimens. Two regions specialising in reds are Muntenia and Oltenia. Other red wines worth investigating are found at Dobrudja, Banat and Arad. In all cases, both French and native varieties are individually used.

Romanian wines tend to be sold under the name of their grape variety, that is, as varietal products. ❧

The wines of Bulgaria

The viticulture history of Bulgaria is similar to that of Romania. The industry can boast a very ancient tradition, survival of many wars and occupations, destruction by Phylloxera and a new, relatively modern outlook. Another similarity is the continental climate with hot summers and cold winters. However, contrary to Romania, rainfall is high, leading to humidity and problems of rot. On the other hand no irrigation is necessary.

Unlike Romania, Bulgaria exports the great majority of its wine production. Although the demise of the Soviet Union, hitherto an important customer as well as political influencing agent, has led to an upheaval in its selling organisation, exports still amount to around 85% of the total output, which make it the fifth largest exporter in the world.

Lying due south of Romania, the weather is hotter and therefore the best wines are red rather than white. Again a strong tendency towards French noble varieties exists, as exemplified by the Cabernet Sauvignon plantings, which although less in area than in Romania, are still four times as much as those in California.

Bulgaria's vineyards can be very easily classified into five geographical divisions. These are the North, East, Southern, South Western and Sub-Balkan regions. The first-named runs along the River Danube and specialises in reds made using mainly French grapes. On the other hand, the Eastern Region, which lies close to the Black Sea coast, is far better known for its whites, although some reds and an interesting rosé are also made. The grapes tend to be French, but some German varieties are also used.
The Southern Region, lying below the Balkan Mountains, is another red wine stronghold, however using indigenous grapes as well as French. The South West, next to the Serbian border, makes the country's best local-variety red with the indigenous Melnik grape. The fifth region lies south east of the Balkan Mountains.
It produces roughly equal quantities of white and red. Again, both French and local varieties are used.

Although a fair number of East European varieties are included in the list below, the amounts planted are decreasing.
Predictably, they are being replaced by French and to a lesser extent German vines. Those likely to survive in the future are Mavrud and Melnik, which make good long-lasting reds, Gamza, another interesting red grape, Pamid a less interesting red used for local early drinking, and Misket, an interesting white variety.
Clearly, the changes mentioned, in the present period of flux, is part of the drive to improve quality and remove the country's image as an exporter of cheap wine. As for Romania, wines are sold with varietal labels. ❧

Principal wines and grape varieties of Bulgaria

REDS
Cabernet Sauvignon, Merlot, Pinot Noir, Mavrud, Melnik, Pamid, Gamza, Saperavi.

WHITES
Riesling, Welschriesling, Sauvignon Blanc, Aligoté, Ugni Blanc, Chardonnay, Traminer, Muscat Ottonel, Misket, Feteasca, Dimiat, Rkatsiteli, Tamianka.

ROSÉS
Burgas Rosé.

The wines of Hungary

Principal wines and grape varieties of Hungary

REDS
- *Varietal Wines: Kadarka, Kékoporto, Kékfrankos, Zweigelt, Cabernet Sauvignon, Cabernet Franc, Merlot, Pinot Noir.*
- *Others of special note: Egri Bikavér, Egri Kádarika.*

WHITES
- *Varietal Wines: Furmint, Hárslevelű, Muskotályos, Sárfehér, Szürkebarát, Mezesfehér, Kövidinka, Kéknyelű, Ezerjó, Juhfark, Leányka, Zöldsilváni, Zöldveltelini, Müller Thurgau, Sauvignon Blanc, Muscat Ottonel, Chardonnay, Sémillon, Cirfandli, Olaszrizling, Riesling, Traminer, Pinot Blanc.*
- *Others of special note: Tokaji.*

Wine production in Hungary is very old, dating from before it became part of the Roman province of Pannonia. Although the industry suffered during a 150 year period of Moslem rule, it was expanded after 1697 when the Turks were defeated at the battle of Zenta and Hungary became part of the Austrian empire. By the time of Maria Theresa's reign, when Der Rosenkavalier is staged, the wines of Hungary had become among the most sought after in Europe. In particular, Tokaji had found great favour amongst the royalty of Russia, Poland and Germany as well as Austria. It is no coincidence that it is mentioned in the second act of the opera's libretto! In common with the rest of Europe, phylloxera struck in the 1870's and although the vines were replanted on resistant stock, the industry failed to do itself justice, primarily because of inadequate wine laws.

In 1990, new regulations that approach those of the European Union have started to produce a renewal, which with stability and time, should lead to great improvements in the future.

Three regions, Kiskun, Csongrád and Hajós contain a large proportion of Hungary's vineyards. These lie on the great plain in the south of the country and east of the Danube. The sandy soil resulted in the area being given prominence after the Phylloxera outbreak. However the continental climate, with its hot dry summers and spring frosts, is a disadvantage that makes the production of top class wine difficult. Both reds and whites are made.

A second area of importance is that associated with Europe's largest lake, the Balaton. Here the presence of water mitigates the climatic conditions, which results in better wines. Six regions are involved. They are Somló and Etyek, which lie to the North of the lake and Balatonfüred-Csopak, Balatonboglári, Badacsony and Outer Balaton, all of which lie close to and around the lake. The soil varies, but volcanic basalt, clay, sandstone and limestone all play a part. Although some reds are produced most of the wine is white.

North Western Hungary has four wine regions: Sopron on the Austrian border and eastwards, Pannonian Sokoróalya, Aszár-Neszmély and Mór. Sopron, a fine white wine producer in the past, now makes mainly reds while the other regions are biased towards whites. The Northern Massif lies towards the eastern side of Hungary. Three regions, Mátraalja, Eger and Bükkalja are to be found here. The most famous product, from Eger, is the red known as 'Bull's Blood', or to the Hungarians, Egri Bikavér. Most of the other wine is white. Yet another area lies in the far south of the country, west of the river Danube. In the regions of Szekszárd, Mecsek and Villány-Siklós, both white and red wines are made, but the lack of rainfall and hot summers result in a greater proportion of reds than elsewhere.

The last area, on the far eastern side, bordering with Slovakia and not far from Russia is the Tokaji-Hegyalja region where Tokaji is made. Here, the volcanic and loess soils provide ideal growing conditions for the Furmint, Hárslevelű and Muscat vines while the sheltering Carpathian mountains together with the Tisza and Bodrog rivers provide warm humid autumns which encourage noble rot to set in, giving dried out, or 'Aszú' grapes. These are harvested between late October and early December.

Tokaji is produced in five levels of sweetness, as follows:

(a) 'Tokaji Ordinarum', an ordinary basic dryish wine made from grapes not affected by noble rot.

(b) 'Tokaji Szamorodni' contains a proportion of noble rot grapes. It comes in dry 'Száraz' and sweet 'Edes' forms.

(c) 'Tokaji Aszú' is a vintage sweet wine made of over 50% of noble rot grapes. These are allowed to ferment to a sweet paste that is then added to one-year-old base wine in controlled quantities, measured in 'puttonyos'. The more the number of puttonyos (25 litre capacity tubs) added, the sweeter and richer the wine. The actual number added varies from three to six, depending on the product required. The wine is then left to mature in barrels for between three to eight years.

(d) 'Tokaji Aszú Essencia' is an intensely sweet wine containing even more sugar then the above. It is made from the best vineyards in exceptional vintages. No basic wine is used and the fermentation process, brought about by using selected yeast strains, is very slow. The wine is then aged for a minimum of ten years in barrel.

(e) 'Tokaji Essencia' is made from juice that oozes from Aszú grapes before they are crushed. This extract hardly ferments and is left to age for a great many years. The product is low in alcohol, exceedingly smooth yet rich and tangy with an incredibly long finish. Supposedly having magical elixir properties it was once given to dying Kings!

Winemaking in former Yugoslavia dates from ancient times, prospering under both Greeks and Romans. The industry suffered two major setbacks throughout the ages: the invasion and lengthy domination by the Ottoman Turks and more recently the Phylloxera epidemic that hit the vineyards between the very late nineteenth and early twentieth centuries.

Wines of Slovenia

Wines of Croatia

Principal wines and grape varieties of Slovenia

REDS AND ROSÉS

Teran (Refosco), Barbera, Cabernet, Merlot, Cviček.

WHITES

Beli Pinot, Sauvignon, Laski Rizling (Welschriesling), Ljutomer Rizling, Renski Rizling, Traminec (Gewürztraminer), Šipon (Furmint), Tokaji, Rumeni Muškat, Radgonska Ranina, Rebula, Malvazija.

Principal wines and grape varieties of Croatia

REDS

Teran, Refoško, Cabernet, Merlot, Gamay, Borgonja (Pinot Noir), Babić, Bol, Dingác, Lastovo, Plavina, Plavac Mali, Postup, Prošek, Vis Brela.

WHITES

Laski Rizling, Graševina, Rizling Rajnski, Traminac, Burgundac Bijeli (Pinot Blanc), Sauvignon, Sémillon, Malvazija, Muškat, Marastina, Pošip, Grk, Vugava, Bogdanuša, Vrnička Zlahtina, Bijeli Klikun, Varazdin, Plavac Beli, Plavac Zulti, Zilavka.

ROSÉS

Opol, Plemenka Ružika.

Nowadays, the total production in Slovenia derives from three main regions. Nearly half comes from the Littoral, on the western side of the country, bordering the Italian Collio district, with which its wines have much in common, except that here more red is made than white. The most interesting wines are those made with Cabernet Sauvignon, Merlot, Barbera and Refosco grapes. The best dry whites contain Pinot Blanc and Rebula, while Malvasia and Muscat Blanc à Petits Grains are utilised in sweet products. An almost equal proportion is produced in the Drava valley, on the north-eastern side of Slovenia. This lies close to the Austrian region of Südsteiermark, and as expected, is responsible for wines that are almost invariably white, being similar in style to those over the border. The most noted are those made from the Sauvignon Blanc, Welschriesling, Riesling, Gewürztraminer, Pinot Blanc and Furmint varieties. The latter is a grape from Hungary, which lies just to the East of this region. The third region is the Sava valley, in the south, where both reds and whites are made. Although production techniques still need to be modernised, cold temperature fermentation is already commonly practised. The country has much future potential and there is good hope that this will be realised, particularly if the present enthusiasm is maintained.

Wines, as they are in the other countries which were part of former Yugoslavia, are generally sold as varietal products. ❧

The vineyards of Croatia are split between two basic regions that correspond to the two main ones in Slovenia.
The western one, starting at the peninsula of Istra (Istria) in the north, and descending along the coastline, past the towns of Zadar and Split and ending at Dubrovnik in the south, includes wines made in the Dalmatian islands. Both reds and whites are produced, using several grape varieties similar to those in the Littoral in Slovenia. For the reds Refosco, Cabernet Sauvignon, Merlot and Barbera are all used, with the addition of Gamay and Pinot Noir. Also, there are a great number of native varieties, Plavac Mali, Prokupac and Babíc being particularly successful. White grapes used are also comparable to those in Slovenia; Pinot Blanc, Muscat Blanc à Petits Grains and Malvasia are all to be found. However, a large number of indigenous varieties are also utilised. Marastina, Plavac Beli, Grk, Pošip and Vugava are examples, mainly grown in Dalmatia.

The eastern region, running from north to south almost parallel to the Hungarian border, also corresponds to that of Slovenia, whites making up almost the entire production. Here again the main grapes are Welschriesling, Riesling, Gewürztraminer, Pinot Blanc and Sauvignon Blanc, with the French Sémillon instead of the Hungarian Furmint. ❧

Wines of Bosnia-Hercegovina

Bosnia produces very little wine, the best probably being the white Zilavka, made in the Dalmatian sector of the country, near the town of Mostar. Reds are also made in the same region, but they are not as interesting. A second region, making both red and white, is found in a small area towards the north east of the country, around the town of Banja Luka. ❧

Principal wines and grape varieties of Bosnia-Hercegovina

REDS
Blatina.

WHITES
Zilavka.

Wines of Yugoslavia

Together with Croatia, Serbia is the biggest producer of wine in the former Yugoslavia. However, in any consideration of the present country, the regions of Montenegro and Macedonia must also be taken into account.

In Serbia, wine making takes place in two regions, to the north east, in Vojvodina and in central Serbia itself. Vojvodina has two areas of major importance. These are in the north, at the intersection of the Hungarian and Romanian boundaries, and in the southeast, again bordering with Romania. Wines from these districts resemble those of the adjacent countries more than those made elsewhere in Serbia. Although some reds are made, mostly using French varieties, the great bulk of the production is white. Here, Welschriesling, Gewürztraminer and Sauvignon Blanc again play a major part, as does a local grape, the Smederevka.
The vineyards in central Serbia tend to follow the Morava River between the towns of Smederevo in the north and Vranje in the south. Unlike Vojvodina, most wines are red. Again, the noble French varieties including Gamay play a major role, but the indigenous Prokupac is probably still the most utilised, either alone or in blends featuring the French grapes. It is also used to make an interesting rosé. White wines are made from the same grapes as in Vojvodina, except that Gewürztraminer does not appear to be used.

Montenegro produces very little wine, almost entirely red. The best-known products are Vranac and Plavka.
The former is potentially excellent, with a velvety taste and a good ageing potential.

Macedonia is the third largest producer among the former Yugoslav states. It possesses some good vineyards scattered all over the region. However, the greatest concentration of viticulture lies in a large area starting roughly in the centre and running diagonally southeast to the border with Greece. As in Serbia and Montenegro, the great majority of wines produced here are red, involving yet again the French noble grapes, the native Prokupac and also the Italian Refosco. A small amount of white is made using Riesling, Smederevka and Zilavka grapes.

Finally, Kosovo has just one area of wine production, on its western side. Typically, mostly reds are made and from almost exactly the same varieties as in Serbia and Macedonia.
The only difference appears to be that Cabernet Franc is used instead of Cabernet Sauvignon. A white wine is produced from Welschriesling. ❧

Principal wines and grape varieties of Yugoslavia

REDS
Cabernet, Merlot, Cokanski Merlot, Burgundac (Pinot Noir), Gamay, Prokupac, Kadarka, Vranac, Plavka, Zupsko Crno, Teran, Muškat Hamburg, Kratosija, Začinka.

WHITES
Sauvignon, Sémillon, Italijanski Rizling, Banatski Rizling, Rizling, Traminac, Muskat Ottonel, Kevedinka, Neoplanta, Ezerjo, Smederevka, Zilavka.

ROSÉS
Oplenačka Ružica, Prokupac Ružica, Zupska Ružica.

The wines of Greece

Principal wines and grape varieties of Greece

REDS

Mavrodaphne, Xinomavro, Agiorgitiko, Limnio, Mandelaria, Cabernet Sauvignon, Cabernet Franc.

WHITES

Savatiano, Rhoditis, Debina, Muscat Blanc à Petits Grains, Muscat d'Alexandrie, Malagousia, Moscophilero, Assyritiko, Robola, Vilana.

ROSÉS

Rhoditis, Moscophilero.

Although having a very ancient wine making tradition and now being the ninth largest producer in Europe, only 10% of what's made is exported. Therefore Greek wine is comparatively unknown to the general public, a rather strange state of affairs when the past is considered.

Most vineyards are planted on very dry rocky or limestone soils. Rain is scarce and sunshine over abundant. Consequently the grapes tend to acquire a high sugar content leading to wines that are strong in alcohol. As a result, much of the produce is made up of powerful and full-bodied reds that tend to lack finesse and sweet dessert whites. These drastic climatic conditions are more prevalent in the south and it is here that most Greek wine is made. However, the production rate in the north, which has a greater potential for good table wines, is increasing.

In the past the Greek wine industry has suffered from a lack of quality control. Fortunately this changed when Greece joined the European Union. Now twenty-six wine producing areas have been given appellation status and control is applied rigorously. Greek wine-making dates from roughly the seventh century B.C. Later, during her golden age, she was responsible for introducing the wine to a host of Mediterranean countries. Now at last there is a chance that she could recapture some of the fame of her glorious wine traditions of the past.

The region of Attica is very arid but much wine is produced, presumably due to the commercial advantage of Athens being within it. All types are made, using the Mandelaria grape for heavy, full-bodied reds and the Savatiano for whites. These are 'Retsina' wines, that is, wines that have been resinated by adding pine resin to the must during fermentation; this is said to improve the taste.

Peloponnisos is the southernmost region of the Greek mainland and is responsible for almost one third of all wine production in the country. The region has five wine appellations, most important of which are those of Patras and Nemea. All types are made: robust reds using Xinomavro, Mandelaria and Agiorgitiko grapes and rosés and light dry whites from the Moschophilero variety. This is also produced in another appellation area, Mantinia. In addition to the dry wines some very interesting sweet ones are made. The whites are made from Muscat at Patras and Rion, but much more unusual is the red, a dark, concentrated phenomenon with long ageing potential on the same lines as Recioto from the Veneto region in Italy. It is made from a grape variety called Mavrodaphne.

In the north, the most important region is Makedonia. Here the reds are not as heavy and more refreshing to drink. As part of the trend to modernise, change and expand, a Cabernet is made. Very little white seems to be made here. An exception is in Sithonia, one of the Khalkidiki peninsulas where some is made as well as the expected red.

The other northern regions, Thessalia and Ipiros are less important. The former produces red wine, the latter white.

 Opera **Les Troyens** - see page 81

The wines of the Greek Islands

As far as wine is concerned, the Greek Islands produce a very mixed picture, which is hardly surprising as there are so many of them! For simplicity they have been divided into five sectors.

(a) The Ionian Islands

The most important, Cephalonia and Zakinthos, specialise in white wines, particularly from the Robola grape. Also, both white and red dessert wines are made. Corfu and Levkas tend to produce reds but are less important.

(b) The Cyclades

The Island of Paros makes some interesting Mandelaria reds. However, the other main members of this group, Naxos, Milos, Andros and Santorini, also make white wines. Particularly interesting among these are those made using the Assyritiko grape.

(c) Crete

The Island has four designated areas for making red wine from Mandelaria, Liatiko and Kotsifali grapes. The products tend to be intense in colour, robust and high in alcohol. Some white wine is made using the indigenous Vilana grape.

(d) Rhodes

Both reds and whites are made here, Mandelaria and Muscat being the main varieties utilised. Muscat is also used to make a sweet wine.

(e) The Aegean Islands

The sweet wines of Samos are among the best made anywhere in Greece. The Muscat Blanc à Petits Grains is used to make three distinct types of dessert wines of interest.
Other islands in this area which make wine are Lemnos and Ikaria which specialise in red, and Thasos and Kos which make both red and white.

Principal grape varieties of the Greek Islands

REDS

Mandelaria, Mavrodaphne, Kotsifali, Liatiko, Limnio.

WHITES

Muscat Blanc à Petits Grains, Assyritiko, Robola, Athiri, Monemvasia, Vilana.

The wines of Cyprus

Principal wines of Cyprus

REDS

*Commandaria, Afames, d'Ahera,
Amathus, Buffavento, Cornaro Carignan,
Cornaro Grenache, Cypressa, Grenoir,
Heritage, Hermes, Kolossi, Laona,
Nectaria, Olympus, Orpheo Negro,
Othello, Semeli, Troodos.*

WHITES

*Arsinoe, Alkion, Amathus, Anthea,
Aphrodite, Arsinoe, Bellapais, Danae,
Daphne, Eldorado, Duc de Nicosie,
Kolossi, Laona, Muscat, Nefeli,
Olympus, Palomino, St. Hilarion,
Santa Marina, St. Pantelimon, Thisbe,
Troodos, White Lady, Cyprus Fortified
(Dry, Medium and Cream), EMVA
Matured (Dry, Medium and Cream).*

ROSÉS

*Amorosa, Bellapais Rose, Coeur de Lion,
Kokkinelli, Laona, Mirto, Rose Lady.*

Cyprus has been a land of wine since legendary times; it is said that Aphrodite, the goddess of love, was born there. Records of the island's viticulture date back to ancient Greece when a sweet wine called Nama was produced. Later, in the eleventh and twelfth centuries, there were many references to wine making during the occupation of Richard the Lion-heart and the knights Templar while they were involved in the Crusades.
In the fifteenth century Cypriot vines were used, together with those from Hungary and Sicily, to plant the Madeira vineyards of Portugal. The advent of Islam in the island led to a steady decline, and it was British rule, towards the end of the last century, that saw wine production restored to a prime place in the economy.
In the last twenty years, an enlightened and innovative approach has led to the opening of a large export market for Cyprus wine. At present over 10% of the cultivated land is taken up by vines, giving a production that makes the island the most successful wine country in the eastern Mediterranean.

Although Cyprus is dry and hot, the Troodos Mountains attract rain, making viticulture possible. The vineyards lie in green valleys along the hills and are at an altitude of around 900 metres.
The best lie on the southern slopes, between Limassol and Paphos. The island has so far escaped the phylloxera scourge so growers tend to use indigenous grape varieties. The most notable among these is the Mavro, which accounts for nearly 80% of the grapes; others are the Ophthalmo, the white Xynisteri and the Muscat of Alexandria. Recently however, a number of new types have been introduced with much success, the Cabernet Sauvignon, Cabernet Franc, Carignan, Grenache, Merlot, Riesling, Chardonnay, Sémillon and Jerez Palomino being cases in point.

The most important Cyprus wine is a liquorous sweet wine called Commandaria. This is made from dried grapes using both the red Mavro and the white Xynisteri. The ancient tradition was to dry the grapes in the sun giving a dark golden coloured product with a velvety texture and containing as much as fourfold the sugar content of Port. At times the concentration was so high that the wine needed diluting with water. A very tiny amount of this is made nowadays, and most modern Commandaria is a less concentrated pleasant dessert wine. A range of fortified wines made from the Palomino grape and generally known as dry, medium and sweet Cyprus Sherry are also produced.
In spite of the fame of Commandaria, the major production of the island is now red and white table wine. Cyprus is an important exporter of grape concentrate for the production in England of British wine. Also much basic wine is exported for blending, vermouth manufacture and other purposes. ❧

The wines of Turkey

Turkey is, in all probability, the viticultural birthplace of the world. Barrels over four thousand years old have been found in central Anatolia, where grapes have grown since man can remember.

In the more recent past, Turkish vineyards prospered when phylloxera devastated European vines in the last century. Understandably, the vacuum created was filled by wines from the Middle East and those of Turkey in particular were much appreciated in Europe. This state of affairs came to an end with the Greco-Turkish war of 1921-2 and the consequential departure of the Greek communities from Thrace. Wine production quickly dropped by about fifteen fold! In an attempt to halt the decline, Kemal Atatürk did all he could to encourage a resurgence in the industry but even now, with the fifth largest vine growing area in the world only 5% or less is made into wine. The bulk is used for table grapes, raisins and the production of grape juice.

Turkey can be divided into four basic wine-producing regions. Anatolia, in the south, traditionally makes the best, while Thrace, Marmara and the Aegean coast between them produce the most, around 60% of the country's total. The other two are the areas surrounding Ankara and the slopes bordering the Black Sea to the north. Much of the wine making in Turkey is under state ownership and all is subject to state control.

The wines are generally quite good but are low in acidity. All kinds, including sparkling are made. Due to the hot climate, reds tend to be alcoholic, while whites are inclined to oxidize. Both indigenous and French grape varieties are used. Local red grapes are Boğazkere, Cubuk, Dimrit, Horozkarasi, Kalecik, Kimklareli, Oküzgüzü and Papazkarasi. French varieties used are Carignan, Gamay, Grenache and Pinot Noir. White indigenous grapes include Emir and Narince, while the West European are Clairette, Muscat, Riesling and Sémillon. ❧

Principal wines of Turkey

REDS

Buzbağ, Dikmen, Marmara, Trakya, Villa Doluca, Yakut, Pembe Köpük.

WHITES

Izmir, Köroğlu, Trakya, Altin Kopuk, Inci Damlasi, Efsane, Sultaniye, Çankaya, Özel Beyaz, Muskat.

ROSÉ

Kavaklidere Rosato.

The wines of Malta

Principal wines and grape varieties of Malta

REDS

Gellewza, Cabernet Sauvignon, Merlot, Syrah, Grenache, Carignan.

WHITES

Ghirgentina, Gennarua, Chardonnay, Sauvignon Blanc, Chenin Blanc, Pinot Blanc, Pinot Gris, Muscat, Trebbiano.

ROSÉS

Gellewza.

Vine cultivation in Malta possibly began while the island was under Phoenician influence, but it was the Romans who turned this into a wine producing industry. The fall of the Roman Empire resulted in a series of setbacks but matters improved during the time Malta came under Spanish dominion through the kingdom of the two Sicilies. However it was not until a 280-year period between the sixteenth and eighteenth centuries, when the island came under the administration of the knights of the order of St. John of Jerusalem, that the production and drinking of wine became a popular activity. Nevertheless, at the turn of the last century, wine making was generally carried out on an amateur basis and mainly used for self consumption. Larger companies with modern technical know-how are now starting to put the island on the international map.

The Maltese archipelago consists of three islands, Malta itself, Gozo and tiny Comino. There are no mountains or rivers; only low hills. The weather is warm with no biting winds, frost or snow. Rainfall is low, particularly in the summer. However, hot summer days and nights are tempered by cool sea breezes making viticulture possible.

Malta has three main indigenous grape varieties. These are Gellewza, which is used to make medium bodied red wines and very good fruity rosés, Ghirgentina, which produces fresh dry white wines of good flavour and character and the white Gennarua.
However, in order to meet demand, French and Italian grapes are imported from Italy. More recently, modern irrigation methods and improved fermentation techniques have led to the planting of a number of French noble varieties, with promising results. Experiments with upgraded indigenous clones are also encouraging.

So far, the exporting of Maltese wines is in its infancy but attempts are being actively pursued to expand this in the near future. Many of Malta's wines are varietal, being sold under the name of the wine's dominant grape variety. 🎋

The wines of France

France has been making wine since ancient times. It appears that vine growing was initiated by the Phoenicians and Greeks 500 years before the birth of Christ. However, the great French vineyards alongside the rivers Gironde, Loire, Marne, Rhine and Rhône were planted during the Roman occupation, some five centuries later.

Although the range of her climates and soils is extremely diverse, yet always favourable, this is not the principal reason why France is the undisputed Queen of wine production. Not only does she have excellent wine growing conditions and hence vineyards, but probably even more important, she keeps them continuously under strict quality control. A league table of the best sites was started some 200 years ago. This was later extended as the result of the great phylloxera epidemic that devastated the vines in the second half of the nineteenth century. Nowadays, with the world interest in wine on the increase and the need for consumer protection, France has found it increasingly important not only to define and classify her vineyards, but also to control them as to the quality of their products.

The wines are divided into four essential categories. The most important is that of Appellation d'Origine Controlée (AOC). These are subject to strict controls relating not only to the grape growing region and the variety of grape used but also to the yields, the methods of production and the alcohol percentage. All the important French wines, including the 'Premiers Crus' of Bordeaux and Burgundy, fall into this category. The second division is the Vin Délimité de Qualité Supérieure (VDQS) category. It is subjected to the same controls as those listed above and is used for areas that make wines that are distinctive enough to warrant identification and protection. The third rank is the Vins de Pays. These also come from a specific region but are more humble. However they must have a minimum alcohol content of 10% by volume and are guaranteed not to be subject to blending. This grade was introduced in 1973 to set it apart from the fourth division, the simple Vins de Table or table wines, an E.U. category to which France must adhere and in which blending is permitted.

Excluding the brandy making regions of Cognac and Armagnac, all other wine production in France can be divided into eleven distinct areas. These are briefly described as follows:

(a) Bordeaux

The wines of Bordeaux include the great 'Premiers Crus' of the 1855 classification. The region, near the sea and possessing several rivers, boasts a moderate and stable climate. Forests on the ocean side reduce rainfall as well as protecting it from salt bearing winds. The soils are varied but the bedrock is rich in minerals giving old, well-established wines a big advantage over younger ones as well as causing the great diversion of product from vineyard to vineyard.

The majority of wines are red, which are also vastly superior to the whites, although the sweet Sauternes is a notable exception. The major red denominations are Pauillac, Pomerol, St. Estèphe, St. Julien, Margaux, Graves, St. Emilion, Haut Medoc, Bourg and Blaye. The number of grape varieties used is small, the main ones being Cabernet Sauvignon, Cabernet Franc and Merlot. White appellations include Graves, Sauternes, Barsac and Entre-deux-Mers. The varieties used are mainly Sauvignon Blanc and Sémillon Blanc. Other varieties used are Malbec and Petit Verdot for the reds and Muscadelle for the whites.

(b) Bourgogne

Although the province of Burgundy contains at least three of the very greatest vineyards in France, it remains a bewildering contradiction when it comes to classify the region using a quality yardstick. There are an infinite number of growers and most vineyards have many sectors belonging to different people. Consequently, much of what is sold is done so as the wine of a particular district, and is often a blend made from the products of the different growers there. On the other hand there are red wines that fetch prices even the most expensive in Bordeaux cannot match. Thus, a vast and confusing quality range is soon apparent.

The almost continental type climate, the hills that shelter the vineyards from the wind, the mainly limestone soil and the chosen grape varieties combine to give great wines.

However, given the relative northerly situation of the area and the relative difficulty of managing the Pinot Noir grape, the equation for success is harder to achieve than in Bordeaux and hence poor vintages are more common.

The grape varieties used are even fewer than in Bordeaux, just Pinot Noir (and Gamay for Beaujolais) for the reds and Chardonnay (with the occasional Pinot Blanc in some areas) for white. Although some extremely fine whites are made, it is mainly the red wine produced that has made Burgundy famous.

The main Burgundy area is the Côte d'Or, near Dijon. This can be divided into the Côte de Nuits, which almost exclusively produces red wine (including the very best), and the Côte de Beaune, where mainly red is made but some really superb white as well. A second area lies to the south much closer to Lyon. This includes the Chalonnais and the Mâconnais, both of which produce red and white wine. Still further south and very close to Lyon is Beaujolais country. Here red wine that is meant to be drunk young is produced. Finally, far to the north, near Auxerre and some 160 km from the Côte d'Or, is Chablis, which specialises in fine and long lasting dry white wines.

(c) Champagne

The region of Champagne is close to Rheims. Here, the world's finest sparkling wine is made. Three grape varieties are used, the red Pinot Noir and Pinot Meunier and the white Chardonnay, the red grapes being pressed very rapidly so as not to impart any colour to the product. There are three main areas of production. These are the Montagne de Rheims, the Vallée de la Marne and the Côte des Blancs. The first two use mainly the red varieties while the third tends to avoid them.

Such Champagnes, based wholly on Chardonnay are often sold as Blanc de Blancs and do possess a certain freshness, but it is the red grape blended Champagnes which have the extra fullness and roundness of flavour that make the wines so memorable.

(d) Loire

This encompasses the wines made along the Loire valley, an extremely widespread and scattered region that can be conveniently divided into four basic areas. These are, starting at the western end and proceeding eastwards, the Pays Nantais, Anjou-Saumur, Touraine and the Nivernais. The great majority of the wine produced is white although some red is made, mainly in the style of Beaujolais for early drinking. The wines produced in the central areas of Anjou-Saumur and Touraine tend to be sweet or sweetish and are usually superior to the drier wines produced at the eastern and western ends. Most whites are made from Chenin Blanc, Sauvignon Blanc or Muscadet while the reds usually contain Cabernet Franc or Gamay.

(e) Alsace

The vineyards of Alsace are planted along the river Ill, a tributary of the Rhine. The grape varieties used are similar to those in Germany, but whereas German wines have a tendency to sweetness those of Alsace are dry and have a much higher alcohol content. However, distinct from the rest of France, wines tend to be sold as varietal products, that is, under the name of the grape variety they contain (instead of the vineyard where they are produced). Apart from the normal table wines some sweet dessert wine is produced using the Muscat and Gewürztraminer grapes. Although not as sweet, these products tend to resemble the German Beerenauslese wines. As for red wine very little is made. It is light, tending towards rosé and is made from Pinot Noir. The finest whites are made from Riesling and Pinot Gris grapes as well as those already mentioned.

(f) The Côtes du Rhône

This consists of a 190 km extension of very old vineyards along the river Rhône. Such a long stretch can be divided conveniently into two basic halves, the Northern Rhône and the Southern Rhône. These differ not only in location but also in climate, soil and grape variety used.

The Northern vineyards have a predominantly granite soil. The summers and autumns tend to be hot and the humidity is high. The grape varieties used are almost exclusively Syrah for red wines and Viognier, Roussanne and Marsanne for white wines. The very best products come from Côte Rôtie (mainly red), Condrieu (white), and Hermitage (both red and white). Also some fine aperitif sparkling wines are made at Saint-Peray and Clairette de Die.

The soil of the Southern Rhône consists of sand, covered with an abundance of gravel that provides good heat retention. The summers have a tendency towards draught and the Mistral wind can be a problem. A large number of grape varieties are used, Châteauneuf-du-Pape having as many as up to thirteen! The most important of these are Grenache, Cinsault, Syrah, Clairette and Mourvèdre. These are the (only!) varieties used in making Gigondas, the second major wine in the region. Although white wines, sweet aperitif wines and rosé wines are also made, the vast majority of the production, as well as the most celebrated, are the reds.

(g) Provence, the Eastern Midi and Corsica

Provence is responding to the hot Mediterranean climate and the requirements dictated by the tourist industry by producing an ever-increasing quantity of rosé wine, to be suitably drunk chilled. In spite of this, some fine tannic reds are still made at Bandol while Cassis is notable for its dry full-bodied whites. Reds and rosés tend to be made from Grenache, Cinsaut, Carignan and Mourvèdre grapes while whites contain the Sauvignon Blanc, Clairette and Ugni Blanc varieties.
Much Corsican wine is mass-produced and used for blending purposes. Nevertheless, some fine, full bodied and strong reds and rosés are produced using the Sciacarello, Sangiovese, Grenache and Cinsault varieties. A few sweet wines of quality are also made, particularly using Muscat but also with Malvoisie and Vermentino grapes.

(h) The Jura and Savoie

The Jura makes some good dry and sparkling whites using Chardonnay and less interesting reds and rosés from Poulsard, Pinot Noir and Trousseau grapes. However, this small area, with its vineyards on remote limestone hills about 300 metres above sea level, is renowned for the production of two highly original and unusual wines. 'Vin Jaune', made from the Savagnin grape, is produced using a vinification process similar to that of Sherry. It has a characteristic taste and lasts for ages. It is produced by the appellation Château-Chalon and also at Arbois and l'Etoile. 'Vin de Paille', is made by drying the grapes on rocks, then fermenting very slowly to produce a syrupy, liquorous wine which is again extremely long-lasting.

Savoie produces dry lively white wines with sparkling characteristics. The grape varieties used are the Roussette, Jacquère, Molette and Chasselas. Also, some rather plain reds are made from Gamay, Pinot Noir and Mondeuse, the latter giving the better and less expensive products.

(i) Languedoc and Roussillon; The Midi

This region is the mass production centre of French wine. Although real progress is being made, many producers still go for quantity rather than quality. The Carignan and Clairette grapes, both heavy croppers, are mainly responsible for the lack of interest in the products. Recently, the introduction of new varieties, the Syrah, Grenache, Mourvèdre and Cabernet Sauvignon has led to the production of not merely better but even superb quality.

The region does produce some interesting sweet wines, both white and red. The reds, fairly similar to port, are made using Grenache, Malvoisie, Muscat d'Alexandrie and Maccabéu grapes. Muscat is used to produce very good whites, equally at home as an aperitif or with dessert.

The Midi is the biggest wine-growing region in France and has a history of fine wine making dating from Roman times. Following the great phylloxera outbreak of one hundred years ago, the region developed erroneous ideas concerning the production of wine. Now, at last, as for Languedoc and Roussillon, much progress is being made, auguring a very exciting prospect for the future!

(j) The Southwest

This region, due south-east of Bordeaux, tends to produce full bodied, vigorous wines possibly lacking some finesse. This can certainly be said of the reds produced at the Appellations of Cahors and Madiran. On the other hand the Côtes du Frontonnais makes a fruity product intended for early drinking. Other reds are made at the Côtes du Buzet while Gaillac produces all kinds of wines by using a wide range of grape varieties. One appellation does specialise in white: Jurançon makes both dry full flavoured table wines and a small amount of very good sweet syrupy dessert wine. Generally, Bordeaux grape varieties are used.
However, in the production of reds, the Tannat (at Madiran) and Negrette (Côtes du Frontonnais) are also utilised.

(k) Bergerac

The Dordogne valley, on the back doorstep of Bordeaux, boasts a considerable number of appellations for its small size. Monbazillac and Saussignac produce rich golden coloured sweet wines using Bordeaux white grape varieties. On the other hand the appellations of Pécharmant and Bergerac make red wines which are generally full bodied and well balanced. Table whites are also made at Bergerac as well as at Montravel and Rosette.

In order to encourage her more humble wines to improve, France produced a list of seventy-five Vins de Pays between 1973 and 1976. This consisted of the more identifiable Appellation simple or table wines. She also created a new authority, the Office National Interprofessionnel des Vins de Table, to take care of them. The list is a challenge to growers who wish to build on their local or national traditions. Just as many V.D.Q.S wines have advanced to the AOC category, it is probable that the best Vins de Pays will likewise advance to the V.D.Q.S. rank and given further time, perhaps even higher.

The Vins de Pays Controls include a maximum crop yield and minimum alcohol level. They also lay down appropriate limits for acidity and other analysable components. The wines have to be made from locally recommendable grape varieties or from noble national varieties. Finally, the wines have to be approved by an appointed tasting panel.

By 1985 the list had risen to 140 wines, and has grown since. It comprised, in three separate categories, of ninety-two district, commune or local, forty-five departmental and three regional wines. A large number hail from the South of France, between the Southern Rhône and the Pyrénées. This is the Midi where the greatest potential for improvement is to be found. Clearly there is much promise for greater things to come, a promise that is already beginning to materialise! ✺

The wines of Alsace

The early history of Alsace is German. Taken over by France in the seventeenth century, it was reclaimed by Germany in 1871 but went back to France after the First World War, although it was briefly retaken by Germany between 1940 and 1944.

Alsace's vineyards are situated in a narrow strip of land between one and three kilometres wide. They run between the river Ill (a tributary of the Rhine), and the Vosges mountains to the east and west respectively. The strip is approximately 120 km. in length, starting at Marlenheim, near Strasbourg in the north and ending at Thann, close to Mulhouse in the south. The vines are planted on hillside sites with either a south or south-east-facing location.

The grape varieties used are similar to those grown in Germany. Also, as in Germany, 'chaptalization', the addition of sugar to the must, is widely used. However, this is to increase the strength of the product rather than to sweeten it. Indeed, the wines of Alsace are dry and much more powerful than their German counterparts.

The region is possibly the driest in France, being sheltered from wet west winds by the Vosges Mountains. The winters are very cold, the springs mild and the summers warm and dry, although there is always a risk of hail in isolated spots. The territory has about twenty major soil formations. Clay, gneiss, granite, limestone, marl, sandstone, schist and volcanic soil are all to be found in different places. The topsoil at higher altitudes tends to be less deep than that lower down.

Alsace is divided into two departments, the Haut Rhin to the south and the Bas Rhin at the northern end. The former, being better protected by the mountains, which are higher there, generally gives wine of a higher quality, with more body and power, than the latter. The heart of the Alsace vineyards, which contains 80% of the region's best sites, lies here, on a 40 km-stretch, running from St. Hippolyte, through Colmar, the capital of the industry, to Guebwiller, near the far south.

As in Germany, the vast majority of the wines produced are white and most are named after the grape variety they contain. An exception is Clevner, a blended wine made from Pinot Blanc and Edelzwicker. Also, Pinot noir is used to produce light refreshing reds and rosés. The best of these come from Marlenheim in the Bas Rhin and St. Hippolyte in the Haut Rhin.

The region was awarded the A.C. status 'Vin d'Alsace' in 1962 and later, 'Crémant d'Alsace' for sparkling wines in 1976. Grands Crus for the best sites, only if planted with any of four so designated 'noble' varieties, (Gewürztraminer, Muscat, Pinot Gris and Riesling), were introduced in 1983. This appellation is still under modification as some localities only suit some of these noble vines and only these would obtain the status at that vineyard. Examples, all in the Haut Rhin, are Rangen and Kitterlé for Gewürztraminer, Pinot Gris and Riesling, Kanzlerberg for Pinot Gris and Gewürztraminer, Goldert for Gewürztraminer and Muscat, Rosacker for Riesling and Gewürztraminer and Geisberg for Riesling only.
A fine Bas Rhin site is Kirchberg de Barr, which specialises in three of these varieties excepting Muscat.

However, the greatest sites in Alsace are not the grands crus, but small, enclosed vineyards called 'Clos'. These also specialise in one or more of the four noble grape varieties, producing superlative wines. Examples are the Clos Sainte Hune situated near Hunawihr, for Riesling, the Clos Saint Urbain at Thann, for Pinot Gris, the Clos Gaensbroennel in the vicinity of Barr, for Gewürztraminer and the Clos Rebgarten near Andlau for Muscat. It is interesting and remarkable that Muscat wines made in Alsace are dry and not sweet as might be expected!

A further designation and sub-designation, again for the noble grapes, correspond to the German Auslese and Beerenauslese appellations. These are the 'Vendage Tardive' and the 'Vendage Tardive Sélections de Grains Nobles' classifications, referring to rich and powerful products with very long ageing potential.
The former are dry while the latter are sweet dessert wines, which can be, in the hands of the best producers, comparable in quality to the finest Sauternes that Bordeaux can make. ❧

Principal wines and grape of Alsace

REDS
• *A.A.C. Vin d'Alsace: Pinot Noir.*

WHITES
• *A.C. wines: A.A.C. Vins d'Alsace: Riesling, Riesling Vendage Tardive, Riesling Sélection de Grains Nobles, Gewürztraminer, Gewürztraminer Vendage Tardive, Gewürztraminer Sélection de Grains Nobles, Pinot Gris, Pinot Gris Vendage Tardive, Pinot Gris Sélection de Grains Nobles, Muscat, Muscat Vendage Tardive, Muscat Sélection de Grains Nobles, Pinot Blanc, Edelzwicker, Klevner, Clevner, Sylvaner, Chasselas, Auxerrois, Kipperlé.*
• *A.A.C. Crémant d'Alsace.*

ROSÉS
• *A.A.C. Vin d'Alsace: Pinot Noir.*

The wines of Bordeaux

Principal wines of Bordeaux

REDS

A.C. wines: Bordeaux (also Clairet, Supérieur, Supérieur Clairet), Premières Côtes de Bordeaux, St. Estèphe, Médoc, Haut Médoc, Listrac Médoc, Pauillac, St. Julien, Moulis, Margaux, Blaye, Premières Côtes de Blaye, Côtes de Bourg, Lalande-de-Pomerol, Pomerol, Côtes de Castillon, Côtes de Francs, St. Émilion, Lussac-St. Émilion, Montagne-St. Émilion, Puisseguin-St. Émilion, St. George-St. Émilion, Fronsac, Canon-Fronsac, Graves (also Supérieur), Pessac-Léognan, Ste. Foy.

WHITES

A.C. wines: Bordeaux (also Blanc, Sec, Supérieur), Crémant de Bordeaux, Premières Côtes de Bordeaux, Blaye, Côtes de Blaye, Graves (also Supérieur), Entre-Deux-Mers, Entre-Deux-Mers-Haut-Benauge, Bordeaux-Haut-Benauge, Pessac-Léognan, Ste. Croix-du-Mont, Cadillac, Barsac, Loupiac, Sauternes, Cérons.

ROSÉS

A.C. wines: Bordeaux Rosé (also Supérieur).

Bordeaux is the largest district for the production of fine wine in the world. It is also the most renowned.

The region can be divided roughly into three parts. The areas of the Médoc and St. Émilion lie respectively to the north and north east of the city of Bordeaux. These are noted for their superb red wines based on the Cabernet Sauvignon, Cabernet Franc and Merlot grapes. In the Médoc the main variety is the Cabernet Sauvignon whereas the Merlot is the major vine in St. Émilion.

The second area is known as the Entre-Deux-Mers and lies to the south east of the city. It produces mainly good but unexciting dry white wine. However, recently, increasing quantities of nice reds are being made. Nevertheless, this remains the least interesting part of the region.

The third section is situated south of Bordeaux. This is the Graves and its surroundings. Again much dry white is produced. However the area can boast not only one top class red but also the greatest sweet white wine in the world, the Sauternes. This, based on the Sémillon grape (with the addition of some Sauvignon Blanc), is the fortuitous result of using a mould to the advantage of mankind. Given the right conditions, the 'Botrytis Cinerea' will cause what is known as the 'noble rot', that is, it engineers the escape of water from the grape leaving it more concentrated in sugar and flavour than before. Amazingly the product bears no taste of rot or mould but is smooth, rather oil-like, richly flavoured and intensely perfumed.

Indeed, the first Bordeaux wines to be singled out for quality came from the Graves area. This was long before the early eighteenth century when the Médoc was opened. By then Château Haut Brion had already been famous for a hundred years. The Bishop of Bordeaux, who was to become Pope Clement V, is reported to have owned top class wine producing land in this area.

By the middle of the nineteenth century the Médoc had become the prime area for fine red wine in France. In 1855 the wine producing Châteaux where assigned as first, second, third, fourth and fifth growths and a number of lesser designations. This sort of league table of quality was based on the prices the wines had fetched over the previous hundred years or so. Six first growth tags were handed out. These went to Château Lafite, Château Latour, Château Mouton and Châteaux Margaux, all in the Médoc, Château Haut Brion in the Graves and Château d'Yquem, the top Sauternes.

Nowadays, this old classification does provide a rough guide, but naturally, there are many reasons (changes of proprietor, vineyard alterations) why this order is no longer fully accurate. Indeed a first growth would regularly fetch at least two times the price of a second growth without necessarily being much better. More recently, in 1954, a classification was applied to the St. Émilion area of fine red wine. Here, the Châteaux were divided into different grades of Grands Crus. Twelve Premiers Gran Crus were assigned, the leading two being Château Cheval Blanc and Château Ausone.

Not far away, the small area of Pomerol lacks an official classification. Yet, its outstanding wines, Château Petrus and Château Le Pin, are more expensive than any other in the whole Bordeaux region. Incidentally, Pomerol, like St. Émilion, uses Merlot as its basic grape.

The wines of the regions south of Bordeaux

R E D S

A.C. wines: Bergerac, Côtes de Bergerac, Pécharmant, Côtes de Duras, Côtes du Marmandais, Marcillac, Cahors, Buzet, Gaillac, Côtes du Frontonnais, Madiran, Bearn, Irouléguy.

W H I T E S

A.C. wines: Bergerac Sec, Montravel, Côtes de Montravel, Haut Montravel, Monbazillac, Saussignac, Côtes de Duras, Côtes du Marmandais, Gaillac (also Doux, Mousseux), Pacherenc du Vic-Bilh, Jurançon (also Sec).

R O S É S

A.C. wines: Bergerac Rosé, Côtes du Marmandais, Marcillac, Gaillac, Côtes du Frontonnais Rosé, Bearn, Irouléguy.

Geographically, the reason why the Bordeaux region is able to produce such good wine is not difficult to understand.
Being close to the sea and threaded with rivers, its climate is both moderate and stable. Forests on the ocean side reduce rainfall and also shield it from strong salt winds. Paradoxically, a rather poor and deep topsoil is another advantage. The roots, particularly in older vines, (which are known to produce the better wines), will have burrowed deeply and widely in order to search out nourishment, which they eventually find in bedrock which is well furnished with minerals. All this leads to a greater constancy of environment and a protection against sudden and violent climatic changes. The physical make-up of the soil, which consists of deep gravel beds in much of the Médoc area, results in good drainage and is a further positive factor.

However the above can only be a partial explanation.
Two vineyards, side by side, may appear to have identical conditions and yet produce very different wines. Clearly, the quality factors that cause so much variance over such small distances in this region are extremely complex and not fully understood, even today.

Apart from the grape varieties already mentioned, other vines used in the Bordeaux region are the Malbec for reds and the Muscadelle for whites. Altogether, red wines outnumber whites by about three to one. Also the dry white wine produced, other than a small amount, isn't particularly fine. Certainly, the region's sweet white products are far superior. Nevertheless, Sauternes apart, it is due to the reds that Bordeaux is justifiably famous. These, at their best, display a degree of finesse, a complexity of aroma and flavour and a capacity for ageing unsurpassed anywhere in the world. ❧

The wines of Bourgogne

Principal wines of Bourgogne

REDS

A.C. wines: Bourgogne, Côte de Nuits-Villages, Bourgogne Hautes-Côtes de Nuits, Marsannay, Fixin*, Gevrey-Chambertin*, Clos de Bèze Gr.Cru, Chambertin (also Mazis, Chapelle, Charmes, Griottes, Latricières, Mazoyères, Ruchottes) Gr.Crus, Morey-St. Denis*, Clos St. Denis Gr.Cru, Clos de la Roche Gr. Cru, Clos de Tart Gr.Cru, Clos de Lambrays Gr.Cru, Chambolle-Musigny*, Musigny Gr.Cru, Bonnes Mares Gr.Cru, Vougeot*, Clos de Vougeot Gr.Cru, Vosne-Romanée*, Romanée-Conti Gr. Cru, La Romanée Gr.Cru, Romanée-St. Vivant Gr. Cru, Richebourg Gr.Cru, La Tâche Gr. Cru, Echézeaux Gr. Cru, Les Grands Echézeaux Gr.Cru, La Grande Rue Gr.Cru, Nuits-St. Georges*, Ladoix, Pernard-Vergelesses*, Aloxe-Corton*, Corton Gr.Cru, Savigny-lès-Beaune*, Chorey-lès-Beaune (also Villages), Beaune*, Côte de Beaune (also Villages), Bourgogne Hautes-Côtes de Beaune, Pommard*, Volnay*, Monthélie*, Auxey-Duresses*, St. Romain, Blagny Pr.Cru, Chassagne Montrachet*, St. Aubin*, Santenay*, Maranges*, Mâcon (also Supérieur, village names), Rully*, Mercurey*, Givry*, Beaujolais (also Primeur, Supérieur, Villages, village names as above).

* Signifies that an additional A.C. exists for Premier Cru wines.

The wine-producing region of Burgundy is located on the eastern side of France. It includes the isolated area of Chablis, near the town of Auxerre and then starts at Dijon, running southwards to Lyon. It lies mainly on the western side of the N 74 highway on the northern Dijon end and on the western banks of the river Saône on the southern Lyon side.

Wine has been made in Burgundy since ancient times. Its production is probably of Celtic origin, dating almost certainly from before the birth of Christ. It survived, as successively the region passed under Roman, Barbarian and Frankish rule. During and after the reign of Charlemagne, nobles and monks, initially of the Benedictine and then Cistercian orders, played a leading role in wine making. Later, in 1305, when pope Clement V transferred his see to Avignon, Burgundy attained its particular fame and has never looked back. Even when, centuries later, in the 1870's, phylloxera destroyed all the vineyards, on replanting with resistant American rootstock, only the very best locations were re-used. Thus a calamity was turned into an asset by improving the quality of the product.

A quality classification was standardised in 1861. This was modified in the 1930's to more or less what it is today. However, a number of vineyards have since been able to enhance their status by improving their wines.

The soil consists of a limestone base with differences on the surface. The best sites are between 250 - 300 metres above sea level and on the south-eastern slopes, where they enjoy the greatest sun exposure. The hills provide some protection from wet west winds. The climate is the most uncertain factor. Cold winters are followed by spring frosts and a fair amount of hail. Heavy rainfall is possible in the late spring and autumn. The temperamental Pinot Noir especially resents this, making Burgundy reds very variable from harvest to harvest. The white Chardonnay is less fussy and gives more consistent results.

The region uses very few grape varieties. Apart from the two main ones mentioned, the red Gamay is utilised, particularly in making Beaujolais. Also, to a very limited extent, the white Bourgogne Aligoté is used in a few places.

The vineyards of Burgundy tend to be divided into five or six areas. These are, from north to south, Chablis, the Côte d'Or, which is subdivided into the Côte de Nuits and the Côte de Beaune, the Châlonnais (also known as the Région de Mercurey), the Mâconnais and Beaujolais. One should note that the central areas are most typical of what is generally taken to represent Burgundy wine. Chablis is rather distinct, while Beaujolais is completely different with no more than a geographical connection to the others.

(a) Chablis

This consists of a small enclave around the little homonymous town in east central France. Although nearer Champagne than the rest of Burgundy, it is with the latter that it has the greatest affinity.

The vines grow on soil consisting of equal parts of limestone and clay. The climate is cooler than that of the rest of Burgundy so it is not surprising that only white wine is made. The single Chardonnay grape variety is used.

The wines are divided into four quality grades. First come the Grands Crus. There are seven of these and they are found within 2 km north east of the town of Chablis. They are Les Clos, Vaudésir, Blanchots, Bougros, Grenouilles, Les Preuses and Valmur. An eighth, Moutonne, is generally considered as such but lacks the official status. Second are the Premiers Crus. There are about forty of these, situated within a 4 km radius of the town. Although these can be slightly weaker in alcohol and are generally less intense in flavour and perfume than the grands crus, the best ones are comparable and provide excellent value. The third group are simply called Chablis.

They are found further from the town, surrounding the Premiers Crus area. The last and lowest group are called the Petit Chablis. They are grown, in dwindling quantities, on inferior soils furthest from the town.

The quality of Chablis tends to vary from year to year depending on the uncertain weather. The location and soil is also an important factor, as is the grower. At its best it is a superlative wine, certainly the best for shellfish. It is dry and crisp with an intense and complex mixture of flavours on maturation.
It is greenish in colour, fresh yet mellowing with age, having a huge lasting potential for a dry white wine. A grand cru will last for fifteen years and a premier cru for ten.

Improved wine making techniques have raised the general quality. Taking advantage of this, vineyards that had been abandoned since the phylloxera devastation have now been replanted allowing the industry to better meet the ever-increasing demand.

A number of wines are made south of Auxerre, just outside the Chablis area. These are Crémant de Bourgogne and Bourgogne Blanc as well as full bodied and softer reds and some rosé wines. For the whites Bourgogne Aligoté and Sauvignon de Saint-Bris as well as Chardonnay are used while the reds are made from Pinot Noir and César grapes.

(b)   The Côte d'Or
This consists of a narrow strip of land 50 km. long, overlooking the Saône river valley. The area runs in a south-westerly direction, from the town of Dijon to a few kilometres past the small town of Chagny. The vineyards are on hills on the western side of the valley. They face south-east where they obtain maximum sun exposure.

The area is generally divided into two sections. The northern 20 km. stretch is known as the Côte de Nuits while the 30 km. southern part is called the Côte de Beaune. Due to the prime importance of the whole area each section is treated separately.

(b1) The Côte de Nuits
This northern section of the Côte d'Or produces almost exclusively red wine. There are nine important villages acting as communes to the vineyards.
These are, from north to south, Fixin, Gevrey Chambertin, Morey St. Denis, Chambolle-Musigny, Vougeot, Vosne-Romanée, Flagey, Nuits-St. Georges and Prémeaux-Prissey although wines from the last named are sold as Nuits-St. Georges products.

Between them, these villages produce the finest reds in all Burgundy, a truth reflected in the 23 grands crus and countless premiers crus (the best of which are hardly below grand cru standard) to be found here. It is particularly interesting that nearly all the grands crus come from just four communes. Gevrey Chambertin alone boasts no less than eight.
These pride themselves in producing big, robust wines possessing great depth, which mature and mellow with age to give highly complex flavours and perfumes. The most famous crus are Chambertin and Clos de Bèze. In Morey St. Denis the five grand cru wines are of a similar nature, particularly those from Clos de la Roche and Clos St. Denis. On the other hand the best wines of Chambolle-Musigny are not so grand but gain in delicacy and elegance. The two grands crus here are Musigny and Les Bonnes-Mares.

Although Vosne-Romanée has only five grands crus to Gevrey Chambertin's eight, its wines are, with good reason, the most expensive in the world. La Romanée Conti appears to possess all the attributes sought in a perfect wine. Power, spiciness, depth, elegance, finesse, perfume and long lasting capacity are all present. The other grands crus are not far behind; La Tâche, Richebourgs and Romanée-St. Vivant produce marvellous wines that are only minimally of lower quality, if at all.

Unfortunately one other commune, Brochon, does not figure among Burgundy`s elite. The grape used is not Pinot Noir but the Gamay and quantity rather than quality has been sought, with the result that no appellation now exists.

Principal wines of Bourgogne

WHITES
A.C. wines: Bourgogne, Chablis*, Chablis Gr.Cru, Petit Chablis, Marsannay, Musigny Blanc, Côte de Nuits-Villages, Bourgogne Hautes-Côtes de Nuits, Nuits-St. Georges*, Ladoix, Pernard-Vergelesses*, Corton Charlemagne Gr.Cru, Savigny-lès-Beaune*, Beaune*, Bourgogne Hautes-Côtes de Beaune, Monthélie*, Auxey-Duresses*, St. Romain, Mersault*, Mersault-Blagny Pr.Cru, Mersault-Santenots, Mersault Côte de Beaune, Puligny-Montrachet*, Puligny-Montrachet Côte de Baune, Le Montrachet Gr.Cru, Bâtard-Montrachet Gr.Cru, Bienvenues-Bâtard-Montrachet Gr.Cru, Chevalier-Montrachet Gr.Cru, Criots-Bâtard-Montrachet Gr.Cru, Chassagne Montrachet*, St. Aubin*, Montagny*, Mâcon (also Supérieur, Villages, village names), Rully*, Mercurey*, Givry*, Pouilly-Fuissé, St. Véran, Crémant de Bourgogne.

ROSÉS
A.C. wines: Marsannay Rosé, Beaune, Monthélie.

* Signifies that an additional A.C. exists for Premier Cru wines.

(b2) The Côte de Beaune

The southern part of the Côte d'Or consists of nineteen town or village communes. These are, from north to south, Ladoix Serrigny, Pernand-Vergelesses, Aloxe-Corton, Savigny-les-Beaune, Chorey-les-Beaune, Beaune, Pommard, Volnay, Monthelie, Auxey-Duresses, Saint-Romain, Meursault, Puligny Montrachet, Chassagne Montrachet, Saint-Aubin, Santenay, Cheilly, Dézize and Sampigny.

Typically most of the wine made is red, but it lacks the power, depth and longevity of the Côte de Nuits products. Not surprisingly, therefore, only one grand cru exists. This is Corton from the Aloxe-Corton commune. However a good number of premier cru wines that are excellent in their own right can be found. Their main attributes are delicacy and elegance.

Unexpectedly it is the white wines that are really famous here. The communes of Chassagne Montrachet, Puligny Montrachet, Meursault and Aloxe-Corton produce the finest in the world, the five Montrachet grands crus being particularly renowned. These are le Montrachet, Chevalier-Montrachet, Bâtard-Montrachet, Bienvenues-Bâtard-Montrachet and Criots-Bâtard-Montrachet. A sixth grand cru, found at Aloxe-Corton is known as Corton-Charlemagne. Meursault has no grands crus but its premier cru whites are of an exceedingly high quality as are those of the other three communes.

The Montrachet grands crus possess a golden colour and an intense fruity flavour. They are lively yet mellow and give rise to a lingering perfume. Finally, they have very good ageing qualities. The greatest wine is le Montrachet. The Corton-Charlemagne, for example, although similar in colour, vigour and body, possibly lacks some mellowness in comparison. Also, its taste and perfume is more akin to nuts and almonds than flowers and fruit. It has, as expected, excellent staying potential.

(c) The Côte Chalonnaise

This district lies just south of the Côte de Beaune. It is also known as the Région de Mercurey after the largest appellation in the area. The Châlonnais has five main wine making communes. Between them they make some very fine whites and pleasant reds. The wines tend to be lighter than those of Beaune but do not lack finesse. The villages are, from north to south, Bouzeron, Rully, Mercurey, Givry and Montagny.

Mercurey and Givry produce mainly red Pinot Noirs, not unlike a good villages Côte de Beaune. The Mercurey wines are tougher and age well while those of Givry are softer and more approachable when young. Rully produces equal quantities of red and white. The latter are particularly good, especially the Crémant de Bourgogne which, together with that made at Bouzeron, can be really superb in good years. An interesting point is that these two fine wines have a different parentage. The Rully Crémants are made from the traditional Chardonnay and some Pinot Blanc while those at Bouzeron are based on the Bourgogne Aligoté grape. Montagny produces almost exclusively white wine similar to that made in the Mâconnais area further to the south.

(d) The Côte Maconnaise

Although Macon does produce red wine, most is made using the Gamay grape and is not on a par with those made in the other areas of the region. The whites, which tend to be more full-bodied than those of the Chalonnaise while lacking their refinement, are more interesting. The best wines come from the southern part of the area around the village of Pouilly Fuissé. These are lighter in style than the others but are much more elegant.

Most of the wines in the Mâconnais are produced by co-operatives. They are bottled bearing the name 'Mâcon', followed by either 'Villages' or the name of the village itself. The quality is steadily improving with a few producers already making very fine wines which are still available at a reasonable price.

(e) Beaujolais

The largest single area in Burgundy runs on the western side of the A6 and N6 roads and the river Saône, from just south of the Côte Maconnaise, right down to the city of Lyon.

The northern part of Beaujolais produces the best wines on soil that is a mixture of schist and granite. The vineyards of the inferior southern section are planted on lighter ground containing sand as well as limestone and clay.

The great majority of Beaujolais is red and made from Gamay grapes. A small amount of white is produced using the Chardonnay and Bourgogne Aligoté varieties. A minute quantity of rosé is also made.

The common product is a rather rustic thirst quashing wine. It is meant to be drunk young, but is hardly at its best when 'nouveau'. A little ageing, even in bottle, will improve its character.
Indeed, it is a great pity that the wine has been made famous because of the Beaujolais Nouveau cult. Apart from the basic type there are three higher grades of wine. The first is Beaujolais Supérieur, slightly stronger in alcohol than the ordinary, but with the same ageing limit of about a year. Still higher is Beaujolais Villages, a more interesting wine with a longer life span. The top grade is the cru wine. There are ten of these, all to be found in the northern sector of the area. Happily they express what real Beaujolais really means and manifest a character lacking in the other wines. They will last from two to five years, depending on the cru. A good vintage top cru can even last up to ten years by which time it will start to attain some typical Burgundy characteristics.
The crus, in roughly decreasing order of longevity, are Moulin-à-Vent, Morgon, Côte de Brouilly, Juliénas, Chénas, Fleurie, Brouilly, Regnié, Saint-Amour and Chiroubles. Of these, Moulin-à-Vent is generally considered the best, although Morgon equals it in ageing potential.

Chablis apart, the wines of Burgundy are labelled under a host of cru, village and district names, making it a virtual impossibility to list them all. Therefore, wines produced in very small quantities have been omitted from the lists, which runs approximately from north to south. 🐝

The wines of Champagne

Principal wines of Champagne

REDS
   A.C. wine: Coteaux Champegnois.

WHITES
   A.C. wines: Champagne,
   Coteaux Champegnois.

ROSÉS
   A.C. wines: Champagne, Rosé de Riceys.

The Champagne district lies about 150 kilometres east of Paris, due south of the city of Reims. Three main areas are incorporated. The most northern is the Montaigne de Reims, which contains, among others, the vines around Chigny-les-Roses, Ludes and Mailly. Roughly in the middle lies the Vallée de la Marne with Ay on one side of the river and the principal town of the region, Épernay, on the other. To the south is the Côte des Blancs with the areas around the towns of Cramant, Avize, Le Mesnil-sur-Oger and Vertus.

The average daily temperature of 10° C., the sheltering from the north winds, the reflecting chalk soil and the moisture regulating forests nearby, are the factors that combine to produce the ideal conditions for top quality in the making of Champagne.

It is believed that vines have been cultivated in the district since ancient times. During the Roman Empire the Emperor Domitian ordered the vineyards to be dug up, possibly because he feared competition with wines produced in Italy, but also to enforce the planting of more cereals, in short supply at the time.
However, they were replaced 200 years later, when Rome reversed its vineyard policy in its provinces. Much later, in the Middle Ages, the region was already well known. Its fame had spread to the royal court and its wines were used at the coronation of French Kings in Reims.

It was in the middle of the seventeenth century that Dom Perignon, cellar keeper to the Abbey of Hautvillers, discovered the secret of fermentation control, thus preserving limpidity whilst keeping the sparkle in the wines. He also produced the 'Cuvées', the blending of wines of different growths, which gave a richer bouquet. Then, in the early nineteenth century, Madame Clicquot devised the method of eliminating the sediment formed in the bottle due to secondary fermentation without losing the bubbles in the wine. These and other discoveries have now been modernised and perfected to the standards that are adhered to and appreciated today. There have been many imitations of champagne, but at its best it remains unchallenged as the toast of kings.

Champagne is produced in a number of styles. Most is made from Pinot Noir and Chardonnay grapes with some Pinot Meunier added. Blanc de Blancs, from the Côte des Blancs, is a fresher, lighter wine, made entirely with the white grape, while Blanc de Noirs, a rounder, more mellow variety, contains only red grapes. Lastly, Pink champagne is made, usually by adding a small quantity of red wine to the blend. Clearly, in the use of Pinot Noir, a rapid maceration process is of prime importance, since it must be ensured that no colour is imparted to the product.

Apart from Champagne, the region does produce a small quantity of still wine. Two appellations exist. They are the Coteaux Champenois and the Rosé des Riceys. The former is found mainly as red, the white being extremely rare, while the latter is an interesting, dark pink, rosé wine. All three tend to be used for local consumption.

The wines of The Loire Valley

Principal wines of The Loire Valley

REDS
- *A.C. wines: Anjou (also Gamay, Villages), Saumur (also Champigny), Cabernet de Saumur, Touraine (also Amboise, Mesland), Bourgueil, St. Nicolas-de-Bourgueil, Chinon, Sancerre, Reuilly, Menetou-Salon, Coteaux du Giennois.*
- *V.D.Q.S. wines: Haut-Poitou, Châteaumeillant, St. Pourçain.*

WHITES
- *A.C. wines: Muscadet (also des Coteaux de la Loire, Côtes de Grandlieu, Sèvre-et-Maine, sur lie), Anjou (also Coteaux de la Loire, Mousseux, Pétillant), Bonnezeaux Gr.Cru, Quarts-de-Chaume, Coteaux du Layon, Savennières (also Roche-aux-Moines Gr.Cru, Coulée-de-Serrant Gr.Cru), Saumur (also Mousseux, Pétillant), Coteaux de Saumur, Coteaux de l'Aubance, Touraine (also Azay-le-Rideau, Amboise, Mesland, Mousseux, Pétillant), Vouvray (also Mousseux, Pétillant), Montlouis (also Moelleux, Pétillant), Jasnières, Cheverny, Cour-Cheverny, Sancerre, Pouilly-Fumé, Pouilly-sur-Loire, Quincy, Reuilly, Menetou-Salon, Coteaux du Giennois, Crémant de Loire.*
- *V.D.Q.S. wines: Haut-Poitou, St. Pourçain.*

ROSÉS
- *A.C. wines: Anjou, Cabernet Rosé d'Anjou, Saumur (also Mousseux, Pétillant), Touraine (also Azay-le Rideau, Mousseux, Pétillant), Bourgueil, St. Bicolas-de-Bourueil, Chinon, Sancerre, Reuilly, Menetou-Salon, Crémant de Loire.*
- *V.D.Q.S. wines: Haut-Poitou, Châteaumeillant, St. Pourçain.*

On referring to the wines of the Loire Valley, it must be remembered that what is intended are wines made from all the vineyards that surround the river. The area involved is widespread, having many different climates as well as soils and also a considerable diversity in wine making traditions. Fortunately, there are some reasonably common factors as well. The majority of the wine produced is white and also only about four or five main grape varieties are used.

Nevertheless, when trying to document the wines of the Loire, it is convenient to break up such a large mass of land into four distinct regions. These are the Pays Nantais, the Anjou-Saumur, Touraine and the Nivernais. There is much in common within each region, both geographically and in the grape varieties used and wines produced.

(a) Le Pays Nantais

This is the most westerly region and lies in Brittany. It can be further divided into four basic areas. The Gros Plant du Pays Nantais is the biggest of these but probably the least interesting. The other areas are the Coteaux de La Loire, the Sèvre-et-Maine and the Coteaux d'Ancenis.

Most of the wines are made from the Muscadet grape and are white. They are very dry but soft, being low in acidity and go well with fish and particularly seafood. Some red wine is made around Ancenis using Gamay grapes. All wines made here are drunk young and do not keep. They are charming and inexpensive.

(b) Anjou-Saumur

This region can be described as being on the mid-western end of the Loire basin. Although smaller than the Nantais it is more complex and possesses seven distinct appellations. Therefore, the wines, as one would expect, are of higher quality and more interesting.

The dominating grape varieties are Chenin Blanc followed by Chardonnay and therefore most wines are white.

However, different soils, schist and clay in Anjou and chalk in Saumur, make these far more varied than one would otherwise expect. The best wines are delicious sweet dessert wines while sweetish table wines, not too unlike those in Germany, are also very good. This applies particularly to the appellations Quarts de Chaume and Bonnezeaux and also to the area of Coteaux de Layon, where following a long warm autumn, the product can rival the best Sauternes. Chenin Blanc is also the main variety used in the Savennières area. Again the wine produced is outstanding, but surprisingly, dry rather than sweet.

The wines of Saumur are fruity but acidic. They are transformed into sparkling wines by the Methode traditionnelle. The fine products suggest they are ideal for this purpose.

The last two zones, Saumur-Champigny and Coteaux de l'Aubance produce red wines using mainly Cabernet Franc grapes. Rosé is also made, particularly around the Aubance river. This is sold as Cabernet Rosé d'Anjou and can be as good as any pink wine made elsewhere. It should be noted that the Coteaux de l'Aubance also produces white whereas Saumur-Champigny specialises almost exclusively in red. Most of these are light and drunk chilled but a more full-bodied and tannic red with some ageing characteristics is also made. Although Cabernet Franc is the major grape variety in Anjou, Cabernet Sauvignon and Grolleau are also used in some areas.

(c) Touraine

This region takes up the mid-eastern part of the Loire Valley. Its simple appellation generally refers to rather thin wines, mainly whites but also some reds. The grapes used are mainly Sauvignon Blanc but also Chenin Blanc for white wines and Gamay for red wines. However, the region also boasts five appellations of distinction. Vouvray and Montlouis produce some excellent whites. The grape variety used is the Chenin Blanc, although Arbois grapes are also utilised in Vouvray. Their tendency is to be sweet but less so than those at Anjou. They are light and delicate yet can, at their best, show remarkable ageing characteristics.

The wines of Auvergne

The wines show great differences between vintages, lesser years being used to make some very good sparkling products using the traditional method as in Saumur. Indeed, this area, in the heart of Touraine, is able to produce all kinds of white wines, dry, semi-sweet, sweet, semi-sparkling and sparkling, a remarkable feat. Jasnières, located north-west of Tours, makes wines which are fairly similar to those of Vouvray, again using the Chenin Blanc variety.

The last three areas, Bourgueil, St. Nicolas-de-Bourgueil and Chinon specialise in making red and rosé wines. The grape variety used is the usual Cabernet Franc, with Cabernet Sauvignon added in Bourgueil, but most of what is made is far closer to good Beaujolais than to Claret and is intended to be drunk cool. However, Bourgueil does make a light Médoc style product that can be aged for up to ten years. In addition to the reds, some very good rosé wines are produced from the same grape.

(d) Le Nivernais

The most easterly region of the Loire Valley, similar to the Nantais in the west, tends to make dry rather than sweet wines.

There are five appellations in this sector, all making exclusively or mainly white wines using the Sauvignon Blanc variety. Sancerre and Pouilly-Fumé are greenish wines that are fresh, spicy and pleasant when at their best. Sancerre also makes some reds and rosés from Pinot Noir but as with the whites, of rather uneven quality. Also, the white wines tend to suffer from too much acidity and need a very good vintage to be really worthwhile. Quincy, Reuilly and Menetou-Salon also use the Sauvignon grape and make fruity white wines that do not keep and are drunk young.

(e) Other wines

Two recently promoted appellations are Cheverny and Coteaux du Giennois. The former produces wines from the Romorantin grape as well as those made by using the Sauvignon Blanc variety. A number of V.D.Q.S. wines, mainly in the Nivernais, of which St. Pourçain, Châteaumeillant and Haut-Poitou are the most interesting, make up the total produce of this part of France. 🦅

Although under the auspices of the Loire region, Auvergne wines have more in common with those of the northern section of the Rhône Valley. The main grapes are Gamay for reds and rosés and Chardonnay for whites. There is no appellation wine in the region. 🦅

Principal wines of Auvergne

R E D S   A N D   R O S É S
V.D.Q.S. wine: Côtes d'Auvergne.

W H I T E S
V.D.Q.S. wine: Côtes d'Auvergne.

The wines of The Rhône Valley

Principal wines of The Rhône Valley

REDS

A.C. wines: Côtes du Rhône (also Villages with village name), Côte Rôtie, Hermitage, Crozes-Hermitage, St.Joseph, Cornas, Châtillon-en-Diois, Coteaux du Tricastin, Rasteau, Gigondas, Vacqueyras, Châteauneuf-du-Pape, Lirac, Côtes du Ventoux, Côtes du Luberon.

WHITES

A.C. wines: Côtes du Rhône (also Villages with village name), Condrieu, Château Grillet, Hermitage (also Vin de Paille), Crozes-Hermitage, St. Joseph, St. Péray (also Mousseux), Crémant de Die, Clairette de Die Méthode Dioise Ancestrale, Châtillon-en-Diois, Rasteau (also Rancio), Vacqueyras, Muscat Beaumes-de-Venise, Châteauneuf-du-Pape, Lirac, Côtes du Ventoux, Côtes du Luberon.

ROSÉS

A.C. wines: Côtes du Rhône (also Villages with village name), Coteaux du Tricastin, Rasteau, Gigondas, Vacqueyras, Lirac, Tavel, Côtes du Ventoux, Côtes du Luberon.

Wine has been produced in the Rhône valley since pre-Roman times. The Romans themselves utilised the vineyards fittingly, but little is known about their fate after the fall of the Roman Empire until the French Popes transferred the Holy See to Avignon in the late Middle Ages. The great potential of the region was quickly noted and fully exploited.

The wines soon took a pre-eminent position with the major dignitaries of the time, a status that was maintained even after the Popes had returned to Rome. In fact, Hermitage, the finest Rhône wine, was considered to be on a par with the best that Bordeaux or Burgundy could produce as late as the nineteenth century.

It took the Phylloxera epidemic to deliver a near fatal blow from which the area has recovered but failed to regain its former status. Nowadays, the vineyards lie along a 200 km.-stretch on steep riverbanks. Climatic and soil considerations make it convenient to divide the region into two sections, the North Rhône and the South Rhône.

The North Rhône area runs from the towns of Vienne in the north, to Valence. The climate is humid with hot summers and warm autumns. The soil consists mainly of granite but some localities, reserved for the cultivation of white grapes, are composed of a clay and limestone mixture. As expected, most of the wine produced is red.

The area has ten designated appellations. These are, from the most northerly, Côte Rôtie, Condrieu, Château Grillet, Hermitage, Crozes-Hermitage, Saint-Joseph, Cornas, Saint-Péray, Clairette de Die and Châtillon-en-Diois. Most turn out red wines made from the Syrah grape. Whites are produced either using the Viognier or a mixture of the Roussanne and Marsanne varieties.

The tiny Condrieu and Château Grillet appellations specialize in perfumed fruity dry whites made from the former, while Saint-Péray is particularly known for a sparkling aperitif wine produced from the latter. Another sparkling white, either brut or semi-sweet, is to be found at Clairette de Die. This is surprisingly made from a mixture of Clairette and Muscat à Petits Grains grapes.

The finest red wines are those at Hermitage (which also makes a very good white using the Roussanne/ Marsanne mixture) and Côte Rôtie while Cornas is undervalued and worth exploring. Crozes-Hermitage, Saint-Joseph and Châtillon wines are of a more variable quality and at their best, softer and lighter, lacking the ageing potential of the others.

The South Rhône section lies between the towns of Montélimar and the most southerly, Avignon. The weather is dry with hot summers and draughts being a common factor. The ground consists of fluvial stones over a sandy base. This gravel is an excellent heat retainer, a necessity due to the Mistral wind, which causes a large temperature variation between night and day.

The area has seven designated appellations. These are, from north to south, Coteaux du Tricastin, Gigondas, Vacqueyras, Châteauneuf-du-Pape, Lirac, Tavel and Côtes du Ventoux.
In addition, two 'Villages', Rasteau and Beaumes-de-Venise, have been granted appellations only for a particular type of reinforced sweet wine 'Vin Doux Naturel' made from Grenache and Muscat à Petits Grains respectively. Unlike the north, whose reds are based totally on Syrah, no less than thirteen different varieties are permitted in the south. In practice, only about half of these are used, the most important being Syrah, Grenache, Mourvèdre and Cinsaut for reds and Grenache Blanc, Clairette and Bourboulenc for whites.
The finest wines, which are deep, rich, full bodied, and long lived are those at Châteauneuf-du-Pape, with Gigondas close behind. Similar but less refined reds are produced at Vacqueyras, while those of Tricastin and Ventoux are lighter and best drunk young. Lirac reds are somewhat intermediate in character.
The Tavel and Lirac districts produce some fine, dry, relatively full bodied rosé wines, those made at Tavel being reputedly the very best in France, with Lirac not far behind. Very little white is made, the full-bodied top Châteauneuf-du-Papes being the best.

One rung down in the quality ladder come a group of villages whose wines are deemed superior to the norm. These are designated as Côtes-du-Rhône Villages. Of these, Cairanne is considered universally to be the best.
Also deserving special mention are Chusclan and Laudun, whose rosés are not far below the standard of the best appellation wines. The other Villages are Beaumes-de-Venise, Rasteau, Roaix, Rochegude, Rousset-les-Vignes, Sablet, St. Gervais, St. Maurice-s'Eygues, Séguret, St. Pantaléon-les-Vignes, Valréas, Vinsobres and Visan.

The simple 'Côtes-du-Rhône' designation is given to the ordinary bulk of wine produced in the region and is the lowest tier.
The grapes used are more or less the same as those of the Appellation and Villages areas. Also identical is the very high proportion of reds. Rosés are second with whites a poor third, accounting for less than 5% in the quantity table. Most wines are lighter than those of the higher rungs and need to be drunk when young.

At present, nearly all the wines are labelled using the Appellation, Villages, or simply Côtes du Rhône designation, together with the name of the Château or Domaine, these being too numerous to list below. However, worth noting is the Coteaux d'Ardèche, an exception to this rule, whose Syrah, Cabernet, Merlot, Gamay and Chardonnay are marketed as interesting varietal products, a successful departure from the norm. It remains to be seen if any other district will attempt to follow suit in the future. ❧

The wines of Provence

Principal wines of Provence

REDS

*A.C. wines: Côtes de Provence, Coteaux
d'Aix en Provence, Coteaux Varois,
Bandol, Les Baux de Provence, Cassis,
Bellet, Palette.*

WHITES

*A.C. wines: Côtes de Provence, Coteaux
Varois, Bandol, Cassis, Bellet, Palette.*

ROSÉS

*A.C. wines: Côtes de Provence, Coteaux
d'Aix en Provence, Coteaux Varois,
Bandol, Les Baux de Provence, Cassis,
Bellet, Palette.*

The origin of winemaking in Provence is uncertain but clearly dates from ancient times. The region is France's warmest, enjoying mild winters and fine, sunny summers. The rainfall is low, concentrated mainly in the spring and autumn. Vineyards are given a southerly exposition wherever possible in order to protect the vines from the Mistral wind, which can be a problem at times. The soil does show variation from place to place but tends to be limestone dominated. Clay, shale and Bauxite are found in some areas, the latter giving its name to the Coteaux des Baux appellation.

Provence grows a particularly large number of grape varieties by French standards, some being rather unexpected. Particularly prominent among these are the dark berried Braquet, Folle Noire and Tibouren and the white skinned Bourboulenc, Rolle and Grenache Blanc. There are others that show the influence of Italy and in particular Sardinia. This is no surprise when it is realised that part of the region belonged to the Kingdom of Sardinia and was administered by the Italian royal house of Savoia for over half of the nineteenth century.

The region has eight appellations, the areas of which greatly differ in size. The two largest, Côtes de Provence and Coteaux d'Aix en Provence produce the workhorse wines of the region. These are rosés intended for early drinking. Reds and whites are also made; the latter in small but increasing quantities. A third appellation, the Coteaux Varois, is located towards the centre of the region, on the western side of the huge Côtes de Provence district. Here, some interesting reds and rosés of widely differing styles are produced. Only a small amount of white is made.

Perhaps it is to be expected that the five smallest appellations make the most interesting products. Two of these, Bandol and Coteaux des Baux, both on the western end of the region, produce some very fine and long lasting red wines. These are based on the Mourvèdre grape but Syrah and Cabernet Sauvignon are being introduced with increasingly good results. Rosés are also interesting but whites tend to be less successful. Two other appellations, Cassis and Bellet, lie to the south, the former towards the west and the latter on the eastern hills above Nice. These districts are atypical of Provence as a whole by producing some really good white wines. In Cassis, complex blends containing Clairette, Ugni Blanc, Marsanne and Sauvignon Blanc are used to make interesting whites, while Bellet, enjoying hillside sites that are cooler than the rest of the region, uses Rolle and Chardonnay in its grape mixture. The last appellation, Palette, which is surrounded by Aix en Provence, is the smallest, and not surprisingly, the most consistent appellation. It produces not only fine reds and rosés containing a blend of Syrah, Mourvèdre, Grenache and Cinsault grapes but also interesting whites made from the Muscat and Sémillon varieties. ❦

The wines of Languedoc-Roussillon

Winemaking in this region dates from before the birth of Christ. The Romans first encouraged the industry and then suppressed it. Later, in the Middle Ages, wine production again flourished, thanks to the local monasteries. The wine trade continued to do well for hundreds of years, until a rapid growth in the mid-nineteenth century was tragically cut short by the phylloxera epidemic. However, the region recovered more quickly than the rest of the country and soon became France's major producer. Unfortunately this led to a quantity-orientated attitude and quality suffered accordingly.

Today, the region, which possesses the world's largest wine area, still accounts for about 30% of the French national production. Unfortunately, apart from a very small number of enlightened pioneers, the majority of the vineyards belong to small producers who follow out of date techniques and are unwilling to alter their traditional methods. Consequently the general quality remains of a mediocre standard. The region can, however, rightly claim a number of important assets. The French equivalents to Port and Sherry are made here; Maury, Banyuls and Clairette du Languedoc 'rancio' are all fortified and can be very good in spite of being relatively unknown outside France. Also, the Limoux appellation produces several very fine sparkling wines by the champenoise method. In addition, the region can boast no less than five appellations for interesting fortified white dessert wines made from different Muscat grapes. Lastly a great number of promising Vins de Pays that are aspiring for promotion to a higher classification are produced. The potential for improvement certainly exists, as shown by the increasing number of excellent wines that are continuing to emerge.

Apart from the usual grapes found in the south of France, a number of particular local varieties are used. These are Grenache Noir, Grenache Gris, Picpoul, Fer and Terret for reds and rosés, and Grenache Blanc, Mauzac and Muscat Rosé à Petits Grains for whites. ❧

Principal wines of Languedoc-Roussillon

REDS

A.C. wines: Costières de Nimes, Coteaux de Languedoc, Minervois, St.Chinian, Faugères, Corbières, Maury, Fitou, Côtes du Roussillon (also Villages), Collioure, Banyuls (also Gr.Cru)

WHITES

A.C. wines: Costières de Nimes, Coteaux de Languedoc, Clairette de Languedoc, Minervois, Muscat (de St. Jean-de-Minervois, de Frontignan, de Lunel, de Mireval, de Rivesaltes), Limoux, Crémant de Limoux, Blanquette de Limoux, Blanquette Méthode Ancestrale, Corbières, Côtes du Roussillon, Banyuls

ROSÉS

A.C. wines: Costières de Nimes, Coteaux de Languedoc, Minervois, St.Chinian, Corbières, Côtes du Roussillon, Collioure, Banyuls

The wines of Corse

Principal wines of Corse

REDS AND ROSÉS

A.C. wines: Patrimonio, Ajaccio,
Vin de Corse (also Coteaux du Cap Corse,
Porto Vecchio, Calvi, Figari, Sartène)

WHITES

A.C. wines: Patrimonio, Ajaccio,
Vin de Corse (also Coteaux du Cap Corse,
Porto Vecchio, Calvi, Figari, Sartène),
Muscat du Cap Corse

The island of Corsica is one of the oldest wine producers in Europe. It is known that wine was made in Phoenician times, over 500 years before the birth of Christ. Nowadays, the grapes used show the influence of Italy (Genoa owned the island until 1768) and Provence, the nearest French region.
Happily, several noble varieties have now been introduced from mainland France with success.

Corsica possesses a hotter climate with more sunshine than anywhere on the mainland. In addition, there is little rain during the growing season and the hilly and mountainous terrain provides many excellent vineyard sites. Yet before 1980, the emphasis was on quantity production grown on plains on the eastern side. Since then, a change of direction towards quality has led to a continuous improvement of the island's wines. An important point is that Corsica has a number of different soil types.
Chalk, clay, granite, sand, schist and alluvial soils are all well known. This, as well as some variance in altitude, exposition, sea-influence and wind cover, results in a myriad of microclimates with differences even between neighbouring vineyards. Consequently the correct marriage of grape variety to site is vital if a good result is desired.

Although A.C. wines account for little more than 15% of the total, there are eight appellations on the island. They are Patrimonio, Ajaccio and Vin de Corse, which has five others within it, these being Coteaux du Cap Corse, Porto Vecchio, Figari, Sartène and Calvi. Patrimonio produces a fine red that is probably the best wine made on the island and good reds also come from Figari. Porto Vecchio probably makes the best whites, while Sartène produces interesting wines of all types. A fine sweet white is made at Coteaux du Cap Corse.

It is not surprising, due to the Mediterranean influence, that Corsica produces mainly red wine. A considerable amount of rosés are also to be found but white, although on the increase, only accounts for about 10% of the total. Also, the grape varieties used make interesting reading. Many are now French, but a number of Italian ones are still the most prominent. Red and rosé wines are produced from Nielluccio, Sciacarello, Grenache, Barbarossa, Mourvèdre, Carignan, Cinsault, Syrah, Aleatico, Cabernet Sauvignon, Merlot and Pinot Noir grapes while whites are made using the Vermentino, Ugni Blanc, Muscat, Chardonnay and Viognier varieties. ❧

The wines of Jura and Savoie

These two isolated regions, situated in the French Alps bordering with Switzerland and Italy have wine styles that are particular to the region, bearing little relationship to those of France as a whole. Both regions have a winemaking tradition that goes back to Roman times.

Today the Jura vineyards, situated at a reasonable height on limestone based lower hill-slopes at an altitude of about three hundred metres are suitably exposed to protect them against winter frosts.

As expected, most wines produced are white. However, surprisingly, some reds are also made, Pinot Noir being the variety used. In fact, these are not much darker than rosés made from the same grape. The white wines, both still and sparkling, are made from Chardonnay and Savagnin, a grape of local origin. The latter is particularly used to produce, using a sherry-like vinification process, an interesting speciality known as 'Vin Jaune'.
As the name suggests, the wine is yellow in colour. It is dry and has a typical nutty flavour and can be kept in bottle for many years. Another local speciality is 'Vin de Paille', or straw wine. This is a sweet dessert wine made from Chardonnay, Savagnin and Poulsard, another indigenous variety. In this case, the grapes are either laid to rest on straw mats or hung to dry, so to concentrate their sugar content. The method is reminiscent of the process used in the Veneto to make the Recioto di Soave wines with which they can be compared. As for the Vins Jaunes, these have excellent ageing potential. A third speciality is the curious 'Macvin', an aperitif wine made by a process which appears to be unaltered since it was discovered well over one thousand years ago.

Most of Savoie is too mountainous for the cultivation of vines and consequently the vineyards tend to be found on the lower hillsides, scattered about in localities that offer the greatest protection against the elements. Again, most wines are white, being made from Chadonnay and the indigenous varieties Jacquère, Roussette and Molette. Some areas also utilise Pinot Gris, Aligoté and Chasselas, a variety commonly found over the border in Switzerland. A lesser amount of red and rosé wines are produced, mainly from Pinot Noir and Gamay, together with the local Poulsard and Mondeuse varieties. It must be added that the Vin de Savoie appellation is often followed by a Cru name, there being sufficient distinction to necessitate this procedure. The Savoie also produces a fair amount of sparkling and semi-sparkling wine, that which is made with local grapes in the Seyssel A.C. being particularly good. In addition, a fine Vermouth wine is produced at Chambéry. ✷

Principal wines of Jura and Savoie

REDS
- *A.C. wines; Arbois (also Pupillin), Côtes du Jura, Vin de Savoie (also Arbin, Chautagne, Cruet, Jongieux, Mondeuse).*
- *V.D.Q.S. wine: Vins du Bugey*

WHITES
- *A.C. wines: Arbois (also Mousseux, Pupillin), Château Chalon, Macvin du Jura, Côtes du Jura, L'Étoile (also Vin Jaune, Mousseux), Crémant de Jura, Vin de Savoie (also Abymes, Apremont, Ayze, Chignin, Chignin Bergeron, Cruet, Jongieux, Marignan, Marin, Molette, Montmélian, Ripaille, Mousseux, Pétillant), Roussette de Savoie, Seyssel (also Mousseux), Roussette de Seyssel, Crépy.*
- *V.D.Q.S. wines: Vins du Bugey, Roussette du Bugey*

ROSÉS
- *A.C. wines: Arbois (also Pupillin), Côtes du Jura, Vin de Savoie (also Pétillant).*
- *V.D.Q.S. wine: Vins du Bugey*

The wines of Piemonte

Principal wines of Piemonte

REDS
- *D.O.C.G. wines: Barolo, Barbaresco, Gattinara.*
- *D.O.C. wines: Nebbiolo, Barbera, Dolcetto, Rubino di Cantavenna, Freisa, Grignolino, Brachetto, Brachetto Spumante, Carema, Ghemme, Roero, Fara, Boca, Bramaterra, Lessona, Monferrato Rosso, Sizzano, Gabiano, Spanna delle Colline Novaresi, Ruché di Castagnole Monferrato, Langhe Rosso, Verduno Pelaverga*

WHITES
- *D.O.C.G. wines: Asti Spumante, Moscato d'Asti, Gavi.*
- *D.O.C. wines: Loazzolo, Caluso Passito, Erbaluce di Caluso, Roero Arneis, Monferrato Bianco, Cortese, Moscato, Moscato Passito, Malvasia, Langhe (Bianco, Favorita), Chardonnay, Pinot Bianco Spumante, Pinot Grigio Spumante, Pinot Nero Spumante, Pinot Chardonnay Spumante, Spumante del Piemonte*

ROSÉS
- *D.O.C. wine: Monferrato Chiaretto*

Piedmont is the most important quality wine region in Italy. Although only seventh in Italy, for the quantity of wine produced, it has no less than forty one D.O.C.G. and D.O.C. zones accounting for 40% of its total output.

The region lies at the foot of the Alps to the north and west, the Apennines to the south and the Ticino River and Lake Maggiore to the east. The climate is relatively severe with cold snow laden winters, cool and misty springs and autumns and dry and warm summers. These factors, together with the iron bearing clay and limestone soil and hilly terrain, result in the production of Barolo and Barbaresco, at their best two of the world's greatest wines.

The dark, thick-skinned Nebbiolo is not only rich in tannin and acid, but also extremely late to ripen. This makes it a difficult grape to manage particularly as it is so much dependent on good late autumn weather.

However, given the right handling and conditions it will produce wines of exceptional longevity that will, in time, shed their tannic mantle to reveal a host of flavours, possibly of greater complexity than any other grape variety. Truffles, raspberry, liquorice, tar, violets, roses, prunes and chocolate are among its many essences, which truly make it, as it is said, a wine of kings and a king of wines.

The location of Barolo production centres round the town of Alba in southern Piedmont. There are three areas: around the villages of Barolo and La Morra where Tortonian soils produce slightly lighter and more quickly ripening wines of greater perfume, near the villages of Serralunga and Monforte where poorer Helvetian soils result in fuller, more tannic and longer lasting wines and around the village of Castiglione Falletto whose wines are a compromise between the other two.

Although many excellent cru Barolos exist, some of the best producers blend the grapes from the different areas to obtain, in their view, the best possible product.

The smaller area of Barbaresco lies to the north east of Barolo, around the villages of Barbaresco and Neive. Here, lighter soils and gentler slopes, together with a shorter barrel ageing period contribute to produce a softer, more feminine wine with a slightly lower alcohol content. The Nebbiolo ripens sooner here, avoiding problems of late autumn rain, which often affects the Barolo harvest. Barbaresco is generally a more accessible wine, with however, less staying power than Barolo.

Although the Nebbiolo reigns supreme, Piedmont can boast at least five other interesting indigenous red grape varieties. Foremost are Barbera and Dolcetto, which are used to make lighter, varietal wines utilised for day-to-day drinking purposes by the locals. These are best if drunk when young but well-made Barbera from good vintages will keep and both wines are capable of considerable interest at their best. The other varieties are Freisa, Grignolino and Brachetto, which give rise to slightly fizzy, varietal wines that should be drunk young. Of these, Freisa is usually the most interesting while Brachetto remains the most universally acceptable.
A number of other reds are made in the region. These are blends, mostly combining Nebbiolo with other local grape varieties.

The white wines of Piedmont are of far less importance. However, Asti Spumante and Moscato Spumante, made further north around the city of Asti, are world famous as delicately fruity unpretentious sparkling wines best drunk fresh and young. They are made from the Muscat grape. The region's best dry white wine is Gavi, produced in the south-eastern corner of Piedmont from the indigenous Cortese grape. It is good but not in the class of the best French whites. Other white wines are Arneis and Grignolino d'Asti, each made from the homonymous grape. The former seems to be the more interesting of the two, being excellent when made by committed producers. Yet another white variety, the Erbaluce, is used to make a 'Passito' from the dried grapes. The result is a sweet dessert wine of strong character. A dry product made from the identical parentage lacks the same interest.

Briefly, it should not be forgotten that the world's most famous Vermouth wines, both red and white, come from Turin, the region's capital.

Piedmont, in common with other Italian regions, is increasingly using the noble French varieties (Cabernet, Pinot Noir, Chardonnay, Sauvignon Blanc, Pinot Blanc and Pinot Gris), generally with very good results. Nevertheless, the region boasts a host of excellent native grapes, the produce of which creates the greatest interest. Moreover, an ever-increasing quality drive makes Piedmont one of the most exiting wine regions in the world today. ❧

Wines of Aosta Valley

Living in the Alps with bitterly cold winters, the people of the Valle d'Aosta, Italy's smallest region, practise the art of viticulture in a few well-chosen sheltered sites, on the lower slopes. There is only one denominated wine, yet it exists in a large number of different types, including dessert and sparkling products. A number of local grape varieties as well as some well-known ones are used. Since there are a large proportion of French speakers amongst the population, it is no surprise that the latter include a number of French varieties as well as Italian ones.

Most wines are varietal, but a good number are blends with their own, special name. ❧

Wines of Liguria

Liguria ranks nineteenth of the twenty Italian regions in quantity of wine production. Unlike neighbouring Piedmont 75% of its wine is white. The region possesses just four D.O.C. zones. These are Dolceacqua, a red wine area lying in the extreme west of the region next to the French border; Riviera Ligure di Ponente also on the western side of the region; Cinque Terre, a white wine area on the eastern side of Liguria; and Colli di Luni, which lies by the sea adjoining the Tuscan border.

Strangely, the red Rossese di Dolceacqua is probably the best wine in this white producing region. It is refreshingly light and best drunk young. Unfortunately, it is made in small quantities and is difficult to find. The best of the whites are probably those made from the Vermentino and Pigato varieties. The sweet Sciacchetrà from the Cinqueterre area, another rarity, is worth investigating. ❧

Principal wines of Aosta Valley

REDS
D.O.C. wines: Valle d'Aosta (Rosso, Enfer d'Arvier, Torrette, Nus Rosso, Chambave Rosso, Gamay, Arnad-Montjovet, Donnas, Novello, Pinot Noir, Fumin, Petit Rouge.)

WHITES
D.O.C. wines: Valle d'Aosta (Bianco, Blanc de Morgex et de la Salle, Chardonnay, Nus Malvoisie, Nus Malvoisie Passito, Chambave Moscato, Chambave Moscato Passito, Prëmetta, Petite Arvine, Pinot Noir, Pinot Gris, Müller Thurgau.)

ROSÉS
D.O.C. wine: Valle d'Aosta Rosato

Principal wines of Liguria

REDS
D.O.C. wines: Rossese (di Dolceacqua, della Riviera Ligure di Ponente), Ormeasco di Riviera Ligure di Ponente, Rosso di Colli di Luni, Colline di Levante

WHITES
D.O.C. wines: Vermentino (della Riviera Ligure di Ponente, di Colli di Luni), Pigato di Riviera Ligure di Ponente, Cinque Terre, Cinque Terre Sciacchetrà, Bianco di Colli di Luni, Colline di Levante

ROSÉS
D.O.C. wines: Ormeasco Sciacchetrà della Riviera Ligure di Ponente

The wines of Lombardia

Principal wines of Lombardia

REDS

- *D.O.C.G. wine: Franciacorta*
- *D.O.C. wines: Oltrepò Pavese (many types), Cellatica, Botticino, Valcalepio, Valtellina, Valtellina Superiore (usually sold under the names of the four areas: Grumello, Inferno, Sassella, and Valgella), Valtellina Sfurzat, Riviera del Garda Bresciano, Colli Morenici Mantovani del Garda, San Colombano al Lambro, Capriano del Colle.*
- *Other: Ronco di Mompiano*

WHITES

- *D.O.C.G. wines: Franciacorta, Fracciacorta Cremant.*
- *D.O.C. wines: Lugana, Valcalepio, Valcalepio Moscato Passito, Oltrepò Pavese (many types), Colli Morenici Mantovani del Garda, Riviera del Garda Bresciano, San Martino della Battaglia, Capriano del Colle Trebbiano*

ROSÉS

- *D.O.C.G. wines: Franciacorta Rosato.*
- *D.O.C. wines: Oltrepò Pavese, Riviera del Garda Bresciano (Chiaretto and Spumante Rosato), Lambrusco Mantovano, Colli Morenici Mantovani del Garda*

There is evidence that vineyards were present in Lombardy in ancient times. The wines of the Valtellina and Lake Garda were known to the Romans and referred to with much praise by Virgil, Pliny and the Emperor Augustus. Later, Leonardo da Vinci described the Valtellina as a place surrounded by high mountains, which made powerful wines.

Indeed, the region has been historically very rich in its vineyards, with, however, a sad trend towards quantity rather than quality. Then, when in the nineteenth century Phylloxera devastated the vines, many sites were abandoned and even now, although there is a resurgence in wine making, the region, a prime consumer of the product, is still a second rate producer by Italian standards. At present both the traditional and ancient grape varieties as well as newly introduced French ones are used, sometimes even in unexpected blends. This switch towards quality inspired by innovation has helped raise the standing of the product. Nevertheless the region still has considerable catching up to do.

The wines in Lombardy can be classified as coming from six basic areas. Franciacorta, in the province of Brescia, lies in the centre of the region and its wines are probably the most characteristic of Lombardy. Surprising blends of Cabernet Franc, Barbera, Nebbiolo and Merlot are used to make some fine reds while the whites contain French grape varieties, particularly Chardonnay and Pinot Blanc. A classy metodo classico spumante is of particular interest. In the same province one finds the district of Lugana and Riviera del Garda. Here, in contrast to the above, the best wine is a white which possesses a nutty, floral quality, an astonishing attribute considering the nature of the grape used, the usually bland Trebbiano which seems to do unexpectedly well in this part of the region. Valcelapio, in the province of Bergamo, also lies in the centre of the region. Both reds and whites tend to be made from French varieties. Towards the south west of Lombardy, in the province of Pavia, is the district of Oltrepò Pavese. Here, on the border of Emilia, reds are made from both French and indigenous grapes. There is a rosé made from Pinot Noir while whites contain German as well as French and Italian varieties. As in Franciacorta, a good spumante is produced. To the northeast of the above, again on the Emilia border, is the small San Colombano district where a red made with a blend of Croatina, Barbera and Uva Rara grapes, a particularly strange mixture, is found.

The Valtellina, in the province of Sondrio, consists of a thin strip to the north of the region, along steep slopes on the banks of the river Adda. The vineyards are positioned at an altitude of around 600 metres and are not far from the Swiss border. The wines are red and based on the Piedmont Nebbiolo although French grapes are also used. The district is divided into four areas, the Grumello, Inferno, Sassella and Valgella. A riserva is produced which is richer in flavour and fuller in body than the normal wine. Also, a semi-passito containing about 14.5% of alcohol is made. This wine is called Sfurzat or Sforzato. It is dry and similar to, but not quite in the same class as, the Amarone of the Veneto region.

The wines of Trentino - Alto Adige

Wine production here appears to date from Etruscan times, some six centuries before the birth of Christ.

The region encompasses two provinces, those of Trento in the south and the predominantly German speaking Bolzano (Bozen) in the north. Here, the vineyards are planted along the banks of the rivers Adige and Isonzo, more or less around the city of Bolzano itself. The valleys are narrow with steep hillsides that are often terraced. Due to the proximity of the Alps, the winters are invariably cold, while in the summer, cool nights are followed by unexpectedly hot days. This subjects the grapes to a slow but definite ripening process. Around Trento the Adige valley is wider and the climate is less extreme.

The geographical topography of the region should make it well suited to the production of fine whites, particularly in the north. In fact, the best Alto Adige wine is white whereas the finest in Trento is red. Surprisingly, the region as a whole concentrates more on reds, which account for 70% of the total output. Unfortunately, partly due to overproduction, the quality falls short of the potential, but is pretty good nevertheless. The D.O.C. wines account for no less than 60% of the total and the high level of export, 35%, tells its own story. It must be added that quality is steadily improving with a number of enterprising producers showing the way.

The wines of the two provinces differ considerably but the varieties used have much in common. The region can boast a number of indigenous grapes. These are used to make interesting products, while the usual noble varieties, both red and white, are also utilised to advantage. The red Lagrein and Schiava Gentile grapes are found over the whole region while the Teroldego and Marzemino (referred to in Don Giovanni) are grown only in the Trento province. For the whites, Traminer is cultivated in the whole region but originates from Termeno (Tramin) in the Alto Adige, while the Nosiola variety, indigenous to Trento, is used to produce the region's very good sweet, Vin Santo.

Regarding non-indigenous grapes, the finest Pinot Blanc and Sylvaner wines found anywhere are made here. Also as for the noble varieties, Chardonnay in particular, Pinot Noir, Pinot Gris and Pinot Blanc are used in some extremely good Champenoise sparkling wines.

Many of the wines sold are varietal, but a number of interesting blends with special names also exist. Santa Maddalena and Lago di Caldero (or 'Caldero'), both red wines, are worth discovering. Also, the region produces some characterful rosés, those made from the indigenous Lagrein grape being particularly fine. ❦

Principal wines of Trentino - Alto Adige

*The wines are found in both provinces unless followed by * (Bolzano only)
or ** (Trento only)*

REDS
- D.O.C. wines: Lagrein (Scuro or Dunkel), Schiava (Vernatsch), Cabernet (Sauvignon or Franc), Cabernet-Merlot, Merlot, Pinot Noir, Schiava Grigia (Grauvernatsch)*, Colli di Bolzano*, Santa Maddalena (St. Magdalener)*, Klauser Leitacher*, Lago di caldaro (Caldaro)*, Meranese*, Cabernet-Lagrein*, Sorni Rosso**, Marzemino**, Teroldego Rotaliano**.
- Others: Valdadige Rosso**, Casteller**

WHITES
- D.O.C. wines: Traminer, Pinot Bianco, Pinot Grigio, Chardonnay, Riesling Renano, Riesling Italico, Müller Thurgau, Moscato Giallo, Sylvaner*, Sauvignon*, Malvasia*, Veltliner*, Kerner*, Alto Adige Spumante*, Nosiola**, Trento Bianco**, Trentino Bianco**, Sorni Bianco**, Vino Santo**
- Other: Valdadige Bianco**

ROSÉS
- D.O.C. wines: Moscato Rosa, Lagrein Rosato*, Merlot Rosato*, Pinot Nero Rosato*, Trento Rosato**.
- Others: Valdadige Rosato**, Casteller Rosato**

The wines of The Veneto

Principal wines of The Veneto

REDS
- *D.O.C. wines: Valpolicella, Amarone della Valpolicella, Recioto della Valpolicella, Valdadige, Garda, Colli Berici (Tocai Rosso, Barbarano), Colli Euganei, Bagnoli (Rosso, Friularo, Passito), Bardolino, Lison Pramaggiore Refosco dal Peduncolo Rosso, Montello e Colli Asolani, Raboso del Piave, Breganze, Cabernet, Cabernet Sauvignon, Cabernet Franc, Merlot, Pinot Nero*
- *Others: La Poja, Campo Fiorin*

WHITES
- *D.O.C. wines: Soave, Recioto di Soave, Bianco di Custoza, Vespaiolo, Tocai Italico, Garganega, Gambellara (Bianco, Recioto, Vin Santo), Garda (Corvina, Riesling Renano), Lessini Durello, Breganze, Colli Berici Spumante, Colli Euganei (Bianco, Moscato, Fior d'Arancio, Pinello, Serpina), Prosecco di Conegliano-Valdobbiadene (Bianco, Superiore di Cartizze), Piave Verduzzo, Valdadige, Colli di Conegliano Torchiato di Fregona, Bagnoli (Bianco, Spumante), Chardonnay, Pinot Bianco, Pinot Grigio, Prosecco di Montello e Colli Asolani, Lison Pramaggiore (Riesling Italico, Verduzzo), Sauvignon*

ROSÉS
- *D.O.C. wines: Bardolino Chiaretto, Bagnoli (Rosato, Spumante Rosato)*

There is archaeological evidence that vines were growing in this area about forty million years ago. However, the wine-making is not so ancient. The Arusnati, a people living near the town now known as Fumane, were producing wine in the fifth century B.C. A number of Roman writers, including Pliny and Virgil, wrote about the wines here. Later, in the sixth century A.D., Cassiodorus, minister to King Theodoric and provider of food and wine at his court in the region, described the red Acinatico wines of the region as having a pure and exceptional taste of incredibly gentle sweetness and regal colour. He proceeded to praise the white even more highly, describing it as possessing a beautiful whiteness and a clear purity, and concluding that whilst the red could be said to be 'born of roses', this seemed to originate from lilies.

The most common wine of the region, Valpolicella, possibly derives its name from the words Valle (meaning Valley), Poli (Greek for many) and Cella (Latin for cellar), that is, the valley of many cellars. The name Val Polesela was used in a decree issued by the holy Roman Emperor, Federico Barbarossa, in the late twelfth century. This wine, nowadays made from a blend of Corvina, Molinara, Rondinella, and sometimes also Negrara and Rossignola grapes, is noted as a full and fruity red to be drunk relatively young. Yet the same blend, partially dried and fully fermented produces Amarone, which in the Classico zone, can be a wine of great opulence and longevity, to be served with roasts or cheese or simply for meditation. If the grapes are fully dried and partly fermented, the sweet wine, Recioto della Valpolicella, is produced. This, at its best, vaguely resembles a fine Port, being less intense but possibly more complex, having a touch of bitterness behind its basic sweet character. Another interesting wine, made from the same grapes, is Bardolino, both in its red or rosé forms.

As well as looking to improve its traditional wines by decreasing its yields, the Veneto is at the forefront in introducing and perfecting those made from the classic French varieties. As a result, many have now been granted the D.O.C.status. Reds made from Merlot, Cabernet Sauvignon, Cabernet Franc and Pinot Noir feature strongly here.

The Soave D.O.C. is for the whites, which account for 55% of the total production, what Valpolicella is for the reds. Also, a sweet Recioto, made in a similar way as the red, is produced and can be very good at its best. There is, however, no corresponding white wine to Amarone. Similar to Soave and also worth investigating is the Bianco di Custozia D.O.C. As is happening with the reds, classical French varieties are gaining more and more prominence in the region, with a corresponding greater recognition by the government. Here, Pinot Blanc, Pinot Gris, Sauvignon Blanc and Chardonnay are particularly distinguished. A notable point is that an increase in the prominence of 'Prosecco' sparkling wines, made by the classical method, has accompanied the increasing role played in them by French grapes, Chardonnay and Pinot Blanc in particular.

The success of the Veneto as an innovative and greatly improving region can be measured by the fact that it exports the greatest quantity of Italian D.O.C. wine, that is, even more than Piedmont or Tuscany. Its favourable geographical position is clearly not the only reason for its present success.

As can be seen by the list, many wines from this region are sold as varietal products, bearing the name of the dominant grape variety as well as the 'denominazione' district. This is true for a number of wines made from local grapes as well as those containing French varieties. ❧

The wines of Friuli - Venezia Giulia

This north-eastern region of Italy is possibly the third most important after Piedmont and Tuscany. However, the best wine is white, which accounts for about 55% of the total production. Also the region is unique in that it contains a mix of three cultures, Venetian, Teutonic and Slav. It is almost certainly for this reason that more foreign grape varieties are cultivated than local ones. Much of the wine is sold with varietal labels, a practice not normally employed in Italy.

The northern half of the region is mountainous and unsuited to vineyard cultivation. In the south, on the other hand, there are seven D.O.C. districts and a small part of an eighth, Lison Pramaggiore, which mainly lies in the Veneto region. No less than 45% of the all wines made in Friuli are D.O.C., an abnormally high figure testifying the generally good quality of the produce.

The best two districts by far are the Colli Orientali del Friuli and Collio, both on the eastern side, close to the Slovenian border. Isonzo, just south of Collio also makes interesting wines, while those of Grave, the largest district, and Latisana are normally pleasant but lack the interest and complexity of the others. Aquileia's wines are generally the least satisfying, while those of Carso, a relatively new D.O.C., appear to bear little in common with the rest.

As mentioned above, a large number of foreign grape varieties are grown. The red Cabernet Sauvignon, Cabernet Franc, Merlot and Pinot Noir are planted in most districts and only Pinot Noir is less than successful. Colli Orientali dei Friuli, in particular, produces some stunning Cabernets and Merlots. Those made at Collio and Isonzo are also very good. As for whites, Sauvignon Blanc, Tocai, Traminer, Chardonnay, Pinot Blanc, Pinot Gris and Riesling wines are all very well made, again particularly at Collio and Colli Orientali del Friuli, but with Grave and Isonzo not far behind.

As far as Italian varieties go, the red Refosco is probably the most typical of the region. The best is yet again found in the Colli del Friuli but good specimens are also made at Grave, Latisana and Aquileia. Strangely, it is not grown at Collio. The red Schioppettino grape, near to extinction some years ago, has been revived at Colli del Friuli with remarkable results that show great future potential. Other local reds are the Franconia, grown at Latisana and Isonzo and the Terrano, found only at Carso.

Natural whites include Verduzzo, Malvasia, Ribolla Gialla and Picolit. The first two are grown in most areas while the latter pair only in Colli Orientali del Friuli and Collio. Picolit is used to make sweet wines that are good but apparently very overpriced.

The sweet variety of Verduzzo, at its best, is probably its equal and not so expensive.

It is not surprising that some fine Champagne method sparkling wines are produced. Most of these are made from the traditional Pinot Noir and Chardonnay grape varieties. 🐾

Principal wines and grape varieties of Friuli - Venezia Giulia

REDS

D.O.C. wines: Rosso, Novello, Cabernet, Cabernet Sauvignon, Cabernet Franc, Pinot Noir, Merlot, Schioppettino, Refosco dal Peduncolo Rosso, Franconia, Terrano

WHITES

D.O.C. wines: Bianco, Chardonnay, Pinot Bianco, Pinot Grigio, Riesling Renano, Riesling Italico, Sauvignon, Tocai Friulano, Traminer Aromatico, Müller-Thurgau, Ramandolo, Ribolla Gialla, Verduzzo Friulano, Malvasia (Istriana), Picolit, Chardonnay Spumante, Pinot Bianco Spumante, Spumante

ROSÉS

D.O.C. wines: Rosato (Mostly made of Merlot with added Cabernets)

The wines of Toscana

Principal wines of Toscana

REDS

- *D.O.C.G. wines: Chianti Classico, Chianti Rufina, Chianti (Colli Senesi, Colli Fiorentini, Colli Pisani, Montalbano, Colli Aretini), Brunello di Montalcino, Vino Nobile di Montepulcano, Carmignano*
- *D.O.C. wines: Bolgheri (Rosso, Sassicaia.), Rosso di Montalcino, Rosso di Montepulciano, Parrina, Pomino (Rosso, Vin Santo Rosso.), Morellino di Scansano, Colli dell'Etruria Centrale, Val di Cornia, Barco Reale di Carmignano, Montescudaio, Monteregio di Massa Marittima, Colline Lucchesi, Sant'Antimo (Rosso, Merlot, Pinot Nero, Cabernet Sauvignon), Montecarlo, Elba (Rosso, Aleatico)*
- *Others: Solaia, Ornellaia, Tignanello, Nemo, Ghiaie della Furba, Cepparello, Le Pergole Torte, Tavernelle, Fontalloro*

Winemaking in Tuscany dates back to the Etruscans, whose territories partly corresponded to the present region. Their flourishing wine trade was allowed to slide by the Romans, who preferred the heavier products from the south, and was later destroyed by the Barbarian invasions. It was restored by monks in the Middle Ages and grew greatly in stature during the Renaissance, when wines from the region flourished, not only in the major Tuscan cities, but also all over Europe. This position of eminence was maintained for the next two hundred years when the region was well ahead of its time in wine making skills. In 1716, the Duchy of Tuscany named Europe's first official wine areas, two of these being Chianti and Carmignano. Methods of viticulture, fermentation and ageing unsurpassed anywhere in the world were developed and the region continued to flourish.

Unfortunately, a combination of this ready success and devastation caused by the phylloxera epidemic led to a marked degeneration of what all the wines, but particularly Chianti, stood for. When the vineyards were replanted, in a misguided effort to make good all losses, the areas of production were expanded to include places that failed to live up to the name. Moreover, the wines became coarse and cheap, often diluted in order to serve a mentality that put quantity above quality. The sale of the wines in attractive looking flasks became more important than the quality of the product inside! Eventually, supply came to exceed demand, leading to a crisis in the industry. This, together with the introduction of the D.O.C. and D.O.C.G. laws in 1963 and 1980 respectively, has led to more and more producers seeking to recapture the standards that had been lost. Now, great strides have been made although there is still someway to go. The laws have not been able to clear up confusion in the style and type of the wines. Also, although they lay down certain standards for viticulture, production and ageing, they are not always able to discriminate between, for example, a well made Chianti and an inferior one. Consequently it's up to the consumer to know whether a producer is reliable or otherwise, a slow and painstaking process often carried out by trial and error. Given fierce competition from France, the region is facing an uphill battle to regain its former prestige.

The territory of Tuscany consists of approximately 67% hills, 25% mountains and 8% plains. The soil shows a great diversity; limestone, dolomite, volcanic soil, sand, clay, schist, flysch and marl all make an appearance in different places. The climate depends on the altitude and distance from the sea. It can be temperate in some places but continental with large temperature differences between day and night in others. All this results in a varied and complex morphology and consequently a region that is able to grow thirty-five red grape varieties and thirty white ones successfully and produce well over one hundred and fifty recognised wines.

The most typically Tuscan of all these wines is Chianti. This is produced in the centre of the region, more or less between the towns of Siena and Florence. Chianti itself is subdivided into seven area types. These are Classico, Rufina, Colli Senesi, Colli Fiorentini, Colli Pisani, Colli Aretini and Montalbano, of which the first two are by far the best known. In every case the wine is made principally of Sangiovese with a little Cannaiolo added and although the law allows the use of up to 10% Malvasia Bianca, a white grape, the best producers tend to use only the red varieties.

Further south, in the province of Siena, two other important Tuscan style reds are produced. These are Brunello di Montalcino and Vino Nobile di Montepulciano. Both are made from the Prugnolo Gentile grape, a Sangiovese clone, the former exclusively while the latter has some Cannaiolo and Mammolo added. As for Chianti, the Vino Nobile is legally allowed some white grape but the better firms ignore it. Both these wines can be superb, particularly the Brunello, which has a great ageing potential.

Although Sangiovese is the standard Tuscan grape, much use is made of the noble French red varieties. To the north of Florence one finds Carmignano, made from a mixture of Sangiovese and Cabernet. The reserve of this wine, aged in oak for two years, is particularly fine. Many other reds, similar to the four above, are made either using Sangiovese alone or mixed with white grapes, or Sangiovese mixed with Cabernet and /or

Merlot. Some of these include many Vini da Tavola (Table wines) not recognised by the Italian government, but which are products with style and finesse and command a high price in the bottle. A small but increasing number of wines are being made using only French varieties, particularly Cabernet Sauvignon, Cabernet Franc and Merlot and to a lesser extent Pinot Noir and Syrah. Some of these table wines, especially those containing the Bordeaux grapes, are serious rivals to the very best produced in France.

White Tuscan wines are far less impressive than the red. The most typical is probably Vernaccia di San Gemignano, made from the homonymous grape variety. Many other whites are based on Malvasia and Trebbiano and are of lesser interest. However, as for the reds, there is an increasing trend to use non-indigenous and particularly French varieties, with the resultant production of increasingly interesting wines. Special mention should be made of Chardonnay, but Pinot Blanc, Pinot Gris, Sauvignon Blanc, Riesling, Grechetto, Greco and Vermentino all play a part.

By far the finest white wine made in the region is the sweet 'Vin Santo'. Although traditionally produced from Malvasia and Trebbiano, a number of winemakers are now adding other, mainly French, grapes to the blend. At its best it is a wine for meditation, commanding a very high price. It should be noted that Vin Santo comes in three distinct main types, dry and semi-sweet, as well as sweet. It can also be found as a rosé 'Occhio di Pernice' and in the single case of Pomino, a red wine. ❦

Principal wines of Toscana

WHITES
- *D.O.C.G. wine: Vernaccia di San Gemignano*
- *D.O.C. wines: Moscadello di Montalcino, Candia dei Colli Apuani, Bianco della Valdinievole, Colli dell'Etruria Centrale, Bianco dell'Empolese, Pomino, Parrina, Bianco Pisano di San Torpè, Monteregio di Massa Marittima, Vin Santo, Vin Santo del Chianti Classico, Carmignano Vin Santo, Vermentino, Colline Lucchesi, Bianco di Pitigliano, Montecarlo, Bolgheri, Ansonica Costa dell'Argentario, Val di Cornia, Sauvignon, Sant'Antimo (Bianco, Chardonnay, Pinot Grigio), Montescudaio, Val d'Arbia, Bianco Vergine Valdichiana, Elba (Bianco, Ansonica, Ansonica Passito)*

ROSÉS
- *D.O.C. wines: Colli dell'Etruria Centrale, Bolgheri (Rosato, Vin Santo Occhio di Pernice), Monteregio di Massa Marittima (Rosato, Vin Santo Occhio di Pernice), Parrina, Val di Cornia, Vin Santo del Chianti Classico Occhio di Pernice, Sant'Antimo Vin Santo Occhio di Pernice, Carmignano (Rosato, Vin Santo Occhio di Pernice), Montecarlo Vin Santo Occhio di Pernice, Elba (Rosato, Vin Santo Occhio di Pernice.)*

The wines of Emilia - Romagna

Principal wines of Emilia - Romagna

REDS

- *D.O.C. wines: Colli Piacentini (Barbera, Gutturnio, Pinot Nero, Cabernet Sauvignon, Bonarda), Rosso dei colli di Parma, Lambrusco di Sorbara, Lambrusco Reggiano, Lambrusco Grasparossa di Castelvetro, Lambrusco Salamino di Santa Croce, Colli Bolognesi (Barbera, Cabernet Sauvignon, Merlot), Bosco Eliceo (Merlot, Fortana), Sangiovese di Romagna, Cagnina di Romagna*

WHITES

- *D.O.C.G. wine: Albana di Romagna*
- *D.O.C. wines: Colli Piacentini (Monterosso Val D'Arda, Val Nure, Trebbiano Val Trebbia, Malvasia, Sauvignon, Chardonnay, Ortrugo, Pinot Grigio.), Colli di Parma (Malvasia, Sauvignon.), Bianco di Scandiano, Montuni del Reno, Colli Bolognesi (Bianco, Pignoletto, Riesling Italico, Pinot Bianco, Sauvignon, Chardonnay), Bosco Eliceo (Bianco, Sauvignon.), Trebbiano di Romagna, Pagadebit di Romagna, Pagadebit di Romagna Bertinoro, Romagna Albana Spumante*

ROSÉS

- *D.O.C. wines: Lambrusco di Sorbara, Lambrusco Reggiano, Lambrusco Salamino di Santa Croce, Lambrusco Grasparossa di Castelvetro*

This region, which almost cuts across northern central Italy, takes up much of the fertile Po River Valley. Here, the richness of soil allows for the successful production of both crops and livestock, but also results in a quantity orientated wine industry. The result is Lambrusco, made from grapes growing in high-trained 'tendoni' vines.

Lambrusco is a pleasant, slightly fizzy, unpretentious wine that should be drunk young and slightly chilled, as an accompaniment to the rich local food. Most is light red in colour, although rosé forms can also be found. White Lambruisco also exists, but most is hardly commendable. Superior varieties bear the D.O.C. label. These are from Sorbara, Castelvetro and Santa Croce, all around the town of Modena and also Reggiano from Reggio Emilia.

The Romagna part of the region, on the eastern Adriatic side, has one D.O.C.G. and two D.O.C. wines. The former encompasses the different styles made from the white Albana grape, dry, amabile and spumante, while the latter consist of a red, Sangiovese di Romagna, which at its best can rival most that Tuscany can offer, and a white, Trebbiano di Romagna.

Other D.O.C. wines in the region come from Emilia around the city of Bologna and the towns of Piacenza, Parma and Scandiano.

An interesting development, particularly in the Emilia hills, has been the production of wines using foreign grapes, some of which have already attained the D.O.C. status. Examples are Cabernet Sauvignon, Merlot and Pinot Noir for reds, and Sauvignon Blanc, Pinot Gris and Pinot Blanc for whites.

The success of these innovations, coupled with the fact that an increasing number of growers are moving in the direction of quality rather than quantity, earmarks the region as one with great future potential. ❧

The wines of Marche

The castle of Gradara, where the unfortunate Francesca da Rimini died, is in the province of Pesaro, in the Marche region and not in Rimini or Romagna as is commonly believed.

The Marche region lies on the eastern side of Italy, between the Appenine Mountains and the Adriatic sea. It borders with Romagna to the north and Abruzzo to the south. Although the terrain is hilly with fertile calciferous and clay soils and the weather is temperate with hot dry summers, the region has not yet realised its full wine producing potential; unlike Emilia-Romagna innovation has been slow to take place.

Three wines of note exist, two reds and one white. These are Rosso Conero from Ancona, Rosso Piceno from Ascoli Piceno and Verdicchio from Jesi. The best red, Rosso Conero, is made from the Montepulciano grape with a little Sangiovese added, while in Rosso Piceno the proportions are more or less reversed. Verdicchio is produced using the homonymous grape variety with the addition of some Malvasia and Trebbiano. The latter grape seems to find its way into many of the region's whites, most of which, unfortunately, lack interest. ❦

Principal wines of Marche

REDS

D.O.C. wines: Rosso Conero, Rosso Piceno, Colli Pesaresi (Sangiovese, Rosso, Focara), Lacrima di Morro, Vernaccia di Serrapetrona, Esino

WHITES

D.O.C. wines: Verdicchio dei Castelli di Jesi, Verdicchio di Matelica, Bianco dei Colli Pesaresi, Roncaglia dei Colli Pesaresi, Bianchello di Metauro, Falerio dei Colli Ascolani, Colli Maceratesi, Esino

The wines of Abruzzo and Molise

These regions lie due south of the Marche, again being sandwiched between the Appenines and the Adriatic sea. Molise was formerly part of Abruzzo, but is now administrated separately.

In common with the Marche, the Montepulciano and Trebbiano grape varieties are widely used. On the other hand, the Sangiovese is not utilised to the same extent.

The vines grow on hills just inland from the sea and mostly use the high 'tendoni' system of vine training. However the Montepulciano d'Abruzzo D.O.C. wines show complexity of character as well as good ageing potential. At their very best they are unbelievably good. Although the same cannot be said for the Trebbiano wines, one producer turns out what is certainly one of the best whites in Italy, almost equalling the very best that Bordeaux and Burgundy can offer. A very fine deep rosé, Cerasuolo, is also produced and should not be missed. ❦

Principal wines of Abruzzo

REDS

D.O.C. wines: Montepulciano d'Abruzzo, Montepulciano d'Abruzzo Colline Teramane

WHITES

D.O.C. wines: Trebbiano d'Abruzzo

ROSÉS

D.O.C. wines: Montepulciano d'Abruzzo Cerasuolo

Principal wines of Molise

REDS

D.O.C. wines: Biferno Rosso, Pentro (di Isernia) Rosso

WHITES

D.O.C. wines: Biferno Bianco, Pentro (di Isernia) Bianco

ROSÉS

D.O.C. wines: Biferno Rosato, Pentro (di Isernia) Rosato.

The wines of Umbria

Principal wines of Umbria

REDS

- *D.O.C.G wines: Sagrantino di Montefalco (also a sweet variety), Torgiano Rosso Riserva*
- *D.O.C. wines: Torgiano Rosso, Torgiano (Cabernet Sauvignon and Pinot Nero.), Colli Altotiberini, Colli Amerini, Colli del Trasimeno, Colli Martani Sangiovese, Colli Perugini, Montefalco*
- *Other: San Giorgio*

WHITES

- *D.O.C. wines: Orvieto, Torgiano, Torgiano (Chardonnay, Pinot Grigio, Riesling Italico and Spumante.), Colli Altotiberini, Colli Amerini, Colli Almerini Malvasia, Colli del Trasimeno, Colli Martani (Grechetto and Trebbiano), Colli Perugini, Montefalco*

ROSÉS

- *D.O.C. wines: Torgiano, Colli Altotiberini, Colli Amerini, Colli Perugini*

Wine was made in Umbria, the green heart of Italy, over 2000 years ago, when the Etruscans and Umbri occupied the territory. Unfortunately, the Romans didn't take to the product and it wasn't until the late middle ages that wine making in the region became renowned again.

Umbria, set around the Appenine Mountains, consists of gentle verdant uplands. The soil is rich in lime and the temperature is cool. These conditions seem ideal for wine making and yet the region is well down the list in Italy's wine production. The reason is probably a lack of local initiative, as those who have tried have achieved very promising results.

The wine areas of Umbria can be divided into two broad zones: a large one around Perugia, the regional capital, starting at the far north and reaching southwards just to the town of Spoleto, and a smaller one around the town of Orvieto, bordering onto Lazio on the west. About 80% of the product is white, of which the majority is ' Orvieto', a pale crisp wine, which can also be found in a sweet golden form. The region's whites are based on both local and imported grape varieties. Malvasia bianca lunga, Trebbiano (Spoletino and Toscano), Grechetto, Garganega and Verdello are more or less local, while Chardonnay and Sauvignon are French in origin.

Although red wine is made in lesser quantity, some products are surprisingly good and even first class. Those wines made in Torgiano, just south of Perugia, deserve particular mention. Just as the whites, modern French varieties are used as are traditionally proven fairly local Italian ones. Of particular importance are the Italian Sangiovese, Cannaiolo, Montepulciano, Sagrantino and Ciliegiolo and the French Merlot, Cabernet (Franc and Sauvignon) and Pinot Noir. ✎

The wines of Lazio

Lazio has produced wine since at least Roman times. Nowadays the region is slowly trying to reverse a trend towards quantity, as an improvement in quality is becoming the main priority of an increasing number of producers.

The major Lazio wine-growing region lies south of Rome, in the Castelli Romani. This is where Frascati and Marino, the two best whites are made. North of Rome, the wine country is more scattered. Here, the most famous area lies around the lake of Bolzena where the renowned 'Est! Est!! Est!!! di Montefiascone' is made.
The story as to how the wine got its strange name goes as follows. It is said that in the twelfth century a wine-loving German Bishop was travelling to Rome. The cleric was in the habit of sending his servant ahead to sample what wine each tavern could offer. The word 'Est!' marked on the tavern door would tell the Bishop the wine was good. At Montefiascone the servant was bowled over and wrote the fatal word three times, with an increasing number of exclamation marks each time. It seems that the Bishop didn't get to Rome. He had found his destiny in the tavern and there he stayed! Unfortunately, the present Est! Est!! Est!!! wines contain a high proportion of Trebbiano and are rarely inspiring.

The region is primarily known for its whites although the production of red is slowly gaining ground. Traditionally, the region's white wines are made by a full skin fermentation of a Malvasia-Trebbiano mixture. This is to maximise the product's taste and improve its perfume. However, the production of a fruity wine, intended for early drinking, is accompanied by a major drawback, namely a marked tendency to oxidise. The wine does not travel well and on keeping turns brownish and acquires a flat taste.
Happily, an increasing number of producers are overcoming these problems by improving their manufacturing techniques in all the distinct phases of wine production. In the vineyard, less Trebbiano and more Malvasia, particularly Malvasia of Latium (as opposed to Malvasia of Candia) is being used. Also, stricter quality control, as to which bunches should be excluded from the wine, is applied in harvesting the grapes. However, most important of all, a carefully managed low-temperature skinless fermentation is applied in the cellar.

The result of these improvements is a fruity wine of good consistency and with a far greater resistance to oxidation.
The use of Chardonnay has also caught on and is increasing.

The production of red wines in Lazio is of secondary importance but on the increase. The grapes used tend to be Sangiovese and Montepulciano, but Merlot, Cesanese (comune and d'Affile.), Barbera, Cannaiolo, Ciliegiolo and Cabernet Franc, are variously utilised by different producers. Much of the D.O.C. made is of moderate quality but more recently some firms have made surprisingly good Vino da Tavola products. Unfortunately, the better reds are far more expensive than whites of an equivalent quality. ✺

Principal wines of Lazio

REDS
- *D.O.C. wines: Aleatico di Gradoli (Sweet and often fortified), Cerveteri, Cesanese del Piglio, Cesanese di Olevano Romano, Cori, Merlot di Aprilia, Sangiovese di Aprilia, Velletri, Vignanello, Genazzano, Colli Etruschi Viterbesi (Rosso, Grechetto Rosso, Sangiovese, Canaiolo and Merlot.)*
- *Others: I Quattro Mori, Vigna del Vassallo*

WHITES
- *D.O.C. wines: Frascati, Marino, Bianco Capena , Cerveteri, Colli Albani, Colli Lanuvini, Cori, Est! Est!! Est!!! di Montefiascone, Montecompatri Colonna, Trebbiano di Aprilia, Velletri, Zagarolo, Vignanello (Bianco and Greco.), Genazzano, Colli Etruschi Viterbesi (Bianco, Grechetto Bianco and Moscatello Secco.), Orvieto (Essentially a wine from Umbria, but produced in Lazio as well.)*

ROSÉS
- *D.O.C. wines: Vignanello, Sangiovese di Aprilia, Colli Etruschi Viterbesi*

The wines of Campania

Principal wines of Campania

REDS

- D.O.C.G. wine: Taurasi.
- D.O.C. wines: Taburno, Ischia, Solopaca, Falerno del Massico (Rosso, Primitivo.), Vesuvio, Capri, Lacryma Christi del Vesuvio, Castel san Lorenzo (Rosso, Barbera.), Cilento, Sant'Agata de'Goti, Guardiolo, Campi Flegrei, Costa d'Amalfi, Costa d'Amalfi Ravello / Furore / Tramonti, Aglianico, Aglianico del Taburno, Penisola Sorrentina, Penisola Sorrentina Gragnano / Lettere / Sorrento, Piedirosso, Montevetrano.
- Other: Gragnano

WHITES

- D.O.C. wines: Greco di Tufo, Greco, Fiano di Avellino, Ischia (Bianco, Forastera, Biancolella.), Capri, Falerno del Massico, Vesuvio, Lacryma Christi del Vesuvio, Castel san Lorenzo (Bianco, Moscato.), Campi Flegrei, Sant'Agata de'Goti, Guardiolo, Penisola Sorrentina, Penisola Sorrentina Sorrento, Asprinio di Aversa, Solopaca, Costa d'Amalfi, Costa d'Amalfi Ravello / Furore / Tramonti, Cilento, Taburno (Bianco, Coda di Volpe.), Falanghina

ROSÉS

- D.O.C. wines: Aglianico del Taburno, Vesuvio, Lacryma Christi del Vesuvio, Solopaca, Guardiolo, Castel san Lorenzo, Cilento, Costa d'Amalfi, Costa d'Amalfi Ravello / Furore / Tramonti, Sant'Agata de'Goti

Whereas every region in Italy can claim at least one indigenous grape variety, Campania boasts no less than four: the red Piedirosso and the whites Coda di Volpe, Fiano and Falanghina. In spite of this, the two best-known varieties used, the Aglianico and Greco, both have Greek origin. The former was originally called Vitis Hellenica, then Ellenico and finally Aglianico. It was brought to Basilicata from ancient Greece by settlers in pre-Roman times. Subsequently it spread to Campania and other neighbouring regions.

Campania has grown vines since ancient times. The wine Falerno was the best known in the days of the Roman Empire. How close (or otherwise) this was to the modern Falerno del Massico, now grown to the north of the region near the border with Lazio, is very uncertain, however. More recently, Pope Paul III's bottler, Sante Lancerio, recorded in his chronicles that he held the wines of the kingdom of Naples in greater esteem than those of any other part of Italy. Indeed, this reputation was maintained right up to the middle of the nineteenth century. But then a decline, which even now is showing only very slight signs of recovery, set in.

At present, the best wines are made in the provinces of Avellino and Benevento. Indeed, the former is the home of one of the oldest enology colleges in Italy and also boasts the production of Taurasi, probably the best and most renowned of all the region's wines. The vineyards are found in wooded uplands, coastal hills and other areas of fairly high altitude, where the cooler temperature is more suited to the growing of vines.

Unfortunately there are several promising locations that still need exploiting. Also many vineyards are being run down and even abandoned. Campania is, in fact, one of the very few Italian regions that imports more wine than it exports. This is a dubious distinction, particularly when one considers the region's former eminent position as well as its fertile, volcanic soil and large number of indigenous varieties. 🐌

Wines of Basilicata

As with Puglia, wine making dates from ancient times. However, in contrast, whereas Puglia can boast as many as 24 DOC wines, Basilicata has only one.
This is the Aglianico del Vulture, a powerful red made from the Aglianico grape, brought to the region by the Greeks in the sixth or seventh century before Christ. The vineyards lie in volcanic soil, 750 metres above sea level on mount Vulture, approximately fifty-five kilometres north of the city of Potenza. Strangely, this is, at its best, a better wine than anything Puglia can produce! It possesses great intensity of both perfume and flavour, is smooth and rounded and has great ageing potential. At lower altitudes where the climate is hotter, the Aglianico grape is not so successful, as seen from its other wines.

Other reds are made using Aleatico, Bombino Nero, Ciliegiolo, Montepulciano, Sangiovese and Primitivo grapes. White varieties include Bombino Bianco, Asprinio, Fiano, Malvasia, Trebbiano, Moscato Bianco, Pinot Grigio and Chardonnay. The region does not appear to make any rosé wine of note but sweet wines and sparkling wines, both white and red, are produced. ❧

Wines of Calabria

In common with the rest of southern Italy, wine production in Calabria is of Greek origin.

Due to its mountainous nature, the region offers many variations in microclimates, ranging from hot coastal areas to chilly inland heights. Also there is a great diversity of soils; clay, marl, sandstone, gravel, alluvial and volcanic being found in different places. Consequently there is plenty of high ground with temperate conditions having a range of soils to choose from, which should provide suitable situations for the plantation of many different grape varieties. Yet the region has fallen away badly with only about 5% of its area used for wine production.

The most important grape is the Gaglioppo, used to make Cirò red, a powerful dark coloured wine with good ageing potential. This and Savuto, grown on steep slopes at an altitude of approximately 150 metres are the best the region makes.
Other grapes used are Greco Nero, Nerello Capuccio, Nerello Mascalese and Sangiovese for reds and Greco Bianco, Trebbiano and Moscato for whites. French varieties have also been planted, but with only a few good results.

As with Puglia and Basilicata the overwhelming majority of the wine produced is red. Nevertheless some very good rosés and sweet whites are made. Unfortunately however, in common with its neighbours, the general standard is only moderate in quality. ❧

Principal wines of Basilicata

REDS

- D.O.C. wine: Aglianico del Vulture.
- Others: Aglianico dei Colli Lucani, Aglianico di Matera, Montepulciano di Basilicata, Canneto, Metapontum

WHITES

Asprinio, Metapontum, Malvasia del Vulture, Malvasia della Lucania, Moscato del Vulture

Principal wines of Calabria

REDS

- D.O.C. wines: Cirò, Donnici, Lamezia, Melissa, Pollino, Sant'Anna Isola di Capo Rizzuto, Savuto, San Vito di Luzzi, Scavigna, Verbicano, Bivongi

WHITES

- D.O.C. wines: Cirò, Greco di Bianco, Melissa, Lamezia, San Vito di Luzzi, Scavigna, Verbicano, Bivongi

ROSÉS

- D.O.C. wines: Cirò, Sant'Anna Isola di Capo Rizzuto, Lamezia, San Vito di Luzzi, Scavigna, Verbicano, Bivongi
- Others: Cerasuolo di Scilla

The wines of Puglia

Principal wines of Puglia

REDS

*D.O.C. wines: Salice Salentino
(Rosso, Aleatico Dolce.), Cacc'e Mmitte
di Lucera, Rosso Barletta, Rosso Canosa,
Castel del Monte (Rosso, Pinot Nero,
Aglianico.), Nardò, Rosso di Cerignola,
Alezio, Leverano, Aleatico di Puglia,
Copertino, Gioia del Colle (Rosso,
Primitivo, Aglianico Dolce.), Lizzano
(Rosso, Negro Amaro, Malvasia Nera.),
Brindisi, Matino, Orta Nova, Ostuni
Ottavianello, Primitivo di Manduria,
San Severo, Squinzano, Monte Vetrano*

WHITES

*D.O.C. wines: Locorotondo, Castel del
Monte (Bianco, Chardonnay, Sauvignon,
Pinot Bianco, Bianco da Pinot Nero),
Gioia del Colle, Gravina, Leverano,
Lizzano, Martina Franca, San Severo,
Moscato di Trani, Ostuni,
Salice Salentino Bianco, Pinot Bianco)*

ROSÉS

*D.O.C. wines: Salice Salentino,
Castel del Monte (Rosato, Aglianico),
Squinzano, Gioia del Colle, Leverano,
Alezio, Brindisi, Orta Nova, Copertino,
Lizzano (Rosato, Negro Amaro),
San Severo, Matino, Nardò*

The Greeks and Phoenicians brought the art of wine making to this region. In spite of many invasions after the fall of the Roman Empire, the Puglia has constantly been one of Italy's most copious producers of wine and olive oil. Now it vies with Sicily as the country's top quantity wine supplier.

The region is fortunate in having a good soil, rich in calcium and iron, but not so lucky with its climate, which is rather too hot for the production of consistently good white wine.
Consequently reds easily outnumber whites, but surprisingly, some very good rosé wines are made. Although some hilly ground to the north and cooling sea breezes (together with the greater rainfall they bring), in the southern Salento peninsula offer better conditions, much of the production takes place on less attractive sites.
There the emphasis is on quantity, with a corresponding quality reduction.

The principal red grape varieties are Negroamaro, Uva di Troia, Malvasia nera, Primitivo di Manduria (also used as a blending variety in Vermouth production), and Bombino Nero.
Although Sangiovese and Montepulciano are also used, they are less successful than in Tuscany and Abruzzo respectively.
The best of the reds are probably Salice Salentino, Castel del Monte, Squinzano and Rosso di Cerignola.

In spite of the difficult conditions a successful white wine, Locorotondo, is produced from both Bianco di Alessano and Verdeca grapes. Other whites are made from Malvasia, Trebbiano and Bombino Bianco but are less successful. Some fine sweet wines are also made. In this category, the red Aleatico di Puglia and the White Moscato di Trani are noteworthy.

A recent attempt to use noble French varieties has proved to be a difficult enterprise. There have been a few surprising achievements but only the future will show if this is more generally successful. 🕏

The wines of Sardegna

Wine making in Sardinia is said to date from the eighth century, B.C., mainly because of Phoenician traders. However, it didn't prosper fully until the thirteenth century, when the settlers from Spain brought many new varieties to the island. Even today, the traditional wines produced have a character which is more Spanish than Italian.

Although hills, mountains and plateaux, all very suitable for vine growing, account for around 85% of the total area, most vineyards are to be found in the more accessible lower ground. The climate of the island tends to be very warm and dry with little rainfall. The soil has an underlying rock consisting of basically granite or volcanic deposits, usually mixed with varying amounts of sand, limestone, chalk and clay.

The grape varieties used show a wide range of character and origin. The traditional grapes of Iberian provenance, Bovale, Cannonau, Carignano, Girò and Monica for reds and Torbato for whites, often give rise to strong (at time fortified) dessert wines, or to powerful products suitable for blending, a practice which, however, has now mainly ceased on the island. About thirty years ago, in response to the worldwide demand for lighter, fruitier and fresher products, co-operatives promoted a rapid change towards this direction. More recently, the introduction of a host of French, Italian and German grape varieties, both red and white, is complicating the situation; many new products are being made as well as the traditional ones.

Sardinia can be divided into four basic wine zones. Generally, the hottest parts are those to the south and west, facing North Africa, while those to the north and east, influenced by breezes from the Tyrrhenian Sea, are somewhat cooler. Rainfall is low, particularly in the south, a factor that has led to the irrigation of many vineyards.

The northern zone consists of three districts, Gallura, Sassari and Alghero. Cooler conditions in Gallura results in the production of mainly white Vermentino and Muscat wines, while elsewhere whites and reds (from Cannonau) are made in about equal amounts. The Torbato grape, grown at Alghero, can produce some of the finest dry white wines of the island. The eastern hills of Gennargentu produce mainly red wines, but although Cannonau is the main grape variety, Bovale and Monica are also used. The west central zone around Bosa and Oristano is hot and dry at the southern end but milder towards the north, where the white Malvasia di Bosa is produced. The most typical of all Sardinian white wines, Vernaccia di Oristano, produced from the indigenous homonimous grape, is made in the hotter, southern part of the zone. Other varieties used are Nuragus and Trebbiano for whites and Bovale and Sangiovese for reds. The southern zone of Campidano and Sulcis, due to its very hot and dry climate, is suited to the production of dessert wines made mainly from Malvasia, Cirò, Nasco and Moscato grapes. Dry reds are made from Cannonau, Monica and Carignano while the Nuragus, a grape of Phoenician origin is used to make whites.

Unlike Italian practice, most Sardinian wines are sold under varietal names. Exceptions are Campidano di Terralba, Mandrolisai and Anghelu Ruju. ❧

Principal wines of Sardegna

REDS

- *D.O.C. wines: Arborea Sangiovese, Campidano di Terralba, Cannonau di Sardegna, Mandrolisai, Carignano del Sulcis, Girò di Cagliari, Monica di Cagliari, Monica di Sardegna, Cabernet di Alghero Sangiovese di Alghero, Cagnulari di Alghero, Alghero.*
- *Other: Anghelu Ruju*

WHITES

- *D.O.C. wines: Vernaccia di Oristano, Nuragus di Cagliari, Moscato di Sardegna Spumante, Moscato di Sorso-Sennori, Moscato di Cagliari, Vermentino di Sardegna, Vermentino di Gallura, Arborea Trebbiano, Malvasia di Bosa, Malvasia di Cagliari, Nasco di Cagliari, Torbato di Alghero, Chardonnay di Alghero, Sauvignon di Alghero, Vermentino di Alghero, Alghero, Sardegna Semidano*

ROSÉS

- *D.O.C. wines: Arborea Sangiovese, Cannonau di Sardegna, Carignano del Sulcis, Mandrolisai, Alghero*

The wines of Sicilia

Principal wines of Puglia

REDS

- D.O.C. wines: Marsala Rubino,
  Cerasuolo di Vittoria, Faro, Etna,
  Eloro (Rosso, Nero d'Avola, Frappato,
  Pignatello, Pachino.), Menfi Bonera,
  Sanbuca di Sicilia (Rosso,
  Cabernet Sauvignon.),
  Santa Margherita di Belice
  (Rosso, Nero d'Avola, Sangiovese.)
- Others: Rosso del Conte, Vino Fiore

WHITES

- D.O.C. wines: Marsala (Oro, Ambra.),
  Moscato di Noto, Malvasia delle Lipari,
  Moscato di Pantelleria,
  Moscato di Siracusa, Bianco d'Alcamo,
  Etna, Contessa Entellina
  (Bianco, Sauvignon.), Menfi
  (Bianco, Ansonica, Feudo dei Fiori.),
  Sanbuca di Sicilia, Santa Margherita
  di Belice (Bianco, Catarratto, Ansonica.),
  Chardonnay, Grecanico.
- Others: Nozze d'Oro, Prima Goccia,
  Colomba Platino, Sanbuca di Sicilia

ROSÉS

- D.O.C. wines: Etna, Eloro

The art of wine making was brought to Sicily by the ancient Greeks. Since then, the island has been ruled by the Romans, Byzantines, Arabs, Normans, Germans, French, Spanish and Austrians before eventually becoming part of Italy. Thus it comes as no surprise that Sicilian wines have less in common than those of the rest of Italy than one would otherwise expect.

In contrast to most Italian regions, 95% of the product is white. This seems rather strange for a hot Mediterranean island but becomes more understandable when a closer look is taken. Most of the wine produced is sweet, much of it fortified. In this, an interesting comparison with Andalusia in southern Spain can be seen. Actually, Sicily's climate and terrain go a long way in offsetting its southerly position. Ideal hills with hot sunny days but cooler than expected nights are excellent for good viticulture. Also, the region can boast a number of indigenous grape varieties with real character.

Unfortunately, the island's potential was wrecked by massive overproduction and although this trend has now been reversed and an increasing number of growers are putting quality first, only 2.5% of the output is granted D.O.C. status. In the past much of the produce was exported to France for blending purposes, a market that stimulated high yields. A drop in demand for this has encouraged the production of better wines.

The region can be divided into six major wine making areas. These are in the provinces of Trapani (where Marsala is made), Agrigento, Ragusa, Messina, The Aeolian Islands and the island of Pantelleria. Each tends to make its particular wine from one or more dominant indigenous grape varieties. White grapes of character are Ansonica and Catarratto. Red varieties with high potential are Nero d'Avola, Frappato and Nerello Mascalese. Other indigenous grapes are Grillo and Grecanico (whites) and Perricone (red).

The best-known wine in Sicily is undoubtedly Marsala. It is sweet and sometimes fortified. Unfortunately much of what is made is an inferior product aimed for use in the kitchen. The top quality wine can be found in the Marsala Vergine and sometimes the Marsala Superiore categories. Strangely, the wine was discovered by an English merchant some 200 years ago. Less well-known sweet wines of real interest are the Malvasia delle Lipari, the Moscato di Pantelleria and the rarely seen Moscato di Noto. Dry whites include Bianco d'Alcamo and Contessa Entellina, while major reds are Cerasuolo di Vittoria, Faro and Rosso del Conte. The hills around mount Etna produce white, red and rosé wines. Finally, it should be noted that some of the best Sicilian creations do not have D.O.C. status. These are included in the list on the left. ❧

The wines of Northern Spain

Northern Spain can be divided into three basic wine making regions. These are Rioja in the centre, Catalonia on the eastern side and Galicia in the west, north of Portugal.

(a) Rioja

When phylloxera devastated the Bordeaux vineyards in the 1870's, a number of French producers crossed the Pyrenees into Spain and set up in Rioja. Later, when the bug also attacked Spain, they returned to France.
However, the locals had learnt their ideas and methods, which in time gave them a big advantage over other wine producing regions in the country. Not surprisingly, Rioja was, in 1926, the first region in Spain to get any kind of quality control.

The Rioja vineyards lie along both banks of the river Ebro, and take up an area about 120 km. long by 40 km. wide. The soil throughout the region consists variously of clay, chalk, limestone, and alluvial deposits. The climate, especially on the higher ground, (the vineyards average about 500 metres above sea level), is temperate by Spanish standards. Moreover, the mountain chain, the Sierra de Cantabria protects the region from cold northerly winds.

In Rioja, red is much more important than white. The main variety is the Tempranillo, which is used in conjunction with Garnacha, Mazuelo and Graciano grapes. Traditionally, too much emphasis was placed on longevity and strength. More modern techniques are producing softer and fruitier products, the best of which seem to age just as well.

The Rioja region is divided into three basic areas, the Alta, Alavesa and Baja. The Rioja Alta, situated south of the Ebro on the western end, is the finest and most celebrated. The soil is mainly clay but also has chalk in places and is rich in iron containing minerals. The climate is the coolest in the region. Given these favourable conditions, the wines are the most refined and the longest lived. The Rioja Alavesa lies north of the river. It has a predominantly limestone soil and a warmer climate.

It produces mainly aromatic reds of a light and pleasant nature. The Rioja Baja lies on both sides of the river on the eastern end. It has the hottest climate and heaviest soil. Typically, its reds are robust and rather coarse, with a high alcohol content. Most is drunk locally or used for blending.

The region does produce some dry white wines using mainly the Viura grape variety and also a few rosés. As with the reds, the Rioja Alta makes the best.

Very close to Rioja lie Navarra to the north and Cariñená to the south. The former, at its best, is increasingly producing reds on a par with the finest Riojas while the latter, traditionally the maker of heavy and powerful wines, is now modernising to yield lighter, softer products.

Principal wines of Northern Spain

REDS
- D.O. Ca. wine: Rioja.
- D.O. wines: Catalonia, Ampurdán-Costa Brava, Conca de Barberá, Costeres del Segre, Penedès, Priorato, Tarragona, Terra Alta, Calatayud, Campo de Borja, Cariñena, Navarra, Somontano, Rias Baixas, Ribeiro, Valdeorras, Chacolí de Guetaria.

WHITES
- D.O.Ca. wine: Rioja.
- D.O. wines: Cava, Catalonia, Alella, Ampurdán-Costa Brava, Penedès, Priorato, Tarragona, Terra Alta, Calatayud, Cariñena, Navarra, Somontano, Chacolí de Guetaria.

ROSÉS
- D.O.Ca. wine: Rioja.
- D.O. wine: Catalonia, Ampurdán-Costa Brava, Penedès, Priorato, Campo de Borja, Cariñena, Navarra, Somontano.

(b) Catalonia

This is a high yield region running along the Barcelona coast, mainly due south of the city.

Winters are mild and summers hot, but sea breezes help stop the temperature rising too high. Also, the vineyards lie at high altitude, and this helps keep them cool. The region has a wide variety of soils and is therefore able to produce a wide range of wines. The seven denominations are, thanks to the different soils, much more distinctive than those in Rioja.

By far the most important area is that of Penedés, just south of Barcelona. Here, big-bodied fruity reds in a similar style to Rioja are produced. Although traditional varieties such as Monastrell, Mencia and Bobal are used as in the rest of Northern Spain, an increasing number of growers are using Cabernet and Pinot Noir grapes, with very promising results. In the same innovative vein, Chardonnay and Gewürztraminer are being used to make some excellent whites. However, the most celebrated products of the area are the Champenoise sparkling wines known as Cava, which is made from blends of Viura / Macabeo, Parellada and Xarel-Lo grapes. Regarding still wines, too much emphasis was formerly placed on ageing. Fortunately, modern ideas have resulted in products intended for early drinking, when they are still delicate and fruity. A recently created denomination, Conca de Barberá, produces reds similar to those of Penedés, using both traditional and French grape varieties.

Further south, lie the areas of Tarragona and Priorato. In the latter, a combination of rocky volcanic soil and the Garnacha grape produce a red which is very strong and almost black in colour, and also a golden sweet dessert wine which is aged and made to oxidise in order to develop a so-called rancio flavour. Tarragona produces reds that are robust and high in alcohol content. As those of Priorato, they are used mainly for blending. More interesting is a sweet red wine rather reminiscent of port. Similar products are made in Terra Alta, a third denomination in this area.

The last two denominations lie north of Barcelona. Alella, close to the big city, is getting smaller. It produces mainly white wines of which the medium sweet ones are the most interesting. Finally, Ampurdán, on the Costa Brava, produces mainly rosés. It also makes same light red and sparkling wines worth investigating.

(c) Galicia

This region lies in the extreme northwest of Spain, bordering on Portugal to the south and the Atlantic Ocean to the west. Although its citizens are by far the biggest consumers in the country and the region boasts no less than five local grape varieties (Albariño, Godello, Loureia, Torrontés and Treixadura), only the two most southerly provinces, Pontevedra and Orense make any wine worth mentioning. The climate, granite soil and some of the grape varieties used are similar to those in Portugal, but the quality of the product is disappointing by comparison. Pontevedra contains the Rias Baixas region, which itself has three demarcated areas, Condado de Tea, El Rosal and Val de Salnes. The best products are pleasant sparkling wines and some very dry greenish whites, similar to but not as good as the 'Vinho Verdes' of Portugal. Orense has three regions, Ribeiro, Valdeorras and Monterrey, the first two having D.O. classification. Heavy, alcoholic reds, predominantly used for blending, are produced. More recently, however, some lighter products have been made with encouraging results. This improvement is especially true for Ribeiro, which also makes a satisfying Portuguese style white. ❧

The wines of Central Spain

For convenience, central Spain can be divided into five wine producing regions. These are the Ribera del Duero and the Rueda, both north of Madrid, La Mancha and its surrounding districts due south of the capital and the areas around Valencia and Alicante, both near the sea on the eastern side of the country.

The Ribera del Duero is particularly famous for its red wines that include Vega Sicilia, the best in the country and fully equivalent to the best Bordeaux products. Although the region specialises in the Tinto Fino (Tempranilla) and Garnacha Tinto grape varieties, these very special wines include Cabernet Sauvignon, Merlot and Malbec in their blends. The vineyards lie along the banks of the river Duero at high altitude where the summer days are very hot but are followed by cold nights. This, combined with the chalky soil, seems to be the key to the successful viticulture. The Ribera de Burgos, an adjoining area, produces light red wines that are good but hardly great.

The Rueda, home of the white Verdejo grape, is traditionally known for its production of fortified wines, similar but inferior to Andalusia's sherry. Nowadays, popular demand has resulted in an ever-increasing switch towards fresh table wines. The outcome has been a number of fruity, aromatic characterful whites. Neighbouring districts produce powerful dark reds, light reds and interesting rosés, none of which have the Denominación de Origen classification.

La Mancha (Don Quixote country) is Europe's biggest wine making region, having four D.O. areas, which, however, account for only 10% of the total wine produced. These are Valdepeñas, Manchuela, Méntrida and La Mancha itself. Curiously, although the major grape variety planted in Valdepeñas is the white Airén, most of the wine produced is red. This is because the Airén is blended with the highly pigmented Cencibel red grape. Méntrida and Manchuela both produce heavy reds, mainly sold for blending. Some lighter red wines and rosés are also made. La Mancha has traditionally been the home of powerful white wines, but as with the Rueda, modern ideas are resulting in the production of an increasing quantity of fruitier and less alcoholic products.

The two D.O. areas near Valencia are Utiel-Requena and Valencia itself. The former uses the Bobal grape to make extremely dark reds and fresh , delicately aromatic rosés, while the latter employs the Merseguera variety in making whites of limited interest and at times rough and alcoholic. Again, modern requirements and techniques have led to improved products. The Valencia D.O. is split into three sections of which the most southerly borders onto the Alicante region. This has four areas: Almansa, Yecca, Jumilla, and Alicante. The first three are responsible mainly for heavy alcoholic reds much used for blending. However, Jumilla also makes very reasonable whites and much pleasant rosé wine. The Alicante D.O. is similar to that of Jumilla except that more white is made. Also, an interesting sweet wine is produced from the Muscatel grape. As with the rest of central Spain a move away from highly coloured powerful wines and towards softer, fruitier products lower in alcohol, is taking place.

As is evident from above, Central Spain can boast many local grapes, some of which are mentioned above. Garnacha Tinta, Monastrell, Garnacha Tintorera and Jaen are other much used dark-skinned varieties, while Viura and Pedro Ximénez are whites. The general drive for improvement has seen the introduction of Chardonnay and Sauvignon Blanc as well as the French red grapes mentioned in the text. ❧

Principal wines of Central Spain

R E D S

D.O. wines: Bierzo, Ribera del Duero, Toro, Almansa, Méntrida, La Mancha, Valdepeñas, Alicante, Jumilla, Utiel-Requena, Valencia, Yecla

W H I T E S

D.O. wines: Rueda, Toro, La Mancha, Valdepeñas, Alicante, Jumilla, Valencia, Yecla

R O S É S

D.O. wines: Cigales, Ribera del Duero, Toro, Méntrida, La Mancha, Valdepeñas, Alicante, Jumilla, Utiel-Requena, Valencia

The wines of Andalusia

Principal wines and grape varieties of Andalusia

WHITES

*Jerez (Palomino Fino), Málaga
(Pedro Ximénez, Moscatel de Málaga /
Moscatel de Alejandria),
Montilla-Morilés (Airén, Pedro Ximénez),
Condado de Huelva (Zalema)*

This, the most southern region in Spain, contains four D.O. wine-producing areas. They are Jerez, Montilla-Moriles, Málaga, and Condado de Huelva. The most important of these is Jerez, whose name is synonymous with Sherry. In fact, the word 'Sherry' is an English corruption of the name.

Wine production in Jerez is ancient, originating as long ago as ten centuries before the birth of Christ. It survived many wars and occupations to attain its present position, that is, one of the most important wine centres in Spain.

The Jerez vine growing area is situated at the southernmost tip of the country, facing the Atlantic Ocean, just west of the Straits of Gibraltar. Weather conditions tend to be fairly uniform throughout the territory, which has much sunshine and little rain. However, there is greater variety in the soil, there being three main types. The finest, producing the best wines, is a mixture of clay and chalk or limestone known as 'Albariza'. The second, also a clay soil, contains less chalk and is less able to absorb humidity. It is called 'Barro'. Lastly, 'Arena', is a sandy soil that came into prominence towards the end of the nineteenth century during the phylloxera epidemic when it was discovered that the bug was unable to thrive in sand. However since this is the worst soil in which to grow grapes needed for sherry production, sites containing it are nowadays being abandoned in favour of those with clay.

All types of sherry can be placed into one of two distinctive pedigrees. The first is 'Fino' a pale elegant and delicate wine reinforced to between 15% and 15.5% alcohol. The wines are stored in butts that are exposed to the air. Very soon a layer of yeast, 'flor', forms and protects the wine from oxidation. Since the containers are continually topped up with younger wine of the same style, the yeast is kept alive for a number of years. Periodically, some of the wine is transferred from container to container, each replenishing an older wine and being itself topped up with a more recent one. This, the Solera system of ageing, ensures a constant product and consequently no vintage year on the bottle. True 'Amontillados' are old Finos which have lost their flor and been subjected to some oxidisation. They are less elegant but softer and more powerful than Finos. They have a darker colour but are equally dry.
Unfortunately most commercial so-called Amontillados are blends of 'Rayas' (inferior quality Sherries made from grapes grown on sandy soil), and sweet wines. Manzanilla is a type of Fino sherry that is made from grapes grown near the sea. The wine is crisper than Fino but has a slightly lower alcohol content.

The second type of sherry is 'Oloroso'. Whereas the Fino range of Sherries are made from grapes grown on Albariza soils, the Oloroso class uses grapes grown on Borro clay. These also undergo the Solera ageing process, but being reinforced to an alcohol level of 18%, do not form the protective layer, as this is inhibited by the extra alcohol. A true Oloroso sherry is brown in colour and increases its concentration with age. It is a dry wine but is often sweetened commercially. Blending is also used to convert it into the various Cream Sherries. Commercial specimens of these usually contain the inferior Raya, as described above.

The area of Montilla-Moriles lies inland, north east of Jerez. Montilla is similar to sherry, having the same basic styles. There are some differences however. Firstly, the main grape is the Pedro Ximénez instead of the Palomino used at Jerez. Secondly, the hotter conditions result in the Finos reaching the appropriate alcohol content without any need to fortify them. (Olorosos are fortified as at Jerez). Thirdly, fermentation takes place in characteristic earthenware 'Tinajas' rather than in the more common modern steel vats. Generally, the products are not as fine as those of Jerez.

Málaga lies to the east of the Straits of Gibraltar, facing the Mediterranean Sea. As in Montilla, the intensely hot, dry climate favours the Pedro Ximénez grape. However the Moscatel de Málaga is also widely used in the cooler mountainous northern part of the area. The wines are fundamentally dark and very sweet.
The best are probably the 'Lágrima' wines made from the Moscatel grape. Other sweet wines bear the names of the two principal grape varieties. Some dry wines are also made but generally lack the interest found in the sweet traditional ones.

The fourth area, Condado de Huelva, lies towards Portugal, north west of Jerez and also faces the Atlantic Ocean.
Its main wines, Condado Palido and Condado Viejo are fortified and similar but inferior to a Fino and Oloroso sherry respectively. Both are aged by the Solera method but lack the finesse of their Jerez counterparts. A table wine, Vino Joven, intended for early drinking, is being produced in increasing quantities. ❧

The wines of Portugal

Principal wines and grape varieties of Portugal

REDS AND ROSÉS

*Alfrocheiro Preto, Azal Tinto,
Baga (Tinta Bairrada), Bastardo,
Borraçal, Castelão Frances, Camarate,
Espadeiro Tinto, Jaen, Moreto,
Moreto do Dão, Mourisco Tinto, Ramisco,
Sousão, Tinta Amarela, Tinta Barroca,
Tinta Miuda, Tinta Negra Mole,
Tinta Pinheira, Tinta Roriz, Tinto Cão,
Touriga Francesa, Touriga Nacional,
Trincadeira, Vinhão.*

WHITES

*Alvarinho, Arinto, Arinto do Dão,
Avesso, Azal Branco, Barcelo, Bical,
Boal, Bucellas, Diagalves, Cerceal do Dão,
Encruzado, Fernão Pires, Folgazão,
Loureiro, Malvasia Babosa, Malvasia Fina,
Malvasia Candida, Malvasia Rei,
Manteudo, Moscatel strains (e.g. Moscatel
de Setúbal), Perrum, Rabigato,
Roupeiro (Codega), Sercial (Esgana Cão),
Talia, Tamarez, Terrantez, Trajadura,
Vital, Verdelho (Gouveio), Viosinho.*

*In addition to the above and some others,
Portugal has begun to use some foreign
varieties in its wines. Examples are Cabernet
Sauvignon and Merlot for reds and
Chardonnay, Gewürztraminer and Riesling
for whites.*

Portuguese wine making dates from pre-Roman times. Having survived the Moorish occupation, production and prestige increased, attaining a maximum with the country's period of greatest influence in the world, the fifteenth and sixteenth centuries.

The wines became popular in England in the seventeenth century, thanks to the trade wars with France. It was then that Port was discovered and its method of production perfected. The importing of Portuguese wine to England continued, but flourished particularly at times such as those of Nelson and Wellington, when the British were at war with their main supplier across the channel.

Badly hit by the phylloxera epidemic in the late nineteenth century, only the Port making industry has fully recovered. The table wine sector has mainly gone for quantity and local mass consumption, a surprising attitude for a country with such an illustrious wine making tradition as well as favourable climate. Indeed, it is fortunate in enjoying long sunny summers, and thanks to the proximity of the Atlantic Ocean, a lower temperature and a greater rainfall than Spain. Only now are there signs of the innovation and enterprise needed to meet international expectations.

In discussing the wines of Portugal, it is convenient to divide the country into three sections, the North, the Centre and the South.

Northern Portugal

(a) Port

The grapes are grown along the extremely steep banks of the river Douro. The ground, made up of rocky schist, is stony and seems totally unsuitable. However, over the centuries it has been worked into a soil of sorts in which the vines seem to thrive. Although Port can be made from many grape varieties, five or six are deemed to be the best. The top five are the Touriga Nacional, the Touriga Francesa, the Tinta Barroca, the Tinta Roriz and the Tinto Cão.

In the cellar, brandy (approximately 20% of the final mixture) is added to block the fermentation. Apart from increasing the alcoholic content of the wine this results in the product being very sweet. However the loss in fermentation time would result in a poor extraction of colour and tannins. Therefore a rapid skin maceration process is carried out to compensate for this. The wine is then brought to Vila Nova de Gaia, a suburb of Oporto (from which Port derives its name), where its future is decided before being shipped abroad.

The very best product in vintage years is made into Vintage Port. Here, the single wine is aged for about two to three years and then put in bottle where the ageing process is allowed to continue for up to twenty years or more. A thick deposit forms, with the result that great care will be needed in decanting and serving the wine.

A good product in a good year could be turned into Late Bottled Vintage Port. The single wine is made to complete its ageing process in cask and then bottled.
These wines are slightly lighter and do not need decanting. They are a compromise between the vintage and cheaper blended styles.

Alternatively, a number of good wines might be blended and kept in wood for a greater length of time. This would result in Aged Tawny Port, a wine that is less sweet and concentrated than the vintage varieties, but offers a delicacy of taste and a mellowness missing in these.

Finally, the wines could be blended and aged for a shorter time before being bottled. Deep coloured, big wines result in Ruby ports, while lighter wines are used to make the commercial run-of- the-mill Tawny Ports.

White Port is made in a similar way to the red, but uses white grapes. Several styles exist, running from the extremely sweet 'Lagrima' wines to the drier 'Leve Seco' ones.
Grape varieties used include Esgana-Cão, Rabigato, Malvasia Fina and Verdelho.

(b) Table wines of the Douro

Port accounts for about 50% of Douro wine. Most of the rest is table wine. Vineyards on the outer parts of the Douro valley, further from the river, seem less suited to Port production so normal wine is made instead. Most is red and very good, the Barca Velha being the best in Portugal. Not surprisingly it is made from the same grapes as Port, Touriga Nacional and Tinta Roriz being the most prominent. The result is a rich, complex wine with very good ageing potential. White wines, made from Malvasia and Viosinho are regrettably not up to the same standard.

(c) The Vinho Verde region

This is the largest wine-producing region in Portugal. The name refers to the youthful state of the wines and not their colour. Indeed, as much red is produced as white. The vines are trained along wires held in position by poles. This pergola system has taken the place of the traditional method of training them along trees. Being a densely populated region, as much space as possible is saved for other crops.

Also, this method provides the vines with plenty of circulating air, thus reducing the risk of rot, otherwise possible due to dampness caused by the proximity of the Atlantic Ocean.

The white wines are dry with a slight sparkle. They have a crisp and pleasant fresh taste. The reds, on the other hand, are coarse and far less approachable.

(d) Other Northern Regions

More reds are produced than whites. The further east one goes, the hotter and drier the climate and the greater the proportion of heavy alcoholic reds that are made.
Lighter red and white wines are produced in the cooler, more westerly places.

Central Portugal, between the Douro and Tagus rivers

(a) Bairrada

This region, on the western side, produces mainly heavy tannic reds from the Baga grape, planted on clay soils. Recently, however, some firms have developed methods of making softer wines. Also, some interesting white and rosé sparkling wines are made.

(b) Dão

Lying to the east of Bairrada, this region boasts long warm summers and abundant winter rainfall. Moreover it is sheltered from Atlantic winds, thus making the region ideal for wine making. Unfortunately this potential has yet to be realised although some good reds are now being made from the Port grapes Touriga Nacional and Tinta Roriz. Most whites, other than some made from the Encruzado grape, are unexciting.

(c) Oeste

This region, running along the west coast north of Lisbon, is the largest wine producer in Portugal. Unfortunately, quantity has been put before quality and although there have been improvements, few really good wines are to be found.
More white is made than red.

(d) Other Central Regions

Most of these are to be found around the city of Lisbon. The most interesting is Colares, which survived the phylloxera epidemic due to its sandy soil. Here a powerful red with good ageing characteristics is made from the indigenous Ramisco grape. Also worthy of note is a white wine made at Bucelas from the Arinto, also a local grape. Other regions either lack interest or are in decline.

Southern Portugal

(a) Ribatejo

The second largest wine producer is situated on both banks of the Tagus River, but with the bigger estates on the southern side. Much of the wine produced is harsh but some firms turn out excellent reds and decent whites by judicious blending. The Castelão Frances is the favoured red grape.

(b) The Sétubal Peninsula

This consists of two wine regions, Palmela to the north and Arrábida in the south. Palmela boasts a variety of soils, with clay and limestone giving the best results. The most important red grape is the Castelão Frances, producing rosés as well as red wines. Good use is made of the Moscatel (Muscat) grape in making whites. In Arrábida the vineyards are planted on limestone hills. Here, a famous fortified sweet wine, 'Setúbal', is produced principally from Moscatel grapes. In spite of this tradition, the region has been more innovative than most others in Portugal. Successful wines are now being made not only from indigenous varieties but also using noble red and white grapes of France and Germany.

(c) Alentejo and Algarve

Alentejo is on the eastern side of southern Portugal while Algarve is in the extreme south. Although climatically handicapped due to very hot summers and little rain, innovation in the form of irrigation in the vineyard and temperature control in the cellar have partly compensated for this drawback.

Naturally the production of red wine easily outstrips that of white. Whereas Alenteio shows future promise, Algarve regrettably does not. In common with Alentejo, most wines are red, but without modernisation techniques are high in alcohol and lack interest.

Both regions have one important aspect in common. They grow the trees that produce the corks used for wine bottles, accounting for a large percentage of the world's supply.

(d) Madeira

This volcanic island lying south-west of Portugal has produced wine in amazing conditions for four centuries.
The vines grow on terraces cut into steep slopes in sub-tropical conditions. A system of poles and wires is used to aerate the vines and avoid rotting which is endemic in the island's high level of humidity.

As for Port, but at a later date, brandy spirit was added to improve the travelling resistance of the wine. As a result, the Madeira production technique was perfected to what it is today. However, a double disaster of mildew in the 1850's followed by phylloxera in the 1870's dealt the vineyards two blows from which they have still not fully recovered. Many were rebuilt using American hybrids or the Tinta Negra Mole red variety. The former can only make rough table wines and the latter inferior Madeira. Eventually the original noble varieties were restored, but as yet, still not in sufficient quantities to make enough really good wine to meet demand.

There are basically six types of Madeira, as follows:

(1) Granel, aged artificially by heating up to 50° C. for about four months, then aged for one and a half years before shipping in bulk. Better versions can be aged for longer periods, sometimes in wood, and bottled before exporting. These would be labelled with the words 'Finest' or 'Reserve' on the bottle. However, all are blends using mainly the Tinta Negra Mole grape. Unfortunately some of the 'vintage' wines also contain a small proportion of this grape.

(2) Special Reserve Madeira is aged for at least ten years, normally without resorting to heating. It is a blend containing a high proportion of the noble grape varieties.

(3) Sercial is the driest of the vintage wines, all of which should be made from a single, noble grape variety, in this case from the homonymous grape. It is an excellent aperitif wine.

(4) Verdelho is a rather sweeter vintage wine with a complex smoky flavour. It is made from the Verdelho grape and can be enjoyed before or after a meal.

(5) Bual is a sweet dessert vintage Madeira. It has a rich raisiny taste with a hint of smokiness. It is made from the Boal grape variety.

(6) Malmsey, made from the Malvasia Candida grape, is the sweetest and richest of all the vintage Madeiras and at its best is the perfect dessert wine.

All Vintage Madeiras are aged naturally for at least twenty years. It is an interesting point that they seem to continuously improve with age. Certainly they are the most long-lived wines in the world and resist oxidation even after a bottle has been opened!
A well-made Malmsey is known to keep for over a century, and still improve with age.

Serious efforts are now being made to curtail the use of the Tinta Negra Mole and restrict vintage Madeira to the noble varieties. Hopefully, the wine will attain its former prestige sometime in the future.

Most of the localities that now have the Denominação de Origem Controlada (D.O.C.) classification have been described above. However, the appellation is not necessarily a proof of quality, whilst some of the very best wines do not bear the distinction.
Also, some zones are so tiny they hardly exist. Therefore a list of these seems inappropriate at this point. Since Portugal boasts a huge number of indigenous grapes, often given diverse names in different regions with very confusing results, it seems more useful to list the most important of these, including alternative names in brackets, when these occur. ❧

Principal wines and grape varieties of Russia

REDS

Saperavi, Saperavi Severny, Tsimlyansky Cherny, Khindogny, Donski, Cabernet Sauvignon, Cabernet Severny, Merlot

WHITES

Rkatsiteli, Plavai, Aligoté, Pinot Gris, Muscat Ottonel, Clairette, Riesling, Traminer, Silvaner, Donski

Principal wines and grape varieties of Moldova

REDS

Saperavi, Sereksia Cherny, Negru de Yaloven, Negru de Purkar, Romanesti, Chumai, Cabernet Sauvignon, Merlot, Pinot Noir, Malbec, Gamay, Freaux

WHITES

Rkatsiteli, Fetyaska, Sukhomlinski, Plavai, Aligoté, Sauvignon Blanc, Pinot Gris, Muscat Ottonel, Chardonnay, Gewürztraminer, Riesling, Trifesti, Gratyesti

Wines of Russia

Russia is a very large producer of wine and the largest in the C.I.S. federation. While in the Soviet Union, its vineyard area more than tripled in its last thirty years, yet wine was imported from Eastern Europe to meet the massive demand.

Generally speaking, the country's wine tradition is relatively new, having been initiated as late as the seventeenth or even the eighteenth century. A contributing factor to this is without doubt the rigorous weather situation and although parts of the Caucasus can boast excellent viticulture conditions, much of the country needs vineyard protection against the extremely cold winters. As a consequence the great majority of Russian wine is indeed produced in the Caucasus, which encompasses five vineyard areas. These are Dagestan where wine making dates from ancient times, Krasnodar, Stavropol, Rostov and Checheno-Ingushetia.

Although Russia possesses many indigenous varieties, like other countries there is a growing trend to cultivate the better-known French and German vines. An interesting development has been the breeding of new cold-resistant hybrids, from both indigenous and French grapes. Saperavi Severny and Cabernet Severny, both reds, are examples.

Russia produces a huge variety of different types of wine. Traditionally, sparkling and sweet dessert wines are very popular. The sparkling sweet red wine Tsimlyanskoye is particularly well known. Port, Madeira, Sherry imitations and other fortified wines are also common. The Port style Chyorniye Glaza is a good example. Naturally, a large range of dry table wines are also made.

An attempt to list Russian wines is almost impossible. Many are sold with varietal labels but some bear special names. For example, Rubinavy Magaracha is a Cabernet Sauvignon-Saperavi blend, yet both grape varieties are sold as varietal wines as well. This, coupled with the great number of different grapes used (over one hundred), would make a complete listing extremely difficult. ✿

Wines of Moldova

Contrary to Russia, wine production in Moldova originated in ancient times. Its gentle hills and temperate continental weather make for good viticulture conditions. In addition, unlike most of Russia, there is no need for winter vine protection.

Moldova, although a small country, has a larger vineyard area than Russia. Yet it produces only half as much wine, presumably due to lower yields. The country still lags behind the West in general production techniques but is fully aware of its potential as a major wine producer and is improving them rapidly.

As in Russia, a wide range of dessert wines are made. Interesting examples of these are Trifesti and Gratyesti, both sweet whites, made from Pinot Gris and Rkatsiteli respectively. An unexpected product is the sweet red, Chumai made from Cabernet Sauvignon grapes! However, unlike Russia, there is much more emphasis on dry table wines using Rkatsiteli, Saperavi and also French and German grapes. Three examples of dry wines are the white Fetyaska and the reds Negru de Purkar and Romanesti, the latter being a blend of Cabernet, Merlot and Malbec.

In common with Russia, both varietal and specially named wines are to be found, making a comprehensive tabulation difficult. ✿

Wines of Ukraina

Viticulture in parts of the Ukraina dates from ancient times. The industry has experienced ups and downs throughout the ages, as attempts to expand and improve have been continually hampered by wars, as well as the usual phylloxera epidemic just over one hundred years ago.

Partly because of the temperate continental climate, which does not necessitate the winter protection of vines, the Ukraine is one of the most important wine producers in the C.I.S. Most of the vineyards are found in six areas: the Crimea, possibly the oldest and almost certainly the most important and the regions of Odessa, Kherson, Nikolayev, Transcarpathian and Zaporozh'ye.

As with Russia, a large quantity of sweet, fortified and sparkling wines are made, sometimes from unexpected grape types. These could include Aligoté, Pinot Blanc, Sauvignon Blanc, Riesling, Semillon, Gewürztraminer and Cabernet Sauvignon as well as the usual local Russian grapes. However, in recent years a growing trend towards dry table wines has taken place. The results show much promise and some very good products are sold, generally with varietal labels.

Wines of Georgia

Wine making is an important industry here, viticulture being deeply entrenched in Georgian tradition for over 4000 years. After the devastation caused by the nineteenth century Phylloxera epidemic the country took many years to recover. However, it now plays a leading role in C.I.S. wine production.

Thanks to widely differing soils and weather conditions (temperate to sub-tropical), Georgia is able to produce a huge range of different wine styles from the best of its unbelievable number of native grapes as well as some of the noble western varieties. It is interesting that Rkatsiteli, the most common white grape in the C.I.S. and one of the most widely used in the world, originated here. Dry table wines, sweet dessert wines, semi-sweet, sparkling and reinforced wines are all made, as is most of the Brandy consumed in the C.I.S. countries.

Georgia's vine plantations can be divided into six zones of which the most important are Kakheti, the coolest and where the best table wines are made, Kartli (which includes the capital city of Tbilisi), famous for its brandy and sparkling wines, Racha-Lechkhumi, well known for its sweet and semi-sweet wines and Imereti. As in the Ukraine, none of Georgia's regions need winter vine protection.

Principal wines of Ukraina

REDS
Alushta, Cabernet Kachinskoye, Cabernet Kolchuginskoye, Chorny Doctor, Oksamit Ukrainy, Yuzhnoberezhny.

WHITES
Aligoté, Aligoté Zolotaya Balka, Beregovkoye, Kokur Niznegorsky, Madera Krymskaya, Livadiya, Muscat Massandra, Nadnepryanskoye, Perlina Stepu, Pineau-Gris Ai Danil, Promeniste, Riesling, Riesling Alcadar, Riesling Krymsky, Riesling Xakarpatsky, Rkatsitely Inkermanskoye, Oreanda, Serednyanskoye, Silvaner Feodosiysky, Solnechnaya Dolina.

ROSÉ
Alupka.

Principal wines of Georgia

REDS
Saperavi, Kvareli, Mukuzani, Mtsvane, Napareuli.

WHITES
Rkatsiteli, Gurdzhaany, Mtsvane, Myshako Riesling, Tsinandali, Ehvanchkara.

The wines of Armenia and Azerbaiyan

Principal wines of Armenia

REDS

*Getasham, Areni, Vernashen,
Old Yerevan.*

WHITES

Aigeshat, Ashtarak, Muscat, Oshakan.

Principal wines of Azerbaiyan

REDS

*Akstafa, Kara Chanakh, Kyrdamir,
Matrasa, Sadilly, Shemakha.*

WHITES

Akstafa, Shemakha, Sadilly.

Both these C.I.S. members have ancient wine making traditions. In particular, archaeological evidence has shown Armenia to have possibly been the oldest vine growing country in the world. Although altitude and exposition cause the climatic conditions to differ fairly widely between and even within zones of both states, most of Armenia's vineyards need winter protection whereas the majority in Azerbaiyan do not.

Nowadays both countries tend to specialise in strong sweet dessert wines and also in brandy. However the quantity of dry table wines produced is on the increase, particularly in Azerbaiyan. The Rkatsiteli is still the main grape used for wine making in both countries, but French varieties are being increasingly employed as well, especially in Azerbaiyan, which also grows much Pinot Noir. Other grapes used are Pinot Blanc, Aligoté, Cabernet and also the German Riesling.

Wine is also produced in other C.I.S. states. Kazakhstan, Uzbekistan, Tajikistan and Turkmenistan are possibly the most important. ❧

Wines of Oceania

The wines of Australia

Principal wines of Australia

REDS AND ROSÉS

Shiraz, Cabernet Sauvignon, Merlot,
Malbec, Pinot Noir, Grenache,
Mourvèdre, Zinfandel, Tarrango,
Cabernet Franc

WHITES

Chardonnay, Riesling, Sémillon Blanc,
Sauvignon Blanc, Muscat d'Alexandrie,
Chenin Blanc, Colombard, Taminga,
Verdelho, Tokay, Gewürztraminer

The first Australian vines were planted in New South Wales at the end of the eighteenth century. The state continued to be the foremost wine producer for over fifty years until Victoria took over the prime position, a situation that was unhappily upset in the 1890's when the phylloxera epidemic devastated its vineyards. Strangely, South Australia escaped the disease and by the turn of the century had become the most important wine producing state in the country, a status it still holds today.

Australia's climate is rather hot for successful vine cultivation. This is why all the wine-producing areas are in the southern part of the country where the conditions, although Mediterranean, are cooler, making a reasonable grape ripening time possible. Furthermore, numerous microclimates exist, a situation the Australians have been quick to exploit and are continuing to do so, as more niches are being discovered and utilised.

Prior to about 1960, Australia specialised in fortified wines of the Port and Sherry types. These are still made and indeed are very good. However, they now account for a small percentage of the total production, as the emphasis has shifted towards still table wines, first reds and later whites.

Regarding quantity, the Australians allow higher yields than would be possible in the best European areas. Yet, in spite of light pruning, quality is maintained. Organic viticulture is strong and practised to a greater degree than in Europe. Also, wineries are modern and very well equipped. Refrigeration techniques are advanced, as is research, not only in finding the best grape varieties for any particular site, but also in mixing to get the best blends. This is often achieved by combining grapes grown in different Australian States, a skill almost unheard of in Europe.

Vineyards are to be found in four of the Australian states plus the island of Tasmania. These, in order of importance, are South Australia, New South Wales, Victoria and Western Australia.

South Australia accounts for about 60% of the country's total wine production. There are six regions of viticulture as follows:

(a)   The Barossa Valley, fifty kilometres north-east of Adelaide. A powerful German immigration culture has resulted in the Riesling being the prime grape variety here. However, reds are also successful, as are Port and Sherry style wines.

(b)   The Clare Valley district lies about 100 km. north of Adelaide. It is particularly well known for its superb Riesling and other white wines. However its reds are interesting and long-lived.

(c)   The McLaren Vale / Southern Vales district lies just south of the state capital, running up to the suburbs of the city. It produces a variety of good red and white wines, of which, respectively, the Shiraz and Chardonnay are probably the best.

(d)   Coonawarra is Australia's most southerly wine district and hence the coolest. Lying 350 km. south of Adelaide, it boasts an iron rich soil lying over a layer of limestone, itself resting on a table of water. This, possibly the best area in the country, produces superb Cabernet, Shiraz and Chardonnay.

(e)   Padthaway, an area seventy-five kilometres north of Coonawarra, the potential of which has been discovered more recently, produces some excellent white wines, its Chardonnay and Sauvignon Blanc being particularly good.

(f)   The Riverland is a vast area, running along the Murray River, just over 200 km. north-east of Adelaide. Unlike the other districts, it is a prolific producer of mainly mediocre wines, mostly white, mainly used for boxes or exported for blending. The grape varieties used are Muscat of Alexandria, Sultana and Doradillo.

New South Wales, the cradle of Australian wine making, can at present, claim four major grape growing areas, of which the most important is the Hunter Valley, possibly the most famous of all the country's viticultural zones. Lying 125 km. north of Sydney, it is hot and humid. Fortunately, very frequent afternoon cloud cover and a substantial rainfall combine to allow for sufficiently late grape ripening, thus making the area viable for good wine production. Many different wines are made, but the Shiraz, Cabernet Sauvignon, Sémillon and Chardonnay are possibly the most successful, with excellent ageing potential.

The Upper Hunter Valley is seventy-five kilometres further north, and indeed the most northerly major viticultural district in the country, a disadvantage fortunately offset by the high altitude. Rainfall is low and irrigation essential. The area has a bias towards white wines, the Sémillon and Chardonnay being the best.

Mudgee, another high altitude zone, lies 100 km. west of the Upper Hunter Valley. The hilly situation with its hot days and cool nights results in the production of some very fine reds from Shiraz, Cabernet Sauvignon and Merlot grapes. The Chardonnay is also very good.

The Murrumbidgee-Riverina irrigation area is located 375 km. west of Sydney. Its wines tend to be made from high yielding grapes, mainly white varieties. Recently, some fresh, light wines have been produced. The district has long specialised in Port and Sherry type fortified products.

Victoria, once Australia's biggest wine producer, is now only third in importance, having a fairly large number of mainly small, scattered districts. The Yarra Valley, just to the north west of Melbourne, is undoubtedly the state's best wine making area. The climate is relatively cool and all the noble varieties are utilised: Cabernet Franc as well as Sauvignon, Merlot, Pinot Noir and Shiraz for the reds and Chardonnay, Riesling and even Gewürztraminer for the whites. At their best, the products are excellent.

Four of Victoria's wine districts, that is, Avoca (200 km. north-west of Melbourne), Goulburn Valley (150 km. north of the capital city), Glenrowan (northeast of Goulburn) and Bendigo, located approximately mid-way between Avoca and Goulburn, produce powerful and aromatic, long lasting reds, mainly from Shiraz and Cabernet Sauvignon grapes. Whites, made using Chardonnay, Riesling and Sauvignon Blanc, are fresh and fruity or splendidly intense and long-lived.

The Rutherglen district, on the New South Wales border is well known for its sweet fortified wines. Tokay, Liqueur Muscat and Port style products are particularly good and can age for many years. On the Victoria side of the Murray River lie the Mildura vineyards, long the source of good Sherry style wines. Some interesting table wines are now also made.

The Great Western area situated nearly 200 km. northwest of Melbourne, produces some interesting smooth and fruity reds as well as much of the country's finest Champenois method sparkling wines.

Echuca, in the far north and Geelong, seventy-five kilometres southwest of Melbourne, are two small, new areas of great potential. The former specialises in white wines, its Chardonnay and Riesling being particularly good.

Western Australia has three major viticultural zones. The most northerly and therefore hottest, is the Swan Valley, 200 km. north of Perth. A variety of wines are made, from powerful reds to nice Chenin Blanc and Chardonnay whites. Also, Madeira type products, both sweet and dry, are made using the Portuguese Verdelho grape.

About 250 km. south of Perth, the Margaret River district, being close to the sea, has a much more temperate climate. This permits the use of a multitude of different grapes, including Zinfandel and Hermitage. The best results are probably those obtained using Cabernet Sauvignon, Chardonnay, Sémillon and Sauvignon Blanc.

Even further south, near Albany, is the Lower Great Southern area. Here also, some very good products are made. The grapes mostly used are Shiraz, Cabernet Sauvignon and Pinot Noir for reds and Riesling and Chardonnay for whites.

The island of Tasmania, Australia's most southerly and therefore coolest state, has great viticultural potential, particularly for white wines. Riesling and Chardonnay do exceptionally well, creating light and fresh, delicately perfumed products. There is clearly much promise here, issuing a challenge that the Australians will no doubt take up and exploit in the future.

Australia invariably markets all its wines with varietal labels, naming the principal grape used in the wine. 🦋

The wines of New Zealand

Winemaking in New Zealand initiated in the 1830's and steadily gained ground until phylloxera struck and typically wrecked the vineyards, thus stopping further expansion until Romeo Bragato, an Italian enologist, introduced new techniques at the turn of the century. However, even then progress was slow, being sustained by immigrants from Yugoslavia, France and Germany. In fact, the erroneous belief that the country was unsuitable for the production of fine wine, combined with a local preference for beer, meant that the wine industry failed to take off until after 1970. Since then, however, the rise has accelerated beyond anyone's expectations and is continuing to increase. Today, the country's wine areas can be classified into nine basic regions, five in the warmer but wet North Island and four in the colder but dry South Island. These are described below.

The North Island has a warm and humid climate. Consequently, rot and mould are a problem. Vineyard sites have to be chosen carefully, with particular attention to hill slopes that shelter them from strong westerly winds and the rain these bring. The northernmost region is Northland, where wine production in the country began. Today the best wine comes from near the town of Kaitaia, but most is made in vineyards to the east of Kaikohe, mainly for local drinking. A search for new suitable sites is taking place in an effort to boost the region's contribution to the quality market. Auckland has its major vineyards near the city itself. Again, hot, wet weather is a problem, resulting in wines with herbaceous flavours. In an effort to overcome this problem, vineyard techniques have been improved in the region by the use of canopy management. A trellis system is used to direct shoots towards maximum sunlight. Also excess shoots are removed or trimmed giving the plants greater air circulation as well as strengthening them. Finally, leaves are removed around the grapes where they might cut out the sun. This has happily resulted in the production of some fine red wines, giving the region a boost in the last ten years.

Gisborne lies in the most easterly part of New Zealand. Here, mainly white wines are produced. As often, the most common, which is made by using the Müller Thurgau grape, is not very interesting. The region's best wines are produced from Chardonnay and Gewürztraminer, the former being among the best in the country. Some whites are also made using the Sauvignon Blanc variety. Hawke's Bay lies immediately to the south of Gisborne, again on the eastern side. A mountain backdrop protection provides shelter against wind and rain, making the region one of the very best. Internal climatic variations lead to the production of both whites and reds in different areas. Cabernet Sauvignon is the main grape in red wines, but Merlot is also utilised. In addition, Cabernet Franc is sometimes used in blends. A little rosé is also made. The white wine grapes are Chardonnay, Sauvignon Blanc and Müller Thurgau, the two French varieties giving some very fine products. The region of Martinborough is located at the most southerly tip of North Island and is characterised by its relatively large number of small-scale growers. These tend to make quality their top priority, a fact reflected in the consistently high standard of the wines produced. Both Cabernet Sauvignon and Pinot Noir are used to make excellent reds and a small quantity of interesting rosés.

Contrary to the above, the South Island is very dry and irrigation is generally essential. However, the Nelson region, being at the extreme north-west tip of the island, is wetter than otherwise expected. The wines are basically white, the great majority being made from Chardonnay. Other varieties used are the Riesling and Sauvignon Blanc. To the east of Nelson lies the Marlborough region. Wine production here took off in a very big way in the early 1970's and it is now, together with Hawke's Bay, one of the two best regions in New Zealand. Indeed, the most common wine, the white made from Sauvignon Blanc, is, in the hands of the top producers, the very best in the whole country. White wine is also made by using Chardonnay and Riesling grapes, while red is produced from Pinot Noir, as is some rosé. All types of wines are found here.

Principal wines and grape varieties of New Zealand

REDS AND ROSÉS
Cabernet Sauvignon, Cabernet, Merlot, Pinot Noir

WHITES
Sauvignon Blanc, Chardonnay, Müller Thurgau, Riesling, Gewürztraminer

Sparkling products made by the traditional method are based on Chardonnay, while sweet desert wines originate from the Riesling grape. The soil varies throughout the region, but appears to suit the grapes very well. The cool but sunny weather is ideal, and the lack of rainfall is compensated by modern irrigation techniques.

For many years it was believed that the rest of the South Island was too cold for viticulture. However, experiments to grow grapes in carefully chosen sheltered and sun-orientated sites have been tried fairly recently and with unexpected success.

The result is vineyards in both the Canterbury and Otago regions. In Canterbury, Chardonnay is favoured for whites, which are also made using Riesling and Sauvignon Blanc, while Pinot Noir is used for reds, as it is in Otago. However, the whites in this, the world's most southerly wine region, are made from Gewürztraminer.

As in Australia, wines are sold as varietal products.

Appendices

Detailed index

Opera & Wine

Wine in Opera

Opera & Wine

Wine in Opera

Opera & Wine

Operas for Oceania

Appendices

Wine in Opera

Wines of Oceania

Sydney Opera House, Sydney, Australia.

Proscenia

Teatro alla Scala, Milan, Italy.

Years of production and measurements

Opera and Wine	2001	100 x 90	cm	Otello | 83	1996	81½ x 120	cm
The National Gallery | 2	2002	90 x 130	cm	Die Entführung aus dem Serail | 85	1996	93 x 81½	cm
Wine in Opera | 4	2001	100 x 25	cm	The Tempest | 87	1999	100 x 90	cm
L'Ombre | 6	2001	64 x 84	cm	La Bohème | 89	1997	100 x 120	cm
Portrait Luciano Citeroni | 8	2002	39 x 32	cm	L'Amico Fritz | 91	1998	75 x 81½	cm
Self-portrait Valentino | 9	2002	35 x 29	cm	L'Elisir d'Amore | 93	1994	100 x 120	cm
				Il viaggio a Reims | 95	1999	81½ x 112	cm
Die Zauberflöte | 13	1996	100 x 120	cm	La Traviata | 97	1993	80½ x 112	cm
Samson et Dalila | 17	1997	96½ x 81½	cm	Manon | 99	1997	90 x 100	cm
L'Incontro improvviso | 19	2000	67 x 81½	cm	Mireille | 101	2000	74 x 98	cm
L'Africaine | 21	1997	100 x 120	cm	Iolanta | 103	1998	90 x 81½	cm
Porgy and Bess | 25	1998	100 x 120	cm	Elisa | 105	2001	60 x 70	cm
La Fanciulla del West | 27	1992	80½ x 112	cm	Il segreto di Susanna | 107	2000	100 x 90	cm
Carousel | 29	1999	81½ x 111	cm	Rigoletto | 109	1995	100 x 90	cm
Maria de Buenos Aires | 31	1999	81½ x 107	cm	Don Giovanni | 111	1999	81½ x 100	cm
Il Guarany | 33	1996	100 x 90	cm	La Gioconda | 113	2000	90 x 100	cm
Turandot | 37	1995	100 x 120	cm	Attila | 115	1999	81½ x 100	cm
Madama Butterfly | 39	1995	100 x 90	cm	La Cena delle Beffe | 117	1997	90 x 100	cm
Yu-Zuru | 41	1995	100 x 90	cm	Francesca da Rimini | 119	1999	81½ x 90	cm
Europa Riconosciuta | 45	1995	130 x 150	cm	La Cenerentola | 121	1996	100 x 90	cm
Falstaff | 47	1993	80½ x 93	cm	The Cenci | 123	1997	90 x 100	cm
Die Dreigroschenoper | 49	1993	80½ x 90	cm	L'Incoronazione di Poppea | 125	1996	100 x 120	cm
The Rake's Progress | 51	2000	60 x 81½	cm	Il Campanello | 127	1994	100 x 120	cm
Die Tote Stadt | 53	2000	100 x 120	cm	Così Fan Tutte | 129	2001	81½ x 111	cm
Der Fliegende Holländer | 55	1996	90 x 100	cm	I Pagliacci | 131	1998	81½ x 111	cm
Guillaume Tell | 57	1992	100 x 120	cm	Giovanni Gallurese | 133	1997	100 x 90	cm
La Sonnambula | 59	2000	67 x 81½	cm	Cavalleria Rusticana | 135	1999	81½ x 112½	cm
Tannhäuser | 61	1994	100 x 90	cm	Fidelio | 137	1996	80½ x 90	cm
Der Freischutz | 63	1995	80½ x 90	cm	Don Chisciotte | 139	1999	100 x 90	cm
Les Contes d'Hoffmann | 65	1998	100 x 90	cm	Carmen | 141	1999	81½ x 111½	cm
Faust | 67	1998	100 x 90	cm	Billy Budd | 143	1999	81½ x 80	cm
Undine | 69	1998	81½ x 90	cm	Boris Godunov | 145	2000	67 x 81½	cm
Die Fledermaus | 71	1998	90 x 100	cm	Prince Igor | 147	2000	67 x 81½	cm
Dvě Vdovy | 73	2000	90 x 100	cm	Voss | 151	2000	67 x 81½	cm
Der Rosenkavalier | 75	1999	81½ x 96½	cm	Allegory of New Zealand | 265	1997	84 x 74	cm
Nozze Istriane | 77	2001	75 x 90	cm				
The Bassarids | 79	1998	81½ x 111	cm	Teatro alla Scala | 262	1999	81½ x 80	cm
Les Troyens | 81	1997	100 x 120	cm	Sydney Opera House | 264	1996	81 x 81	cm

Colophon

First published in The Netherlands
in 2002 by Cantor Holding BV
Bolensteinseweg 3
3603 CP Maarssen
The Netherlands

© 2002 by Cantor Holding BV
© 2002 by Valentino Monticello
for the illustrations.

Printed and bound in The Netherlands.
First edition

ISBN 90-807371-1-9

Distributed by:
Mitchell Beazley, 2-4 Heron Quays,
London E14 4JP, United Kingdom

To order in the UK please call 01903 828 800
For further information on Mitchell Beazley
wine titles visit our website at:
www.mitchell-beazley.com

Cantor Holding
ART PUBLICATIONS

Valentino Monticello
Please contact the publisher

Text writer
Luciano Citeroni
Please contact the publisher

Principal sponsor
Jan-Dirk Paarlberg
Cantor Holding BV
Kasteel Bolenstein
Bolensteinseweg 3
3603 CP Maarssen
The Netherlands

Sponsor / concept and design
Oscar van Overeem
Design Consultancy
25 Craven Hill Gardens, no. 4
London W2 3EA
United Kingdom

**Sponsor for the launching of
the book at the National Gallery**
Champagne Jacquesson & Fils
51530 Dizy
France

Assistant copywriter
Judith L. Smyth
Engelandlaan 1176
2034 GJ Haarlem
The Netherlands

Text editor
Lynette Gridley
15 Cherry Grove
Hungerford
Berkshire RG17 0HP
United Kingdom

Text editor
Marjolein van Rooij
Guadeloupestraat 119
1339 MC Almere-Buiten
The Netherlands

Photographer
A.C. Cooper (colour) LTD
46A Maddox street
London W1S 1PB
United Kingdom

Frame maker
Rebecca Bramwell
Art & Soul
g. 14, Belgravia Workshops
157 Marlborough Road
London N19 4NF
United Kingdom

Lay-out and lithograpy
Van Ginneken & Mostaard Group
Anthony Fokkerweg 61
1059 CP Amsterdam
The Netherlands

Printer
Drukkerij Tesink BV
Hermesweg 17
7202 BR Zutphen
The Netherlands